SCENE DESIGN

AND

STAGE LIGHTING

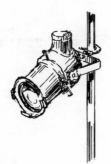

W. Oren Parker

Harvey K. Smith

Yale University

HOLT, RINEHART AND WINSTON, INC.

New York–Chicago–San Francisco–Toronto–London

SCENE DESIGN

AND

STAGE LIGHTING

PREFACE

The stimulation of a professional design philosophy is the focal point around which the chapters in this book revolve. The term *professional* is used not as a symbol of Broadway or commercial theatre, but as an indication of skill and proficiency in execution and pride in good workmanship. A professional attitude toward scene designing, technical production, and stage lighting can and does exist in many community and university theatres across the country. This network of active theatre provides not only the necessary training ground for future artists in the theatre; it also develops theatregoers eager for the best productions possible. It is toward improving and strengthening this vital theatre that this book is directed.

Scene Design and Stage Lighting outlines the background and training prerequisite to designing in the modern theatre. It divides the study of scene design into three parts: first, the concept of scene design as a visual art and its function in the theatre; second, execution of the design, involving all aspects of technical production; and, third, stage lighting as a design element and a theatrical technique. This order of presentation traces the logical sequence of steps in developing a setting from conception to full production. The three parts, although interrelated, are individual enough to be studied separately or in any order.

Part I, the concept of scene design, emphasizes practical application of basic

v

design principles to modern staging methods. It stresses the function of scene design in its relation to the play, and the visual contribution of design to the production as a whole, as well as working procedures and presentation techniques.

Part II, technical production, exposes the reader to construction techniques and methods of moving scenery on the stage. It points out the importance of knowing both the possibilities and the limitations of materials and space.

Part III, on lighting, begins with the principles of electricity and lighting instruments and goes on to analyze the equipment needs of educational and community producing groups. A unique and most important feature is Chapter 20 in which the thinking behind the lighting of five typical production schemes is discussed, step by step, and a complete lighting layout and instrument schedule for each is developed.

This is not a how-to-do-it book in the sense of providing handy hints for the amateur. It assumes in the reader a basic interest in theatre, and the desire for a more specific knowledge in design and production techniques.

Nor is the book filled with "short cuts" and suggestions for home-made equipment. The authors believe emphatically that only the best recognized methods should be taught, that in no other way can a professional approach be encouraged and competence attained. Teaching any but the highest standards is rarely effective. The artist well grounded in the principles of his art can adjust himself to less-than-desirable conditions with relative ease when he has to—if he is truly competent. The unimaginative and superficially trained can rarely apply "handy hints" to the slightly unusual situation.

The expansiveness of scene and lighting design as creative processes makes it impossible to present a completely comprehensive text within one volume; therefore, *Scene Design and Stage Lighting* is by intention introductory and general wherever the authors feel there is sufficient published material to provide detailed reading for further exploration. Carefully selected lists of such books have been provided at the end of the text.

The book emphasizes the principles that lie behind what is generally accepted as good practice in modern stage design. It outlines the reasoning that each designer must go through in planning and executing his concepts, alerts him to technical limitations, and reveals possibilities and opportunities. Above all, it encourages him in an ambition toward the highest professional competence and ideals.

The authors would be exceedingly remiss were they not to express their deep appreciation to the several persons whose assistance, advice, criticism, and encouragement aided them in the preparation of this book. Among the many to whom we extend our grateful acknowledgments are Frank Bevan, Edward C. Cole, George C. Izenour, Stanley McCandless, and Donald Oenslager; David Locklin, Carroll Lusk, and James L. Read, Jr.; Walter S. Dewey, Theodore Fuchs, and William Halstead; Gene Diskey for special photography; the University of Michigan Speech Department and Yale University School of Drama for the use of production photographs; all our students, past and present; and, last mentioned but first in mind, our wives, Thelma Parker and Virginia Smith.

O. P.

H. K. S.

New Haven, Connecticut
1963

CONTENTS

PART 1

THE DESIGN

CONCEPT

1

SCENE DESIGN
AND THE PLAY

INTRODUCTION TO SCENE DESIGN

Any introduction to scene design should begin with at least a nod of acknowledgement to the very reason for its existence, the theatre. The theatrical form, of which scene design is a vital part, combines many related arts into the very intricate, sometimes frustrating, but always fascinating art of the theatre. The written words of the playwright are transformed by the director and his fellow artists into an audible and visible expression of the author's ideas for an audience. In the presentation of a play, scene design exists solely to bring, through the stage setting, visual substance to the dreams of the playwright.

In the simplest terms, scene design is the designing, executing, and lighting of a stage setting. It is a very limited and specialized area of design based upon a wide background of semi-related knowledge as well as specific training in modern theatre practice.

3

THE TOTAL VISUAL EFFECT. Scene design in the modern theatre is concerned with the total visual effect of a dramatic production. In any production the total visual effect is the sum of all the elements that depend upon being seen to make their impression on the audience. The scenic background is the largest and most obvious visual element that supports the spoken word of the dramatic form. The designing of a setting, however, is not confined to creating the color and shape of framed pieces of scenery alone. It also includes the planning of the quality and intensity of the lights that reveal the scene; the selection and styling of the furniture and set-dressings; the careful consideration of the actors' costumes to blend or contrast with the background; and, because a dramatic production is not a static form, scene design must provide for the easy movement of actors. The combination of all these visual elements represents the total visual effect.

The visual requirements of a script may be as simple as those of *Our Town* which all but eliminates physical elements of scenery, or as complicated as those of *Aida* which requires vast quantities of spectacular background. In either case the visual elements, simple or complicated, have to be designed or composed, prepared and lighted by someone.

THE SCENE DESIGNER. The esthetic responsibility of the total visual effect is normally in the hands of the scene designer although his importance and influence may vary with the extent of his talent, experience, and personality in comparison to those of his fellow artists. A beginning designer is frequently dominated by a more experienced director until he develops enough ability and confidence to warrant full membership on the production team.

There are so many things a beginning designer is expected to know almost at once that he may be puzzled as to where to begin. He will soon find that if he wishes to design for the stage, he must have or quickly develop three qualities that are directly related or influenced by the specific demands of the modern theatre. He needs the vision and imagination of the creative artist; the ingenuity and the skills of the stage artisan; and above all the knowledge and sense of theatre of the actor, director, and playwright.

To be a creative artist in the theatre, he must be talented and articulate in line, color, and form. Through the visual arts he must be able to bring meaning and visual significance to the stage picture. He achieves this through his imaginative or creative quality backed by training in design, drawing and painting techniques, and the study of period decoration.

As a stage artisan or craftsman he must be able, through the use of unique materials and theatrical techniques, to bring substance to his own ideas with skill and dispatch within the structural limitations of his medium. This is his practical or technical quality. To create a design that can be wholly realized, he must know the structure of scenery, the limitations of materials, the methods of moving scenery, and lighting techniques.

As a collaborating artist the scene designer should make an important visual contribution to the dramatic form. Through his knowledge of dramatic structure and directing or staging techniques he can bring proper visual expression to support the action of the play. This is his theatrical quality. He must have a strong sense of theatre to bring a theatrical flare to his designs and keep them in proportion to the dramatic import of the play and the movement of the actors.

DESIGN COLLABORATION. Within the realm of the total visual effect are several areas of design concentration. In this age of specialization, not all productions are designed by one designer. Frequently, the design of a large production is divided between a scene designer, a costume designer, and a lighting designer. In this case the work of the three is a collaborative effort dominated by the basic ideas of the scene designer. The design of the scenery either directly controls or indirectly influences the total visual effect of any dramatic production. The scene designer, however, cannot design a setting without considering costumes and lighting even though their design and supervision may be in the hands of someone else.

A designer also cannot design a scene without thinking of the movement of the actors, although the final action and positioning of the actors is the prerogative of the director. The floor plan of a setting influences the ease or effectiveness of the actors' movements whether the director is aware of this influence or not. He is, perhaps, more aware of the restrictions of a poor floor plan than of a successful one. Nevertheless a good floor plan is a highly important part of the total visual effect.

Costume design is another essential part of the total visual effect and, although it directly concerns the actor, it complements or highlights the scene design. But, while deeply engrossed in his own contribution, the scene designer must always remember that to see and hear the actor interpret his role is the main reason the audience comes to the theatre. The costume gives meaning to the individual character, and at the same time places each character in proper relationship to the total visual effect. The major role of the scene design and of the lighting design is to supplement and emphasize the costume or actor in the ever moving stage composition.

Whether the attributes of the artist and artisan are found in one person, or separate individuals, the ultimate goal of scene design is the same. Designing for the stage means working within the limitations of the physical stage (or the limitations of an individual stage) and with the techniques and materials common to the theatre, as well as satisfying the visual requirements of the script.

FUNCTION OF SCENE DESIGN

Scene design, like other kinds of creative design, is the creating of a form to fulfill a purpose or function. The function of scene design is obviously linked with the dramatic form which it serves. Scene design, in providing a visual support to the dramatic form, is an integral part of the modern theatre. Its function, as a result, is woven into the philosophy of modern theatre practice. The basic concept of present-day theatre, as a playwriting and play-production unity, has brought scenery out of the pretty background class into full partnership in the production of a play. The scene designer brings to the production a visual expression of the author's aim. It is a fusing of the visual effect and the basic intent of the play into a single dramatic impression.

The function of scene design can be more clearly revealed by looking at the dramatic form of the play itself, thereby illustrating the relationship of scenery to the action of the play—and in turn to its visual contribution toward placing the action, establishing the dominant mood, reinforcing the theme, and staging the story.

ACTION AND CHARACTERIZATION

ACTION. If scene design is to bring to the play a visual expression of the author's intent, the designer must first examine the action of the play and the kind of people involved in the action. Unless it is completely abstract, every play (or any other dramatic form such as ballet or pantomime) presents a conflict. Out of the conflict, whether of heroic proportions, or of a simple domestic problem, comes the action of the play. The action of the play is the force that moves it forward and makes it a living, breathing form. Dramatic action is a combination of physical or bodily action, visual movement, dialogue, and characterization. Characterization creates sympathy or repulsion for the figures caught in the action. The characters either create the conflict, or are shaped by the conflict in the ensuing action.

The Scene of Action. By incorporating all the elements of the total visual effect, scene design creates in visual terms the scene of the action. At the same time, it is more than just a place; it is an environment for the action. Sometimes the scene or elements of the scene may become a part of the action which can be seen in the frankly theatrical use of scenery in a farce or musical comedy. The scene, on the other hand, may recede into the background and become a witness to the action, to be more felt than seen.

CHARACTERIZATION. Characterization, also, bears a relationship to the environments of the scene. The people in the action react in accordance with,

Figure 1–1.   *YOU CAN'T TAKE IT WITH YOU.*   (Photo-Ouradnik.)

or in opposition to, their surroundings. The influence of the characters on scene design, sometimes subtle, sometimes symbolic, is, on occasions, more obvious. When the place is an interior or dwelling, a study of the people living in the house gives the designer many important clues for details. For example, the family of Grandpa Vanderhof and his bizarre friends in *You Can't Take It with You* certainly contribute a wealth of detail as to the kind of house and collection of curios that make up the environment of the play.

The basic function of scene design, then, is to create the appropriate surroundings and environment for the action of the play. The first function of scene design toward creating an appropriate environment is to place the action of the play in time and locale.

TIME AND PLACE.   The action of the play must take place somewhere. It is usually in a place calculated, by the author, to establish the proper atmospheric surroundings for the action. This place, even though it be in limbo, makes a visual impression on the audience. The author many times visually establishes a mood by where he places the action in time as well as locale. A specific time in the historical past can prepare a state of mind in the audience as much as the absence of either time or place.

Although time and place are linked with the over-all mood, the connection is sometimes rather loose and may merely suggest a place that carries connotations of the atmosphere inherent in the play. The first act of

Figure 1–2. TIME AND PLACE. *Legend of Lovers*. Designer—Eldon Elder, 1951–52.

Anouilh's *Legend of Lovers,* for example, is set in a French provincial railroad station in the early twentieth century. A closer examination of the play shows that it is not a literal station but a point where travelers pause as they come and go between this life and the life hereafter. Time is of very little importance except that it is not contemporary.

Establishing the Mood. The second function of scene design is to establish in the visual elements of the surroundings an expression of the dominant atmosphere, or mood. Scene design aims to create in this first impression, an expression of the mood and its relationship to the action and characters. Mood can be described as the quality of a play that, when properly transmitted, effects a state of mind and emotional response in the audience. It can be expressed in such words as: sparkling, warm, gloomy, violent, earthy, mystic, and so forth. Some more general expressions of mood are: tragedy, comedy, farce, and the like, that are also used to define a type of play.

A play, it can be argued, is the dramatization of a mood, a theme, and a story. All three elements are always present in a play but one may be emphasized over the other two. Hence, a play may be primarily a dramatization of mood with theme and story in a secondary position: the plays with mood dominating seem to be at the extreme ends of the emotional scale. A tragedy is usually a mood-dominated play as is low comedy or farce. The tragedy, *Legend of Lovers*, just mentioned, is an example of dramatization of mood. *Born Yesterday* is another example, although it is in the opposite mood.

Scene design, besides placing the action of the play, creates a visual expression of the mood. It is the ball, sometimes the bouncing ball, the designer must always keep in sight as he moves through the mass of technical decisions and mundane problems that occur during the execution of his design.

The relationship of mood to action is stressed, for on occasion a visual atmosphere is established in contrast to the apparent mood of a play. Comedy scenes are sometimes played in the ghostly surroundings of a haunted house, or tragedy against the gay background of a street carnival. The contrasting moods combine into a single dramatic impression. Hence, fun in the haunted house might turn into farce, and murder at the Mardi Gras may become irony.

Tragedy, of course, frequently begins in a lighter mood which may or may not be expressed in the surroundings. A gay scene, may have an air of foreboding which anticipates the approaching tragedy.

REINFORCING THE THEME. If scene design is a visual expression of the author's intent, the theme of the play is the next area of study. The theme of some plays is clearly apparent, especially if the author is using the dramatic form as a pulpit or soap-box to lampoon society or government.

Theme is, of course, closely linked with mood as well as with the story-telling part of the dramatic form. Comedy often carries a message to an unsuspecting audience as effectively as does the more direct approach of the serious play with a strong story line.

An example of an expression of theme in scenery is found in Shaw's *Heartbreak House*. The living room of Captain Shotover's house is designed

Figure 1–3. *HEARTBREAK HOUSE.* Designer—James Russell (Photo—Shapiro).

like the fantail of an ancient sailing ship. The incongruity of this misplaced bit of architecture is a constant visual symbol of the lack of purpose and aimlessness of the cultured, frank, charming, unconventional people that live in it.

The expression of theme in scenery cannot always be done so pointedly. More often the theme is treated with subtlety and in symbols known only to the designer and his muse. There is danger of overstating the theme in scenery, however, to the point where the actor is only restating what has already been expressed visually. This, of course, is a design mistake and is as inexcusable as the willing exhibitionism of a vain actor.

STAGING THE STORY. Story is the connecting thread that holds together the other elements in a complete dramatic form. It is the train of related incidents that brings continuity to the many events in a play. Story is probably more important to the theatre than to other art forms. The expression of an idea in the theatre is dependent upon having and holding the audience's attention every moment. The theatre audience, if confused, cannot turn back the pages, like a novel reader, and reread a passage for clarification. An engrossing story can hold an audience spellbound as the playwright leads them where he wills. A good storyteller, of course, uses mood to create the atmosphere for his story. He can also use the story to make a point, which is apparent in plays with strong themes. Any good play usually has a good story, but a play that is dominated by the dramatization of story is primarily dedicated to telling an interesting tale, whether it be of love, adventure, intrigue—the list is long and varied. This type of play is fundamentally entertainment which may on occasions have a profound theme, but more often is based on a very simple premise.

As the environment of a story-dominated play is usually real, the designing problem becomes a selection of realistic details and forms that place the action and establish the mood. This, more often than not, has been accomplished by the author, in his choice of realistic location for the scene of the action. A more important contribution of design than the re-creation of a specific locale, is the staging of the action. Staging, or fitting the action on the stage, provides the areas, levels, and properties in such a way as to allow the continuous flow of action so necessary to telling a good story.

The staging can sometimes become complicated as is demonstrated in the three-room apartment of *Voice of the Turtle* or, the cross section of the house in *Desperate Hours*, both examples of story-dominated plays. The designer, as a contribution towards staging in *Voice of the Turtle*, is called upon to divide the stage into the various areas of an apartment all of which must lend themselves to an easy flow of action, to good sightlines and still seem architecturally logical. Staging problems are a part of the scene

Figure 1–4. STAGING. An example involving exterior areas as well as the interior of one of the houses. *At the Seventh Hour.* Designer—John Kurten (Photo—Shapiro).

designer's knowledge of the theatre as a medium and are discussed more fully in the next chapter.

Whether the play is story dominated, mood dominated, or out-and-out propaganda, it is the function of scene design to visually place the action of the play in an environment that will bring significance to the dramaturgical elements. Theatrical form is a complicated medium and a strict taskmaster. It requires of the designer, as well as of his fellow artists, a complete understanding of theatre organization and working methods before he can create freely and imaginatively.

2

SCENE DESIGN
AND THE THEATRE

THE THEATRICAL MEDIUM

Materials and techniques which are the bases of scene design must have a direct influence on the final design form. These materials and techniques evolve a medium through which the design is transmitted. Each medium requires a specific handling which gives it an individual effect. A painting, for example, may be done in an oil, watercolor, or fresco medium. Scene design, however, does not stand alone; it is a part of the over-all dramatic form. As a result the scene designer is not only concerned with the media of canvas, paint, and wood; but, also with theatrical materials and theatrical techniques. A scene designer may draw sketches, or make models, but his designs do not reach a full state of expression until they are on stage in a theatre. If the materials and techniques of the theatre are to be used intelligently, the designer must have an awareness of the theatre as a medium of expression.

13

The basic communicative qualities of scene design are the same as in any other visual art—color, line, and form create the same emotional response on the stage as they do in a poster or display design. Any structural difference traceable to materials and techniques lies in the function of scene design in the theatre. The beginning designer, to understand, at least in general terms, the extent and limitations of the materials and techniques of his medium, must develop an awareness of the theatre as an organization, a show, a machine.

THEATRE AS AN ORGANIZATION.   The preparing of any production requires the close cooperation of many specialists. The theatrical medium brings together the writer, actor, director, designer, and audience. The ultimate success of a play often rests on the efficiency of the producing organization in: (1) selecting a play; (2) procuring financial backing and establishing a budget; (3) securing a theatre; (4) selecting and rehearsing the actors; (5) designing the scenery and costumes; (6) building, painting and lighting the sets; and (7) promoting an audience. Lack of cooperation, or understanding, complicated by faulty planning in any phase of the organization can weaken the production as a whole.

Like any other well-functioning organization, there must be a guiding force. The director or producer is the dean of the production group and the chief interpretive artist for the playwright. His basic, over-all concept of the production brings a unifying control to the visual elements, acting style and literary interpretation.

The designer's contribution towards the production is, of course, a vital part of the visual concept. He is, nevertheless, a part of the organization and its collaborative effort, which may mean subjugating personal triumph many times for the good of the whole. Great moments of unified achievement in the theatre are usually experienced when the goal of the production is placed above individual gain.

The designer, besides being aware of his general relationship to the over-all production plans, needs to know the specific organization of his own area of theatre; design, technical production, and lighting. A thorough knowledge of backstage and scenery-shop organization often leads to a more efficient production as well as resulting in a more faithful reproduction of design ideas. Because of its specialized nature, the personnel organization of designing and technical production is discussed in detail in Chapter 9.

THEATRE AS A SHOW.   The designer's awareness of the theatre as a show emphasizes the temporal quality of scenery, the dramatic qualities of the visual elements, and above all the sense of joining with an audience to give a performance.

As a performing art the theatre has a feeling of immediacy and audience relationship that does not exist as completely in other art forms. It is true that a painting has an audience, or viewers, too, but the painting remains a painting without the viewers. A theatrical performance without an audience, however, is little more than a rehearsal. The audience and its participation are a vital part of the theatrical medium. Consequently, the theatre's need of an audience gives it a temporal quality that becomes an intrinsic part of the medium.

The direct influence of this temporal quality brings about a specific attitude towards scene design and the structure of scenery; for although scenery may look solid for the most part it must be lightweight and portable to move easily from scene to scene or from audience to audience. And, finally, when the production reaches its last curtain, the usefulness of the scenery ends. It is doomed to storage, rebuilding, or destruction.

The dramatic qualities of scenery are, of course, mainly achieved through the versatility of the designer's use of the visual art form. A dramatic quality more specifically related to the theatre is the use of proportion or scale. The theatre, more than other art forms, is an overstatement of life. Even a realistic play is drawn a little sharper and greater than real life. Any idea, no matter how significant, will make little impression on an audience if it is merely stated.

The size and distance of the audience in relation to the performance has an influence on the scale of any overstatement in scenery. If, for example, the theatre is large and the audience is at a great distance from the performance, the scenery has to take on an increased scale just to be in proportion with the size of the auditorium and stage. But whether it is a musical spectacle at Jones Beach, or a drama of intimate proportions in a vest-pocket theatre off Broadway, the electrifying qualities of the theatrical medium are always present.

THEATRE AS A MACHINE. The modern stage is a complex machine which promises to become even more complicated in the very near future. A practical understanding of this machine is of prime importance to anyone expecting to design in the theatre. The designer's use of the physical stage and its equipment means working with theatrical techniques. The influence of these techniques on final design form predicates a scene-designing philosophy. Hence, the scene designer, like the architect, painter, sculptor, must know and use his medium, the theatre, with all the imagination and ingenuity he can bring to bear. To superimpose a design form without regard for theatrical techniques and the limitations of the physical stage is as ill conceived as architecture that forces interior planning into a predetermined exterior shape.

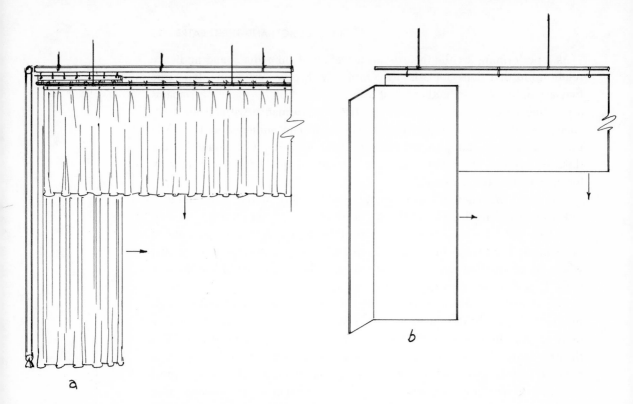

THE PHYSICAL STAGE AND ITS AUDITORIUM

To a beginning designer, the most important step towards learning his new medium is to become acquainted with the physical stage. He needs to know the actual shape and physical make-up of the performance area, for they define the space in which he must work.

THE PROSCENIUM THEATRE. In the contemporary theatre the stage has various forms based upon the relationship of the audience to the stage area. The most common form is the proscenium type of theatre, where the audience is arranged on one side of a raised stage area. The enclosed stage is open to the audience through the proscenium opening. The early concept of this proscenium opening was of a decorative frame to separate the audience from the play in an artificial and often unrelated manner. Modern theatre structure tries to blend the proscenium opening with the auditorium so that the stage and audience are not separated but flow one into the other. The proscenium wall of the modern stage is merely a masking wall to hide the stage machinery, lights, and scenery storage from view.

THE TEASER AND TORMENTORS. As the proscenium opening is a part of the architecture of the theatre, it is of a fixed proportion. There are frequent needs to change the size of the opening to fit the scale of an individual production or setting. For this reason the teaser and tormentors which are

16

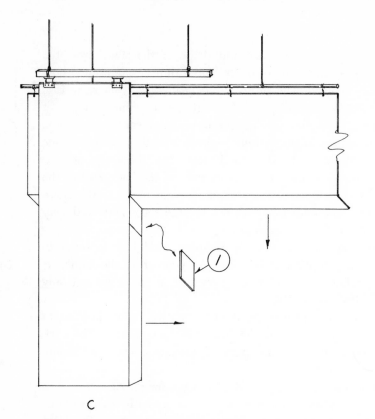

c

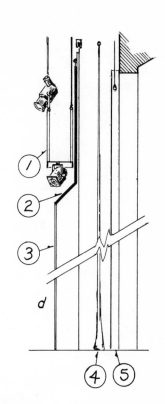

d

adjustable framing members, are located immediately upstage of the proscenium opening.

The tormentors are the right and left vertical frames which move laterally onstage to reduce the width of the opening. A tormentor may be a soft curtain, a flat framed unit, or it may have a beveled edge that gives it a feeling of dimension.

The teaser is the top masking or horizontal frame which is lowered to reduce the height of the opening (Figure 2–1).

Figure 2–1.   THE TORMENTOR AND TEASER.   The proportion of the frame for a stage setting is established by the tormentor and teaser which may assume one of several forms. Shown are three of the more conventional types: (a) drapery border with legs on short traveler tracks, (b) framed border and wings without reveals, and (c) framed with beveled reveals, showing (1) detachable plug to change the height of reveal. (d) This section shows (1) position of light bridge or first pipe, (2) framed teaser with beveled reveal, (3) framed tormentor and beveled reveal, (4) house curtain, (5) smoke pocket. (e) Plan shows (1) right wall of the setting, (2) right return, (3) stage-right tormentor, (4) house curtain, (5) asbestos curtain.

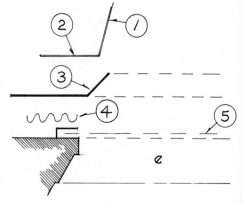

e

SIGHTLINES. Next to knowing the size and shape of the stage area, the designer is interested in the sightlines of the auditorium, to determine how much of the stage is in view. The proscenium theatre has a characteristic sightline problem that varies only slightly with the different patterns of seating arrangement. If the flare of the seating arrangement is very wide, for example, people sitting on the extreme right side of the auditorium see very little of the left side of the stage and vice versa. Similarly, persons sitting in a very steep second balcony see very little of the back wall of the setting. If the auditorium floor is flat without a gradient, or if the stage floor is unusually high the audience does not see the stage floor and very little even of the actor's legs as he walks upstage.

The designer must know these extreme sightline conditions in order to plan his setting to bring important areas into the view of all the audience. It is not necessary to find the sightline of every seat in the house but only of the extreme or critical seat locations.

The extreme horizontal sightlines are drawn from the points farthest to the right and left where a member of the audience can be seated. The horizontal sightlines are located on the plan of the stage and auditorium (Figure 2–2b).

The extreme vertical sightlines are harder to locate for they are found on a sectional view of the auditorium and stage which frequently isn't available to the designer. The vertical extreme sightlines are drawn from the front row upward and from the last row in the balcony downward. On occasion, when a large balcony overhangs a considerable portion of the orchestra, it is necessary to consider a vertical sightline from the last row of orchestra seats (Figure 2–2a).

From the pattern of extreme sightlines, the designer can see how much of the stage is in view to each member of the audience. In Figure 2b, for example, the horizontal sightline (4) shows the designer how far onstage a person sitting in this seat can see and how much of the stage-right wall he can't see. In this manner the designer consults the sightlines of an auditorium in order to efficiently plan the use of stage areas for staging the action of the play.

STAGING. The designer uses the sightlines of a theatre in two different ways: first, when he is studying the staging of the play, to develop the design form, and then later for more technical reasons, to check the masking of the nearly completed setting.

When he is planning the staging, in collaboration with the director, the designer maps out the arrangement of properties, levels, and general floor plan to facilitate the easy flow of the play's action. Because the designer is thinking like a director at this point, the staging is more than a traffic pattern for the actors. Its chief concern is to help bring into focus each scene

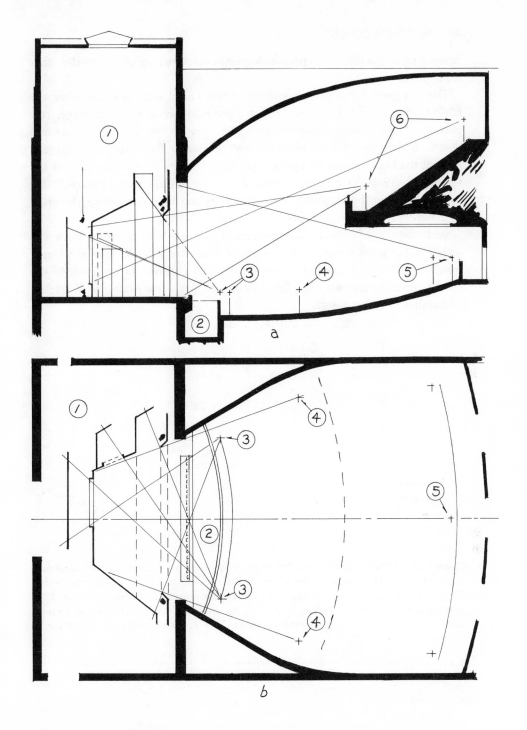

Figure 2–2. SIGHTLINES. **(a)** Sectional view. **(b)** Plan of auditorium and stage: (1) stage area, (2) orchestra pit, (3) front row end seats, (4) widest part of the auditorium which determines the splay of the seating arrangement, (5) back row of the orchestra, (6) balcony seats.

or moment in the play with proper degree of relative importance to the other moments.

The designer, through composition of the visual elements, can alter the basic value of any stage area. Due to their position on the bare stage, certain areas are stronger than others. The very nature of the proscenium theatre makes an actor standing downstage nearer the audience, more important than an actor in an upstage position. The relative importance of the various positions on a bare stage is shown in the diagram (Figure 2–3a) by first dividing the stage into six equal parts and then numbering the areas in the order of their importance.

Such devices as: raking or angling the side walls of a set to force the action in the weak upstage left and right areas towards the center; placing furniture to bring important scenes into good sightlines; using levels in the upstage areas to increase their importance are just a few examples of staging techniques in scene design.

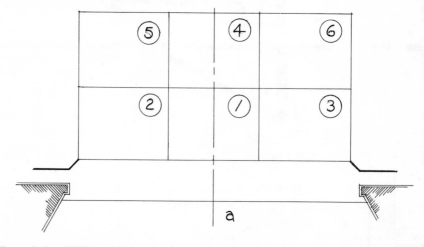

Figure 2–3.   STAGE AREAS.   (a) The stage divided into basic areas for easy identification. They are numbered in order of their relative importance: (1) downstage center, (2) downstage right, (3) downstage left, (4) upstage center, (5) upstage right, and (6) upstage left. (b) A second method of dividing the stage by a series of horizontal planes determined by the location of portals or wings. They are numbered from downstage to

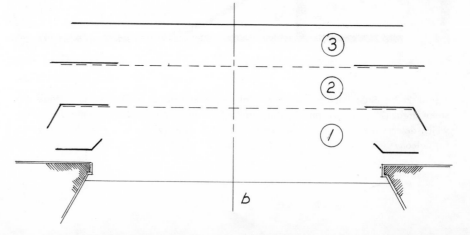

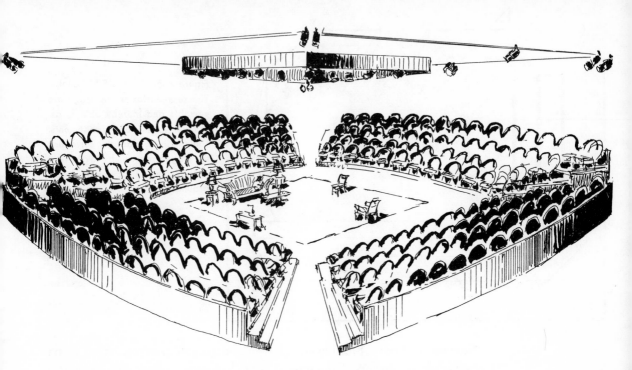

Figure 2–4. THE ARENA THEATRE. The audience surrounds the stage area which may or may not be raised. Any use of scenic elements is limited to properties or an occasional open set piece.

When the stage is cut, left to right, by a series of portals, as in the wing and backdrop type of plan, the staging becomes more two-dimensional. It falls into a series of horizontal planes related to the portals, each traditionally referred to by numbers. Beginning at the apron the downstage strip is number one, the next number two, and so on upstage. The staging can be directed by indicating whether an actor or piece of scenery is to be in "one," "two," or "three," as desired (Figure 2–3b).

ARENA THEATRE. Another familiar stage form is the arena type of staging where the audience encircles the stage area. The scale of arena staging can vary from an intimate theatre-in-the-round to an arena the size of Madison Square Garden, with many sizes and variations in between (Figure 2–4).

Although the sightlines of arena staging are greatly improved over the proscenium type of theatre the stage form is very limiting to the designer in terms of conventional scenery and techniques. The visual elements have to be confined to small low units or open pieces that can be seen through. Design detail becomes more important because of the intimacy of the theatre and the lack of larger elements of scenery in the composition. This type of staging is intentionally simple, depending upon a suggestion of scenery to set the scene and stimulate the audience's imagination to fill in the rest.

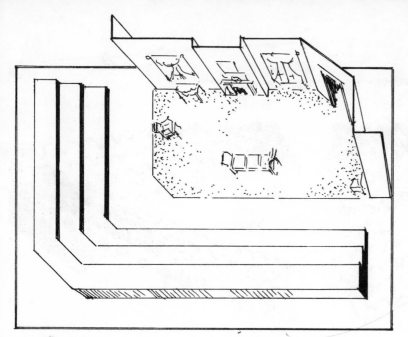

a

FLEXIBLE STAGING. Flexible staging is an outgrowth or expansion of arena staging. It is obvious that arena staging has some advantages over proscenium staging, but on the other hand there are many plays that do not lend themselves to arena presentation.

Flexible staging provides an area for the easy changing of the stage-audience arrangement. Within this flexible space the staging can be altered from arena staging to three-quarters-round, or, to proscenium-type staging (Figure 2–5). Ballroom or cabaret staging is a further variation with the audience on two sides and a small stage or bit of scenery at one end, or both. The sightlines, of course, vary depending on the type of staging. When

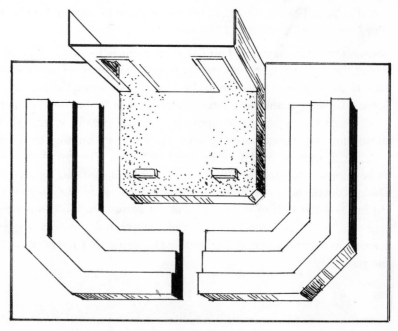

C

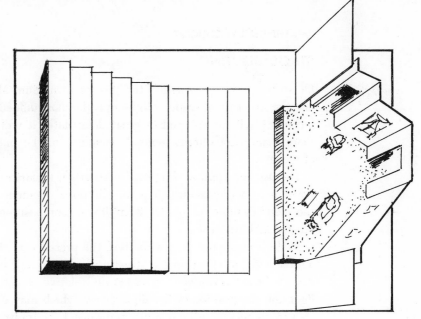

b

the seats are arranged for proscenium-type staging there is a decided improvement in the sightlines over the conventional proscenium theatre. The
seating is usually arranged with a negligible flare thereby creating good
sightlines for the entire house (Figure 2–5b).

Flexible staging offers many exciting designing and directing possibilities.
Its main drawback is the relatively small audience capacity, which limits its
commercial use. A more serious handicap is the loss of time and energy
occurring during the changing of the theatre from one arrangement to
another. It is, however, an excellent staging medium for experimentation in
new dramatic forms.

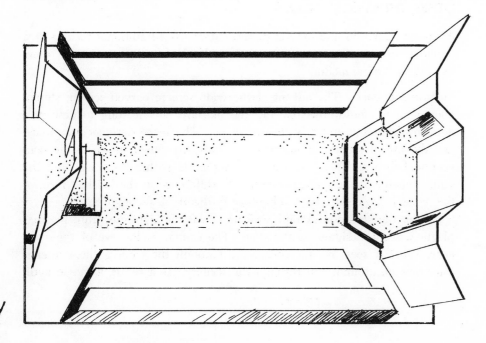

d

STAGE LIGHTING

Of all the techniques within the theatrical medium affecting scene design and the structure of scenery, lighting is the most influential. Because lighting technique will be covered in great detail later it will not be necessary to more than point out its general influence on the materials and structure of scenery.

The use and control of lighting is strictly a theatrical technique, born and developed in the theatre. It is an additional element of design that gives the scene designer a greater flexibility in composition than occurs in any other visual art form.

Aside from its design possibilities, the presence of light on the stage has an unavoidable effect on the structure and materials of scenery. The scene designer must consider in advance the relative changes in the intensity of light and the position of the light source which may determine whether an area of scenery is to be opaque, translucent, or transparent. In the making of transparent or translucent pieces of scenery the pattern of the framing and the location of the seams have to be carefully considered. Frequently the design is altered slightly to conceal or modify a seam or structural element. Conversely, opaque areas should not be neglected, for a strong backing light may reveal an interesting but unwanted pattern of framing.

Often the design of the lighting comes too late in the planning of a setting, almost as an afterthought. It is too important a part of the theatrical medium not to be considered in the beginning along with the other theatrical techniques which condition the design and structure of scenery.

OTHER THEATRICAL FORMS

Although television and motion pictures stem from traditional theatre as a variation of the dramatic form, their individual techniques make them separate theatrical media.

MOTION PICTURES. The advent of the wide screen, curved screen, stereophonic sound, multiprojectors and the like are now leading to new production techniques and new theatre shapes. The scene designer's approach and the use of scenery is nevertheless, basically the same as in the conventional theatre. There are the same signposts within the script and the same demands for visual expression. The difference in the finished form of the scenery is a result of the difference in theatrical techniques.

Motion pictures, for example, do not have the sightline problems that plague a scene designer on the stage. The camera is the eye of the audience. What it sees the audience sees. Through the camera the audience can move in, around, and through the scenery. As a result, a movie audience doesn't have as much of a sense of the whole design as does a theatre audience. For this reason, details in design become much more important in the movie. Details that are hardly seen on the stage are enlarged tenfold on the screen.

There is also, of course, a different audience relationship. Movies, although capable of raising an emotional response in an audience lack the personal contact of living theatre. A moment in the theatre is a moment that will never occur again exactly the same. The next night's performance will vary as the audience varies.

TELEVISION.   Live television combines stage and movie techniques. It has a continuity of performance and a sense of immediacy that is similar to the conventional theatre coupled with the flexibility and dramatic capabilities of the camera familiar in motion picture techniques.

The scene designer's problems are similar to those of motion pictures. The immediate background of a close-up or medium shot becomes important. Details, however, do not assume the degree of prominence due to the size and quality of the reception screen.

There is a considerable difference between the movies and live television in studio procedure and in use of the set. Because of the theatre-performancelike continuity of television technique the action of the play has to flow easily from one set to the next. Space has to be allowed for the movement of cameras, sound booms, lights, wild pieces of scenery, and so forth, with the speed and facility of a scene-change on the stage. Movies, on the other hand, can be shot out of sequence and on widely separated locations. Designing for television employs preliminary staging techniques similar to the stage but unique to the television medium, although the end result is like the motion picture medium.

3

SCENE DESIGN
AS A VISUAL ART

THE FUNDAMENTALS OF DESIGN

The exciting interplay of line, color, and form in a vibrant stage setting or the subtle refinements of an inconspicuous scenic background do not happen by chance. To create them the scene designer uses, either consciously or intuitively, well-established rules and fundamentals of design common to all the visual arts. A knowledge of these fundamentals is of value to the beginning designer as an analytical and constructive aid to the development of the final design form.

The process of designing a scenic form to fit a specific function within the structural limitations of the theatre is a creative process. The steps in the creative process of designing scenery, like those of the other visual arts, begin with a study of the interrelationship of the elements of design and the principles of composition.

COMPOSITION AND THE ELEMENTS OF DESIGN

Composition, in general terms, is the composing or organizing of the elements of design into a unified over-all form. Composition in scene design also brings a unity of purpose or idea to the completed stage setting as well as organizing the physical elements of scenery in space.

The elements of design are the factors that go to make up form, whether it is a two-dimensional shape, a sculptural free form, or an arrangement of many shapes into a unified formation. The elements are line, shape, measure, position, color, and texture.

The term *form* when referring to "design form" implies the use or presence of all the elements of design in a composition. However, because line and color are such strong forces in a composition, it is common practice to refer to form in the somewhat ambiguous yet descriptive phrase, "line, color, and form."

LINE. The basic element of design—line—appears as a formal factor many different ways. First, as a line itself, either straight or curved. Second, as a straight line or a curved line enclosing a space to create a shape. Third, as a shape with the long thin characteristics of a line. And last, as a leadline defined by the eye as it follows a sequence of forms in a composition. The use of line and the line characteristics in a shape become a vital force in any form or arrangement of forms. A composition may use line as a dynamic force with a sense of violent movement, or as a static force with a feeling of strength and stability.

SHAPE. The enclosing of space with line creates a shape. The infinite variety of shapes that are possible is obvious. Shape is a two-dimensional form. Its character comes from the type of line used to enclose that space as well as the use of size, color, and texture within the outline.

MEASURE. The size of a shape is its measure. Measure, as an element of design, is not only concerned with the size of an individual shape but also with the relationship of sizes—large to small, large to large and so forth. In addition, measure includes the amount of the space between shapes in a composition. The interval between shapes has a definite effect on the apparent size or weight of the shape. The prominence of the interval is, of course, further influenced by the use of color and texture.

POSITION. Besides the comparative weight and the interval between shapes, their position in relation to one another has an effect upon the whole. Position brings two things to composition; *direction* and *attitude*. If a shape has one longer dimension it can be given direction by how it is positioned. Standing up, it has a vertical direction, lying down, a horizontal direction, and so forth. The position of the shape also bestows an attitude to the shape itself and toward neighboring shapes. The attitude can be one of opposition or harmony, strength or weakness.

COLOR.   The use of color is a very important factor in the creative process. Like line, it becomes a force of great proportion in the final composition of a stage setting. Color has three variants: hue, value, and intensity or chroma. A specific color can be thought of in terms of its hue, which is the color's wave length, or position on the spectrum; its value, which is the color's black to white relationship; and its intensity, which is the color's degree of purity or saturation. Until it is time to go into the aspects of color in detail (Chapter 7), only the black, white, and grey steps of value will be used to demonstrate the effects of color on a solid area.

TEXTURE.   The textural qualities of a surface are inherent in the material and its structure. Glass, fabric, and stone, for example, have different textures. For this reason materials are often chosen as a design element for their interesting or decorative surfaces. Textures can also vary within the material. Stone, may be highly polished or rusticated; wood may be smoothly planed or rough-hewn. These are examples of real textured surfaces. Unless the real textured surface is deep enough to be seen at a distance it has little value on the stage. Therefore, scene design, to use texture as a design element, depends less on real texture and more on painting a simulated texture.

THE PRINCIPLES OF COMPOSITION

The elements of design are the raw materials ready to be brought together into some order or purpose. Composition, it was said, is the organization of these elements into a unified form. The principles of composition are the various ways the designer can control and use the design elements to bring unity, interest, and meaning to a stage composition. Unity brings into play two controls, *harmony* and *contrast*. The interest or appeal in a stage setting is the direct result of the manipulation of these controls.

HARMONY.   The simplest act of bringing order to disorder is to sort unrelated objects into groups which have some sequential relationship or continuity. The objects may have in common a similarity of shape, color, or texture. Repetition, then, is a basic control. The repetition of one or more of the elements of design shows the presence of outside control. The repetition of line, shape, position, measure, and color are evident, for example, in the common picket fence. Although the picket fence when viewed alone and not as a border is a unified form, it is not a breath-taking example of an exciting composition. This is an instance of too much control. The

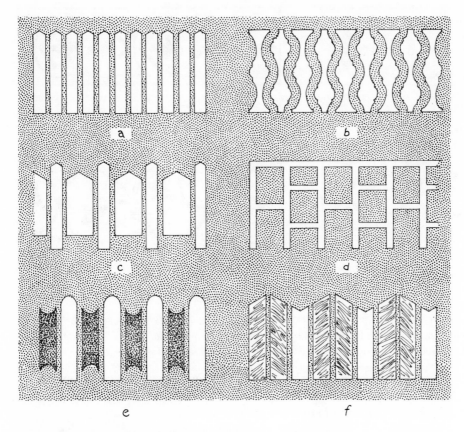

Figure 3–1. VARIATION OF DESIGN ELEMENTS. (a) Repetition of all the elements, (b) variation of shape, (c) variation of measure, (d) variation of position, (e) variation of color, and (f) variation of texture.

monotonous repeating of so many design elements needs to be relieved with a little variation or contrast.

CONTRAST. The designer depends upon contrast to create form. Form cannot be revealed without contrast as is evident in the examples of the absence of contrast occasionally seen in nature. The protective coloration of an animal or bird reduces contrast to the point of making it invisible against the background. This is nature's way of providing protection, but ask an actress in a red dress how she feels when she sits on a matching red sofa. Complete harmony or lack of contrast is as unfortunate as so much contrast as to lose the sense of control. Between the two extremes lies an infinite number of variations.

VARIATION. When a repetition of too many of the elements produces monotony, a variation of one or more of the elements may add interest to the composition. A variation of measure, for instance, would create a little more interest in the aforementioned picket fence by making every other

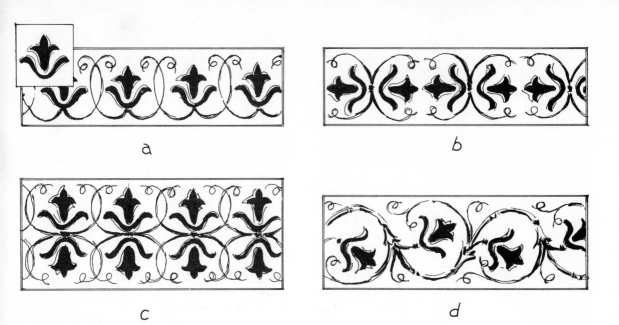

Figure 3–2. PATTERN COMPOSITION. (a) Border motifs in repetition, (b) motifs in opposition, (c) motifs in inversion, and (d) motifs in alteration.

picket shorter, or the space between smaller, and so on. This can be expanded with the variation of the other elements of design into many different compositions or patterns (Figure 3–1).

PATTERN COMPOSITIONS. The injection of variation into composition to relieve repetition establishes a rhythm as the variation itself begins to repeat. This is the basis of most pattern composition which exists in two forms: border and over-all patterns. The rhythm of the variation repeat or "motif," as it is called, is known by the terms of its relative positions. That is to say, the motif may be placed in relative positions of alternation, opposition, or inversion.

The motifs may be placed in alternation, by alternating their position in relation to a central axis without changing the original direction of the pattern.

To place motifs in opposition tends to break the rhythm into a series of static arrangements, creating a feeling of stability.

To place the motifs in inversion takes the direction out of the movement, especially if used in an over-all pattern. Inversion is frequently used in textile patterns permitting the material to hang either up or down without the motif appearing to be upside down.

These arrangements can be combined and compounded into numerous variations of each element of design thereby adding interest to the border or pattern composition (Figure 3–2).

An analysis of border designs may seem unrelated to scene design. However, a border or pattern is a type of composition. It has an obvious control that is easy to see and study. The same control appears with a subtler and less restricted handling in the composition of a setting. Besides, pattern composition as found in wallpaper, paneling, and cornice decorations, still occupies a large part of the scene designer's time.

GRADATION. The variation of motifs within a border composition can, as was shown, establish a rhythm or feeling of movement. The feeling of movement or change is frequently desired in composition of a stage setting where the controls will be less obvious. The sequential controls of a border composition are sometimes too obvious or abrupt. Sharp contrasts can be reduced by the use of the sequence of gradation which by transitional steps, softens contrasting elements and at the same time brings a feeling of movement into the stage picture. The graded wash of a skydrop, as the dark blue at the top gradually becomes lighter near the bottom, is an example of gradation of the value of a color. The use of gradation may occur in line, shape or in any one or more of the elements of design. The resulting feeling of movement in the composition is free of the repetitive rhythm of the pattern composition (Figure 3–3).

COMPOSITION AND SPACE

Space is to the scene designer what a block of wood or stone is to the sculptor. The space in and around the stage becomes an area to enclose or leave open, to light or leave dark, to flatten out or to create the illusion of even greater depth.

Figure 3–3. THE SEQUENCE OF GRADATION. (a) Gradation of shape from a rectangular to oval opening. (b) Gradation of value in the sky and of direction in the steps.

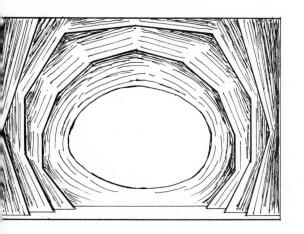

a   b

For the scene designer the perception of space begins in two-dimensional forms with the relationship of *figure* and *ground*. Ground, often background, is a two-dimensional plane. In the simplest example, it can be likened to a sheet of drawing paper. The figure or shape outline has to be in contrast to the ground to be visible. An example of figure is the enclosure of a portion of the ground by an outline. For greater contrast the figure may be filled with a flat tone or color.

The space feeling of a composition made up of a single figure and ground is flat. As figures or large shapes are overlapped, one figure becomes the ground for the other and composition begins to take on depth.

The ground may be simple with a textured or patterned figure, or in reverse, with a complicated ground and simple figures (Figure 3–4).

The composition of a wing and backdrop type of setting is an example of the use of figure and ground in scene design. The flat plane of each wing when contrasted against the adjacent wing, gives an illusion of space that belie their two-dimensionality, especially when other signs of space are used.

Up until now the figure has been thought of as an outline or outline and flat tone. The figure can also represent a solid with not only height and width, but also a depth or thickness. The representation of volume in out-

Figure 3–4.   FIGURE AND GROUND.   (a) Ground, undefined space. (b) Single figure defining a portion of the ground. (c) Several figures. (d) The upstage figures become the ground for the downstage figures helping to establish the planes in space. (e) An example of complicated figures against a plain ground with the reverse in the center.

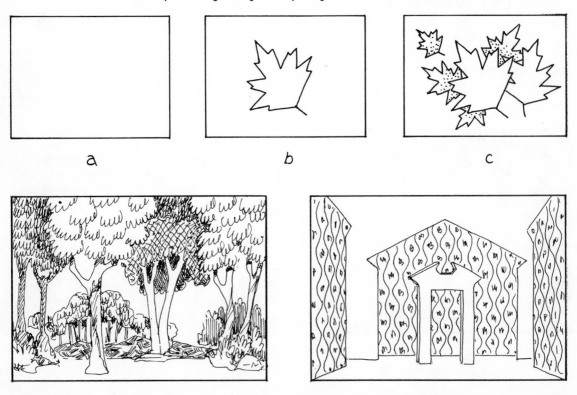

a

b

c

d

e

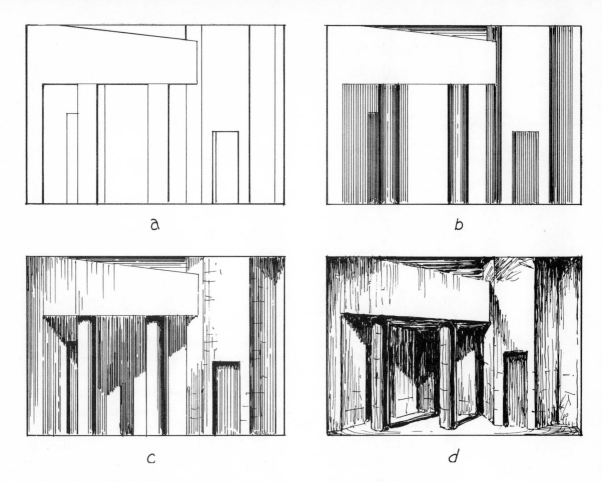

Figure 3–5. COMPOSITION AND SPACE. (a) Outline, or outline and flat tone, is the basic definition of space. (b) Chiaroscuro, or shading, brings out the form within the outline. (c) Cast shadows from an established light source bring out the form with increased feeling of space. (d) Total effect—combines perspective with directional lighting to create the illusion of three dimensions.

line or in solid areas is also an indication of space. The outline itself may be varied in thickness and the ground modeled to accentuate the three-dimensional or plastic qualities (Figure 3–5a).

The figure can be given further plasticity by chiaroscuro modeling, which is to model in light and dark tones without regard for a light source. Chiaroscuro modeling combined with the sequence of gradation emphasizes the structure of solids and gives stronger indication of space (Figure 3–5b).

The next step to heighten the three-dimensional quality of the form is to model it in light and shade as if coming from a definite light source. The direction of the light and the cast shadows help to describe the form and place it in space (Figure 3–5c).

The final exploit of space perception is the illusion of literally breaking through the plane of the drawing paper with the use of perspective. Perspective and the shadows of directional lighting are combined to achieve a total effect, a feeling of space in two-dimensional form (Figure 3–5d).

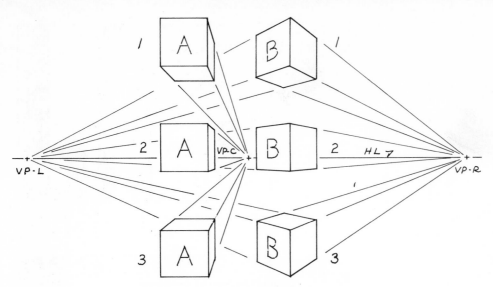

Figure 3–6. GRAPHIC PERSPECTIVE. The front face of cube A is parallel to the picture plane. In this position the sides, top, and bottom of the cube have a single vanishing point (VP–C). A–1 represents the cube above the horizon line (HL); A–2 at HL; A–3 below HL. The corner of cube B is facing the picture plane. In this position the sides have a corresponding right (VP–R) and left (VP–L) vanishing points. B–1 represents the cube above HL, B–2 at HL, and B–3 below HL.

TWO-DIMENSIONAL PERSPECTIVE. The laws of perspective become part of the designer's drawing skill either by observation of normal foreshortening in nature or by knowing the mechanics or graphics of perspective drawing. Figure 3–6 illustrates the basic concept of graphic perspective. It makes two assumptions that differ from perspective in nature: first, that all verticals are perpendicular, although in nature they converge slightly second, that the horizon line (HL) is flat in one plane which, in nature, arcs slightly around the observer.

Shown in the illustration are a combination of views of a cube in simple perspective drawing. "A" represents the cube in a frontal position parallel to the picture plane. The cube in this position has only one vanishing point (VP–C) on the horizon line. "A–1" represents the cube above the HL, "A–2" on HL, and A–3 below HL.

In "B" the position of the cube is angled to the picture plane and therefore has two vanishing points: VPR to the right and VPL to the left. The side walls of the cube converge to their respective vanishing points on the horizon line.

An object with many angled surfaces such as a stage setting has many vanishing points. Figure 3–7 illustrates graphically the development of a perspective drawing similar to the designer's sketch of a simple unit of scenery. The three different results vary with the position of the observation point (OP) and the height of the horizon line (HL).

In the first condition (3–7a), OP is at a proper distance from the object determined by keeping an angle of 30 degrees or less between sightlines

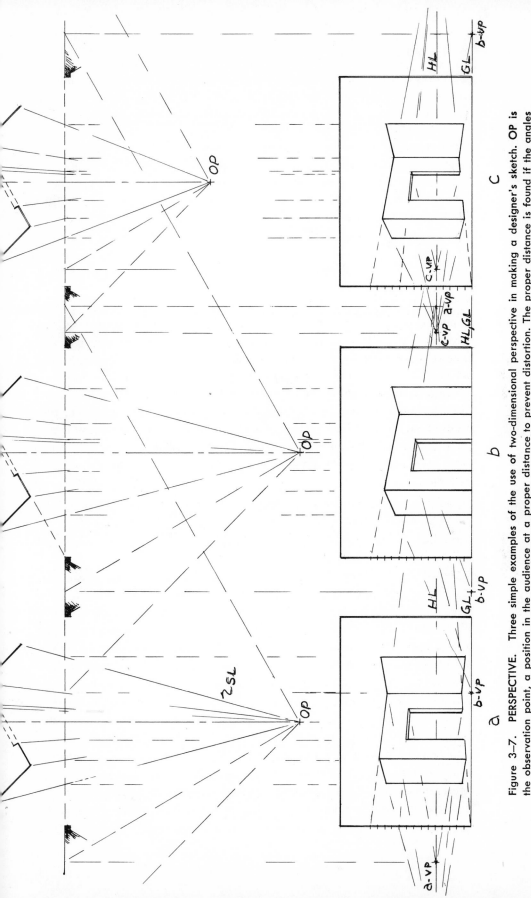

Figure 3-7. PERSPECTIVE. Three simple examples of the use of two-dimensional perspective in making a designer's sketch. OP is the observation point, a position in the audience at a proper distance to prevent distortion. The proper distance is found if the angles between the extreme sightlines (SL) are kept to 30 degrees or less. HL is the horizon line. The distance it is above the ground line (GL) effects the amount of floor that will be seen in the sketch. VP is the vanishing point of each wall. (a) OP is at normal distance and HL is located at about the height of an actor (5'-6''). (b) OP is at normal distance but HL has been dropped to coincide with GL. Many designers prefer this view because it doesn't show any floor. (c) OP has been moved closer to the stage. As a result the perspective angles are sharper and the sketch is slightly distorted.

(SL) drawn from the outside edges of the object to OP. The horizon line is established at a height of about five or six feet above the ground or stage floor. As a result the perspective drawing shows a little stage floor and appears normal.

The vanishing point for each wall is located by drawing a line from OP parallel to the angle of the wall to the picture plane (PP) then projecting it downward until it crosses HL. This point of intersection is the vanishing point (VP) for that wall. The vanishing point for each wall was found in this manner (some of which fall out of view in Figure 3–7).

The conditions in 3–7b are the same as 3–7a except for the position of HL. Some designers prefer not to show any floor in their sketches hence the horizon line is at floor level. All the perspective is shown in the top of the setting.

Figure 3–7c is an example of exaggerated perspective. The position of OP is much closer to the picture plane thus increasing the angle of observation. Although the horizon line is at an average height (same as 3–7a) the perspective in the drawing is sharp and distorted. This type of exaggerated perspective is used more as a design effect than as an illusion of space.

The laws of perspective, as they are used to foreshorten the two-dimensional form into the illusion of deep space, are perhaps more suitable for the theatre than other art forms. The frequent need to create the illusion of more space than is available on the stage forces the scene designer to use not only perspective but all the techniques of space perception in his stage composition.

THREE-DIMENSIONAL PERSPECTIVE. The use of three-dimensional forms on the stage, both architectural and abstract, is the sculptural use of space. It is the use of actual space and not the illusion of space. This is best dealt with in three dimensions with the use of models or real forms.

Sometimes, however, the scene designer has to produce the illusion of more space with three-dimensional forms, or combine two-dimensional with three-dimensional forms to create an illusion of space on a shallow stage. With careful study, the same techniques of space perception applicable to two-dimensional forms can be adapted to three-dimensional forms. Figure 3–8 illustrates a method of foreshortening a three-dimensional form. In this example a structure representing a garden shelter has been foreshortened in perspective into a much smaller space than it actually appears to occupy.

The technique of foreshortening a three-dimensional object is dependent upon two views, the plan and side elevation. View (1) in Figure 3–8 is the plan or view looking down on the structure. The dotted lines designated a, b, c, d represent the actual size of the plan while a′, b′, c′, c′ represent its foreshortened size. Each foreshortened point is located on a sightline drawn from the observation point (OP) to its original position on the actual plan.

Figure 3—8. THREE-DIMENSIONAL PERSPECTIVE. Illustrated are the steps necessary to foreshorten a scenic element (a gazebo or garden shelter) that in reality occupies in plan the space a,b,c,d, to half the depth indicated a', b', c', d' in drawing. (1) Using, jointly, the plan (1) and the side elevation (2) to work out the foreshortened heights of each corner, the four walls are redrawn into their new shapes (4). (3) Is a normal two-dimensional perspective drawing of the gazebo which is the way it will appear if the foreshortened walls are carefully assembled on the foreshortened plan.

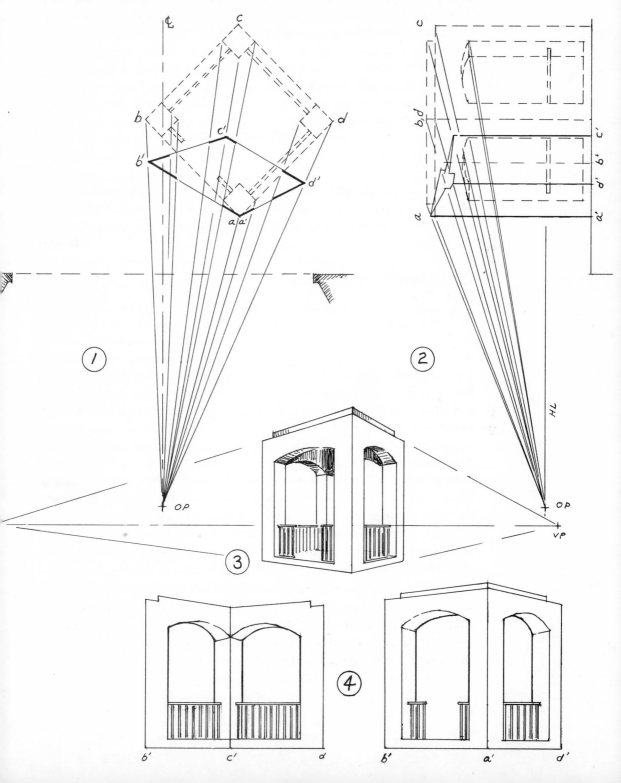

The position of the foreshortened points a′, b′, c′, d′ is arbitrary depending upon how large or small a foreshortened plan is desired.

View (2) is a side view of the structure drawn next to and in alignment with view (1). The points a, b, c, d are shown in side view as well as a dotted line drawing of the rest of the elevation. The side view also shows the height of OP through which is drawn the horizon line (HL).

By projecting each point (a′, b′, c′, d′) of the foreshortened plan into the side view, being careful to relate each to its proper sightline, a foreshortened side view of the structure can be drawn. Because of the height of HL and the theatrical convention of stopping the perspective at the railing, most of the perspective appears at the top of the structure.

View (4) is a development of the four walls of the garden shelter based upon dimensions found in the two foreshortened views, plan and side elevation.

View (3) is a normal two-dimensional perspective drawing with OP and HL in the same positions as in (1) and (2). To a certain extent (3) represents how the foreshortened walls of view (4) will look when they are assembled.

COMPOSITION AND UNITY

The composition of a stage setting is expected to bring a unity to the overall arrangements of the visual forms. Besides the unifying effect of harmony expressed in the sequence of repetition and gradation, scene design needs a greater sense of unity to bring strength to stage composition. The compositional unity of a scene design is dependent in part upon first, balance and movement; and second, proportion and rhythm. At first glance, balance and movement may seem the same as proportion and rhythm; however, a closer analysis will show that they are related but not the same. Balance and movement are the outward, more obvious expressions of the subtler, more sensitive effects of proportion and rhythm.

Unity suggests balance, a balance of the forces within the composition. These forces are the forces of tension, attraction, attention and movement that exist between the forms of a stage design. All scenery forms have mass and size, which means that their proportion must be considered. And lastly, the proportional relationship between forms cannot help but bring rhythm into the composition whether it be static or dynamic in feeling.

BALANCE AND MOVEMENT.   Balance is described as being the balance of forces within a composition. But what is the visual expression of a force? The strong visual pull of attraction and attention are forces. The intense colors of a poster attract the eye. The attention value of the poster contains the interest and meaning that stimulate a response in the viewer.

These two forces, attraction and attention, are of significance to scene design. Many times a setting has to make a telling effect in the opening moments of a play and then have sufficient attention value to sustain interest through the two hours of performance.

A visual expression of tension also exists between forms. The degree of tension is dependent upon the interval or space between forms. The space between the finger of God and Adam as He is giving life to man in Michelangelo's Sistine Chapel ceiling mural is an example of tension. The spark of life can almost be seen. If the fingers were touching, or moved further apart, the tension would be absent. Tension as a force is found in the composition of a setting in the spacing of scenery masses, the grouping of furniture, or in the relationship of the actor to the scenery and furniture.

Another example of a force in composition is the force of gravity, and man's unconscious reaction to it. It has probably the greatest effect on balance. Man reacts to visual signs with an organic sense of balance schooled by a lifetime of living with the pull of gravity. Because of this, an unsupported heavy object may seem to be falling, as does a leaning object, unless its center of gravity holds it in balance. Also a recognizable shape in an unnatural position may cause a feeling of imbalance.

As well as a sense of balance from left to right, and up and down, man has a perception of depth. This allows him to judge whether objects are in the same plane or are receding in proper order. However, it is the same sense of depth on the part of the theatre audience that is fooled, by altering the signs of space perception with perspective foreshortening, into seeing more distance than is actually on the stage.

Movement as a contributor to unity is concerned with *change* and *time*. The harmonious and progressive change of the sequence of gradation is an example of movement as the eye is led, step by step, through the change of color, shape, size, or direction.

A well-organized form has a firmly established movement plan. Some arrangements of form stimulate a greater sense of movement than others. Some cause a different kind of movement such as a precarious balance of tension. The plan of movement within a composition, in any event, is a closed plan, always staying or returning to the over-all form.

In the theatre the element of time in actual movement is quite apparent. The actors move from area to area; the lights dim and brighten; scenery, on occasion, moves in view of the audience. All these are part of the composition of the dramatic form and involve the element of time. The element of time, however, exists in a fixed composition too.

There is an interval of time as the eye follows the pattern of movement through a composition. The interval is minute, of course, when compared to the broader movements on stage. The visual change can lead the eye, abruptly or gradually in terms of time, over the movement plan of a composition.

PROPORTION AND RHYTHM.   The second portion of obtaining unity in a composition is the use of proportion and rhythm. Proportional judgment is probably the beginning or indication of talent. A certain amount can be acquired by training and sharpened by analysis, but the greater portion is intuitive, or sensed, by the artist.

Proportion is the ratio of something to something else. It is natural to relate proportion to the human figure, especially on the stage where the actor is a part of the total composition. If human scale is half of the ratio, the size of a form in relation to the human is a matter of proportion. In the theatre this is referred to as *scale*. The designer is constantly checking the size of a form in ratio to human scale (Figure 3–9). Some productions demand a greater scale, or an increased ratio of the size of surrounding forms to the actor.

Proportion can also be linked to the reason or function of a visual form. The proportion of a chair as a visual form, for example, depends upon how it is to be used. A simple dining-room side chair is small when compared to the scale and grandeur of a canopied throne chair. Stage settings and even entire productions can differ in scale for similar reasons. The proportions of the ballroom scene in *Romeo and Juliet,* for example, are of more significance than the scale of Friar Laurence's cell; similarly, the pageantry of *Henry the Eighth* demands greater scale as a production than *The Merchant of Venice* which is of more intimate proportions.

Many forms and arrangements of forms, however, are not associated with human scale. Besides the concept of proportion as scale there exists a proportional relationship of one form to another, as well as the space between forms. Perhaps more important is the proportional relationship of forms to the surrounding space. The rhythm and proportions of a sculptural arrangement of forms set in an unbound space, for example, may seem different from a similar arrangement of shapes framed or confined within a rectangular shape such as a proscenium opening.

Although scene designing, at least in its formative stages, composes within a rectangular or near-rectangular shape, it is also concerned with the freer compositions of the nonproscenium stage. Designing for nonproscenium theatre approaches the use of sculptural techniques to create a desirable proportional relationship between scenic forms in a more- or less-undefined space. Whereas the composition within a proscenium frame is viewed basically from a frontal direction, nonproscenium scenic forms have to be composed satisfactorily for viewers from all directions.

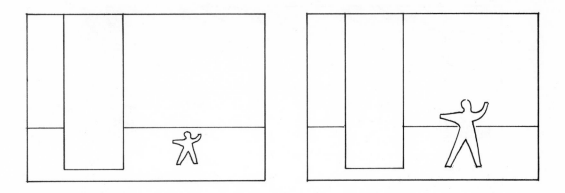

Figure 3–9.   SCALE.   The feeling of scale in a stage setting is linked to the size of the human figure. In the two examples above, the design forms are identical in size. Their scale changes in relation to the size of the figure in the composition.

As balance is linked to movement, so proportion is joined with rhythm. The space between forms and the attitude of one shape toward another creates a rhythm in the composition. Rhythm is a type of movement that repeats or reoccurs at intervals, or completes a cycle. The proportional relationship between forms establishes a rhythm, as does the subdivision of a single form.

The conscious inner relation and rhythm is present in a stage composition in many ways. It may appear in the quiet dignity of a formal arrangement or in the vigorous movement of a dynamic composition. It may be expressed in the rhythmic flow of harmonious forms or in a nervous, staccatolike organization of shapes.

Rhythm, as a unifying factor, is usually expressed in the lines or the linear qualities of a stage composition. The use of actual lines or the feeling of a line caused by the position and direction of one shape to another results in a rhythmic movement that may be as strong or as subdued as the designer desires. Diagonal lines and lines parallel to the diagonals give a greater sense of movement than the use of strong horizontal and vertical lines which tend to stop movement (Figure 3–10).

Although the rhythm of straight lines is more bold and forceful than curved lines, curved lines have infinitely greater variety. The rhythm of a curved line may have the grace of flowing lines, the turbulence of reverse curves, the whirl of a spiral, as well as the repetition and order of interlaced geometric curves, such as circles and ovals.

Whether the rhythm of a stage composition is dominated by straight or curved lines, it eventually becomes a part of the basic movement plan. Likewise, the proportional relationship of forms which determines the rhythm, seeks a balance, all of which results in a greater feeling of unity.

a

Figure 3–10. RHYTHM AND MOVEMENT IN COMPO-
SITION.
(a) A composition based upon diagonal lines has a defi-
    nite sense of movement.
(b) A composition based upon strong horizontals and
    verticals has static feeling.

b

COMPOSITION AND INTEREST

Besides maintaining unity in his stage composition, the designer tries to bring interest and meaning to his setting. Any meaning attached to the scenic forms of the composition is, of course, a part of the designer's interpretation of the scenic requirements of the play as he brings visual substance to the playwright's ideas (Chapter 1).

A stage setting, however, can fulfill all the scenic requirements of the play and still not be interesting. Just what makes one setting for the same play more interesting than another? It can be one of two things, or both.

A setting is interesting many times because of a unique and daring design interpretation which stimulates an intellectual response in the audience. This is possible when the play is a classic or familiar to the audience. Continental scene designers consistently produce exciting and quite different design approaches to well-established classics. Likewise, in university and community theatres, where people are going to see a production or interpretation of a well-known play more often than a new play, the emphasis is frequently on the design idea, or an exciting production scheme.

The designer, unfortunately, cannot take as great liberties with a new play. Here the audience is seeing the play for the first time and will not appreciate too intellectual an approach unless it is a part of the production scheme. It is more important that he first stimulate the proper emotional response to the play.

The second thing that makes one setting more interesting than another is what the designer does to the balance of his composition. A mechanical balance of the design forms may bring unity to a composition but still be monotonous and uninteresting. Any interesting composition varies or stretches the balance into a more exciting arrangement of forms without losing unity.

TYPES OF PROPORTIONAL BALANCE.   There are several arrangements of forms that are organized in a manner to bring a sense of balance or equilibrium to a specific area. The arrangements are classified as axial, radial, and occult balance.

Axial balance is a symmetrical arrangement of forms of equal weight on either side of an axis. The axis may be an actual line or a central-division line. A composition based on such a symmetrical balance may seem dignified and classical in feeling, though rather static and severe in effect (Figure 3–11a).

The formality of the symmetry can be eased a little by using an asymmetric arrangement wherein the basic forms remain in symmetry with a variation of color or detail taking place within the over-all forms.

A stage setting of a formal or architectural nature frequently employs symmetrical balance, both within the composition (individual wall treatment) and as a whole. Sometimes a near-symmetrical arrangement is used to give the effect of symmetrical balance in a softer, freer manner (Figure 3–11b).

Radial balance is a symmetrical balance around a center and the movement is always circular. It is most useful in a decorative pattern or orna-

a

c

Figure 3–11
TYPES OF BALANCE

mental detail, although it may occasionally be seen in the floor plan of a setting (Figure 3–11c).

Occult balance differs from axial balance in the absence of any axis or focal center. It is the balance of unlike elements, the felt balance of mass against space. There are no rules except the judgment of the designer. The result is a feeling of greater movement and excitement which lends itself readily to dramatic uses (Figure 3–11d).

b

(a) Symmetrical
(b) Near symmetrical
(c) Radial
(d) Occult

d

As occult balance is dependent upon the interrelationship of elements within the composition, the use of proportion and rhythm aid the designer to arrive at the delicate balance present in an occult arrangement.

CENTER OF INTEREST.   Unless the composition is an over-all pattern, it is organized about a center of interest or focal point. This is a point in the composition (not necessarily in the center) to which the eye of the viewer is lead by either obvious or subtle means. The leadlines which are present in the movement plan of the composition lead the eye to the center of interest. Besides the focal center there may also be secondary areas of interest as well as intriguing bits of detail within the composition which hold attention yet do not detract from the main point of focus.

A stage setting is usually designed around a strong center of interest with important secondary areas. Although the concept of the setting as a background has its own center of interest, the true center of interest in the total visual effect is on the actor. As was mentioned earlier, a stage composition is a fluid, ever-changing thing with a different center of interest for each scene.

Fortunately, stage lighting, costume colors and the movement of actors all help to make any change of emphasis rather simple. By dimming most of the lights and brightening one area, stage lighting can easily bring focus to a specific point on the stage as can the color of a costume in relation to the setting and to other costumes in the scene. The movement of the actor can also be used to change the center of focus as is so effectively demonstrated in a ballet or group-dance composition. The mobility of the actor allows the director to compose with actor groups or picturization so as to direct the interest of the audience to any portion of the stage setting. The contributions of stage lighting, costumes, and actor picturizations toward the complete stage composition all serve to emphasize the importance of the visual side of the theatre as well as underlining the function of scene design as a visual art.

4

THE DESIGN IDEA

At this point, the beginning designer is conscious of the responsibilities of scene design to the play. He is aware of the influences of the theatrical medium and is familiar with the intricacies of the creative process. But, he may ask, how does one get an idea for a design?

It is impossible to set down universal rules for developing a design idea; there are as many methods as designers. And an individual method is often so subjective and intuitive that it is of little value to another designer as a way of working; each must and usually does develop his own method of reaching his inner reservoir of creative ideas.

Still, it is possible to make recommendations and to point to examples of good design, but the actual conquest of an idea is the designer's individual struggle.

The design idea, of course, doesn't exist until the play becomes a production and the written word becomes dialogue and visible action. It is the individual expression of the artistic imagination, theatrical sense, and technical ingenuity of the designer through the visual control of line, color, and form. The design concept is often evident as a visual theme with variations that weaves through a complicated setting or series of settings, bringing unity of thought to the whole. Many times the theme is so subtle that only the trained eye of another designer can see and appreciate its presence.

The design idea is aimed at stimulating an intellectual or emotional response in the audience. The control of the design elements may be broad and sensational to arouse primitive emotions, or they may be subtle and refined to stimulate an intellectual response. Good design is the result of logical yet imaginative thinking and intuitive feeling expressed through an idea or central theme.

The ideas for many an inspirational setting have been worked out on the back of an envelope during a coffee break, or have been virtually completed before the author has finished the third act. Although this is frequently the pace at which a scene designer is expected to work, it is hardly a practical procedure for a new designer.

ANALYSIS OF THE PLAY

The developing of a concept for a setting begins with the study of the play. Ideally, the play is analyzed from three separate readings. This is assuming that the designer will have the script longer than overnight, or for more than two hours on a train. The three separate readings represent the logical steps towards accumulating information that shapes and inspires the design idea.

The designer's first reading of the play is for its content. He allows himself to react as a member of the audience, avoiding any preconceived image of the background other than the author's description. In this way his first impression is an over-all response that helps him answer two questions: What kind of a play is it? What is the dominant mood?

The second reading is for the play's intent. What is the author saying? It is a more careful reading—between the lines and within parentheses. What is the theme? What is the style? Has the author expressed a point of view through allegorical symbols or in daily-life realism? Has he soared into the realm of epic poetry, or has he dropped into the lusty imagery of sidewalk prose? In the style of the play the designer finds a clue to the degree of reality or unreality of the scenic environment.

THEATRICAL STYLES

The theatre combines many styles. It brings together the literary style of the script; the acting style; the over-all production style of a director; and the visual style of the setting, costumes, and lighting.

Style, among other meanings attached to the word, is a mode of expression or presentation in creative form. The creative forms or elements of scenery, levels, and lightings which make up the stage setting can take on many modes or styles in keeping with the degree of reality or ideality of the play.

SCENERY STYLES. As a visual art, scenery styles can be defined first in terms of the degree of representation of nature. To deal with the extremes, a strictly representational style is imitation. Its main object is to produce a lifelike copy of nature. The design form is represented as near to its natural form as the technical skills of the artist will permit.

The nonrepresentational style, the opposite extreme, is ornamental. Its main object is sensation. The interplay of sheer form and color becomes important. There is no attempt to create a form that bears any resemblance to nature or man-made objects.

In between the two extremes of the representational and nonrepresentational styles lie as many degrees of realism, abstraction, or complete non-objectivity as the designer dares to define.

Most styles, except for complete nonobjectivity, stem from realism. That is to say, the natural source of the abstracted design form is recognizable although it may have been distorted or abstracted in a decorative or "stylized" manner (Figure 4–1).

Secondly, scene design, more than other visual arts, is often subjected to period and national style. A scene designer, for example, may be called upon to produce a Rococo room in French, German, or Venetian tastes. He may, however, vary the degree of realism and simplify authentic detail within the style line and still retain the flavor of the period and country.

Theatre history also has period styles that frequently affect the style of scenery. The painted realism and staging conventions of the nineteenth century and earlier take on a theatrical feeling when compared with the ultrarealism of the box set and removed-fourth-wall style of the early twentieth century. The melodrama revival is a familiar example of the use of a theatrical-period style in scenery.

The third influence on scenery style is that of the individual. The scene designer, as he develops, usually acquires a personal or individual style that creeps into everything he designs. This may change slowly or have phases, but it still exists as a personal stamp on everything he does.

Although style, especially individual style, is a part of each designer's creative ability and therefore is more closely related to the fundamentals of design (Chapter 3), it must at the same time be correlated with the other theatrical styles, acting and writing.

Figure 4–1. SCENERY STYLES. The following six photographs on pages 50, 51, and 53 illustrate realism, stylization, and both fragmentary and suggested scenery types.

REALISM—INTERIOR. *First in Heart.* Designer—William Eckart (Photo—Shapiro).

REALISM—EXTERIOR. *The Three Sisters.* Designer—Alvin Schechter (Photo—Baker).

STYLIZATION—CARICATURE. *American Primitive.* Designer—Peter Larkin (Photo—Shapiro).

STYLIZATION—PAINTED. *Happy as Larry.* Designer—William Bohnert (Photo—Shapiro).

ACTING AND LITERARY STYLES.   With the scenery style, the dramatic form combines the literary and acting styles. They all have an effect on each other and must have some degree of unity or the dramatic form is weakened.

The literary style, reveals through dialogue the degree of ideality represented in the play. The style of a play may capture a cross-section of life, such as Elmer Rice's *Street Scene,* or it may be as expressionistic as the treatment of Mr. Zero's problems in Mr. Rice's *The Adding Machine.*

The acting style of today, for the most part, is believably real when compared to the highly mannered period examples of the seventeenth, eighteenth, and nineteenth centuries. Acting style, however, may vary from naturalism to conform with the style of a specific drama. It takes its cue, as does scenery, from the literary style of the play.

There are many examples of conflicting styles: one illustration is the nineteenth-century conception of opera. A stilted literary style was combined with a presentational acting style of singing dialogue—both set against a conflicting background of painted realism. Today, the style of the scenery has been brought closer to the less realistic acting and writing styles to form a more unified and convincing art form.

Scene design, as a visual art, can reinforce and heighten literary and acting styles. Strangely enough, it can on occasion be a contrast to the acting style without breaking the unity of the production. The designer has always felt that stylized scenery does not necessarily call for stylized acting, as was demonstrated so expertly in Jo Mielziner's setting for *Death of a Salesman.* The reverse, however, is not true. If the acting is stylized, the scenery must be, too. The important thing is that the audience will accept any degree of departure from the real in scenery as long as it is consistent and in good taste.

FINAL READING

After a discussion with the director to reach a mutual understanding of the theme, style, and general interpretation of the play, the designer returns to the script for the third reading.

This reading of the play is for its technique. Close attention is paid to the physical requirements of the plot structure and the changes of locale if there are many scenes. The action and staging requirements are examined to determine such things as: the number of people in a scene, the types of entrances and exits, references in the dialogue to the scene, bits of action hidden from one actor but visible to the audience, and so on, all leading to the development of a basic idea and scheme of production.

SCHEME OF PRODUCTION.   The design solution of a multiscene play, which is known as a "scheme of production," brings scenery-handling techniques

FRAGMENTARY SCENERY.   *Beethoven*. Designer—Ariel Balif (Photo—Shapiro).

SUGGESTED SCENERY.   *Children of the Ladybug*. Designer—George Corrin (Photo—Shapiro).

into the design concept. The design idea is developed around a method of
handling the numerous changes of scene. The kinds of changes and the
methods of handling scenery such as wagons and turntables are discussed
fully in Chapter 8 and indicate the necessity of designing a large production around at least a basic scheme for moving the scenery.

Although discussed separately, a scheme of production is, of course, closely
related to *style*. Many times the designer, through his scheme of production,
establishes certain conventions he expects the audience to accept which,
consequently, create a scenery style. Conversely, a scenery style may dictate
how the scenery is to be handled, thereby becoming a scheme of production.

The Unit Setting. Scenery moving is reduced by the various uses of a unit
setting. This form of setting is based upon the retention or reusing of elements of scenery to simulate a change of scene. This is usually accomplished
by repeating either the plan, design shape, or color in the various settings.
The design shapes and colors, for example, may be varied in each setting
although they are placed in identical floor plans, or the same shape can be
moved to a variety of positions on the stage.

A unit setting can be used in two different ways, either as a cleverly
camouflaged method of reusing scenery unbeknown to the audience, or as
an obvious device that becomes a unifying force for the production, as well
as simplifying scene changes (Figure 4–2).

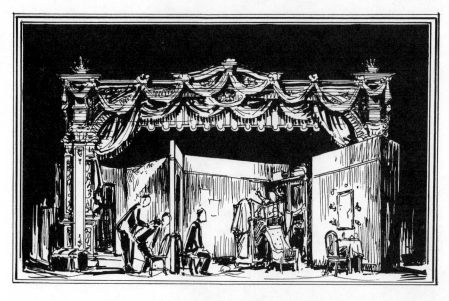

Figure 4–2. THE UNIT SETTING. The production scheme for Anouilh's *Colombe* as it was produced by the Yale Dramatic Association. The repetition of the theatre proscenium form brings a visual and thematic unity to the production.

Figure 4–3. SIMULTANEOUS SCENE SETTING. Four different locales provided simultaneously for the production of *Ribbon Bow*. The action never occurred in all four areas at once as the photograph suggests, but moved from one area to another in sequence. Designer—Lawrence Klein (Photo—Shapiro).

Figure 4—4. FORMAL SETTING. An example of a setting based on an interesting arrangement of steps and levels, providing several acting areas for the fluid action of the play. Changes were achieved by the clever use of lighting to reveal portions of the basic setting in a variety of interesting compositions. *Divine Comedy*. Designer—Peggy Clark (Photo—Shapiro).

Simultaneous Scene Setting.   Sometimes a production scheme can eliminate any actual movement of scenery by placing two or more locales on the stage at the same time. The action moves from one area to the other without a break. The only movement is in the changing of lights. The areas retain their initial identity throughout the show. They may be different rooms in a house, different houses in the same town, or, in some conditions, remotely located scenes (Figure 4–3).

Formal Setting.   A freer example of the simultaneous-scene setting is the use of an arrangement of abstract or architectural forms in such a way as to allow a flow of action over the set, relying on lights to change the composition. Three or four basic areas may be established, but they do not take on the connotation of a specific locale. A formal setting locates the action only in a very general way. It is dependent upon the actor, properties, and dialogue to establish the specific locale of the scene being played. Occasionally a formal setting is dressed with a minimum of moving set pieces to add a little variety (Figure 4–4).

Projected Scenery.   Included with many production schemes for handling multiscene shows is the use of light projections as scenery. The rear projection of a design onto a translucent screen makes the shifting of a scene as simple as the changing of a slide (see Chapter 16 in the lighting section).

Because projected scenery is *light* and not *paint* it has a strong dramatic quality which tends to dominate the scene. It becomes in a sense an actor rather than scenery. Projected scenery when used correctly as an integral part of the play functions best for a nonrealistic or abstract production where the scenery is "acting" and not just background.

In spite of its limitations and dominating characteristics, projected scenery can be used as a highly dramatic and exciting production scheme. Many production designs have been based on projected scenery with successful results (Figure 4–5).

PRELIMINARY STUDIES.   The designer's first impression of a design concept may have been formed as early as the first reading of the play only to be substantially revised or rejected after a closer study of the script in the second and third readings. Often a first impression is right, but sometimes it is wrong and the designer finds it hard to get it out of his mind. For this reason the beginning designer may be wise during the first reading of a

Figure 4–5.   PROJECTED SCENERY.   One slide of a multiscene production of *Snows of Kilimanjaro.* The accompanying diagram shows the screen, projection equipment, and setting relationship. (1) A pair of 5000-watt projection machines. (2) Translucent rear-projection screen. (3) Formal arrangement of platforms. Designer—Robert Thayer (Photo —Shapiro).

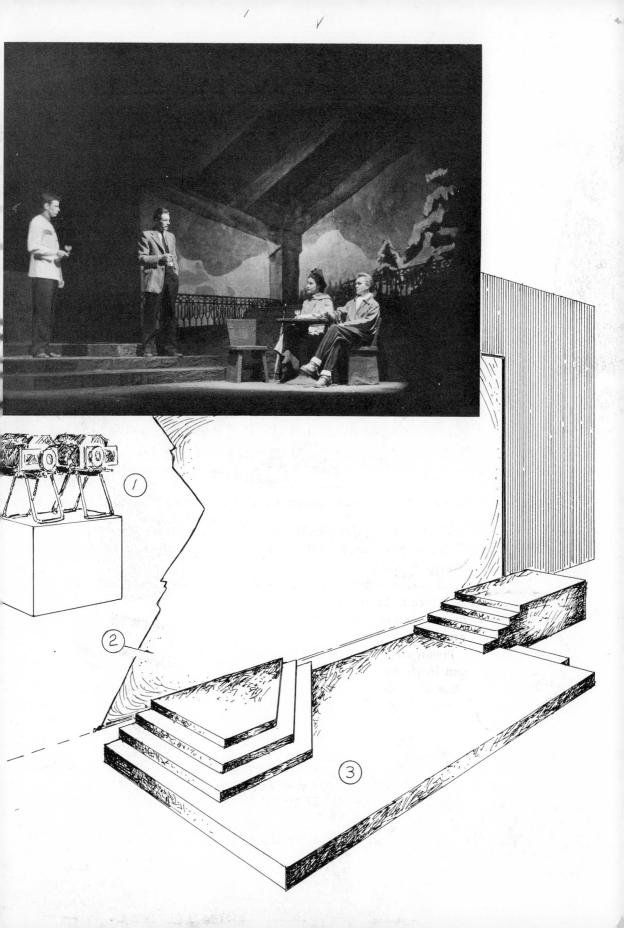

Figure 4–6.
THE DESIGNER'S SKETCH.

new play, to keep his mind open and free of preconceptions until all the facts are accumulated. At that time everything usually falls into place with little or no effort.

An idea may first appear to the designer in the form of an interesting floor plan to be developed later into a related elevational drawing, or the reverse—as a decorative shape or historical form that must be adjusted to a workable floor plan.

Preliminary studies usually consist of small, free-hand thumbnail sketches and rough floor plans. After consultation with the director, the tentative ideas of the designer are ready to be expanded into a more complete form of presentation.

THE PRESENTATION OF THE DESIGN IDEA

A designer may present his ideas in two forms: as a two-dimensional sketch; or, as a three-dimensional model. Sometimes both the sketch and model are used. The sketch is used to "sell" the idea and the model is made later to

more clearly indicate the space relationships and acting areas to the director and builder.

THE SKETCH. Although scene design is essentially a three-dimensional art form, the sketch medium is used to present the design idea. The sketch can be rendered in color and perspective to show atmosphere that would be difficult to accomplish in a model. Many sketches can be made to show changes in lighting, scenery, and composition of the actors. The sketch is light weight, easy to carry around, and therefore more adaptable to selling of an idea.

What is represented in the sketch depends a little on the working arrangement of the designer, such as: an established designer working with a new producer, an established producer working with a new designer, or a producing team, experienced in working together for some time.

The producer views the sketches of an established designer more with a knowledge of what the designer has done in past settings than for what is actually shown in the sketch. He knows that after an agreement on the

Figure 4–7. THE MODEL. (a) Plan for model is the same as floor plan for the stage setting at a smaller scale, usually ¼" = 1' 0". (b) Perspective view of assembled model. (c) Layout of set before corners have been scored or tabs

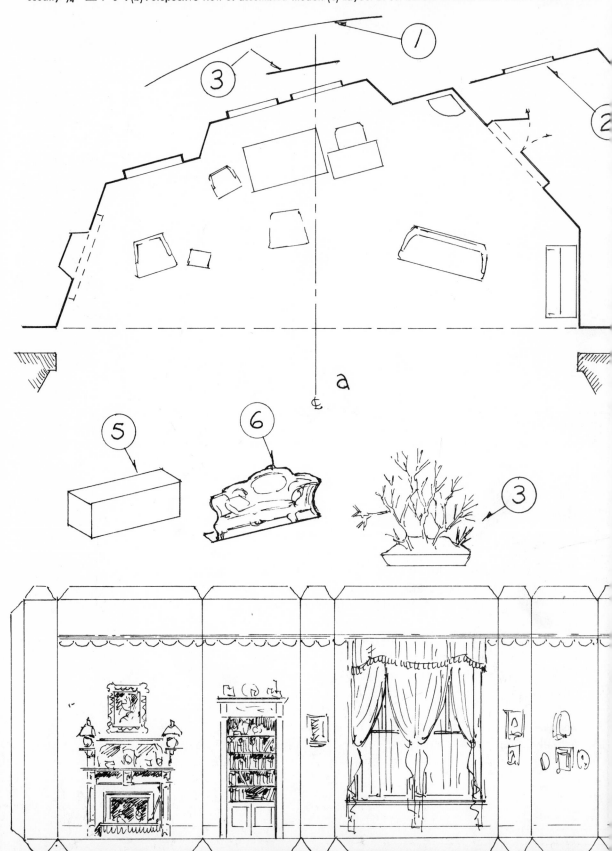

cut prior to folding for assembly. (1) Sky backing. (2) Hall backing. (3) Tree-top set piece. (4) Portal or tormentor-teaser proportion. (5) Block furniture to approximate space it will occupy onstage. (6) Cut-out furniture. (7) Double doors.

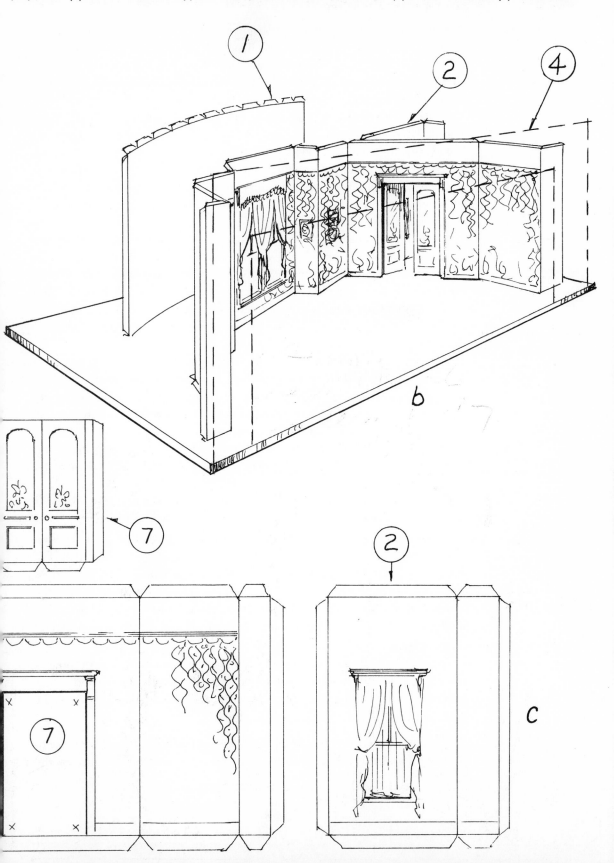

general concept the experienced designer will fill in the details and create a setting to a high standard of excellence in keeping with his reputation.

Because a new designer doesn't have past examples of his work, his ideas are bought or rejected on the strength of his sketch. In addition, of course, he must be able to back up his ideas with faithful execution.

Under either condition, the sketch tries to catch a moment in the play. The designer usually picks a moment that will best show the setting and still express the dominant mood of the play. The sketch is an idealized drawing of the total visual effect which serves as a goal for the execution and guide for the lighting. Supplementary sketches are sometimes needed to show what would happen at another dramatic moment in the play under different lighting and actor grouping.

In the purist sense, however, the sketch is only a means of presenting an idea. It is not the final design and therefore should not be displayed or judged as a complete art form. A stage setting is not complete until it is on the stage, lighted and viewed in context with the action of the play and actor's movements. The judgment of the success or failure of a design, in the final analysis is based on how it functions under finished performance conditions rather than as a beautiful sketch.

The sketch is not meant to be a working drawing. Although it maintains a consistent proportion to show the actor-scenery relationship, it is not necessarily drawn to an accurate scale. It is possible, however, to execute from a carefully proportioned sketch if large portions of the set are parallel to the footlights as in a wing and backdrop setting.

The colors in the sketch are not intended to be the scenery colors, but represent the color as it would appear under the stage lights in the total visual effect.

If the designer is a member of an established producing group such as summer stock or television, his sketch may take on a different character. The designer, director, builder, and painter are so used to working with each other that much is understood without being set down on paper. The designer's sketch becomes schematic with marginal notes. They are carried just as far as is necessary to convey the idea. They are not drawn for the layman but for his professional colleagues. He will resort to a full sketch or model only if he is trying something experimental which needs careful explanation.

The sketch is always accompanied by a floor plan. If the floor plan is drawn to scale and the sketch is in good proportion, the director and others concerned with the production can form an accurate opinion as to how the actual setting will look (Figure 4–6).

THE MODEL.   Although the sketch has been pictured as the prime means of presenting an idea, it is frequently backed up by a model. Because of the

Figure 4–8a. DESIGNER'S SKETCH for *He Who Must Die*, a translation and adaptation of Nikos Kazantzakis' *The Greek Passion.*

Figure 4–8b. THE DESIGNER'S MODEL for *He Who Must Die.*

Figure 4—8c. THE COMPLETED SETTING for *He Who Must Die*.

three-dimensionality of scenery, some designers prefer to work directly in the model form of presentation; it gives a true indication of the space relationships of scenery and actors and is, therefore, of interest to the director when he is planning the staging.

Within the model, each piece of scenery is constructed to an accurate scale, thus giving the designer a miniature preview of how the setting is going to look. Because the model is three-dimensional, composition and sightlines can be checked from all the extreme angles of view.

Besides being a means of presentation, the model also can be used to check construction and effects before making a sketch. In this way the new designer is assured that his sketches can be reproduced in full-scale scenery without technical difficulties.

Figure 4–7 illustrates the steps in making a simple paper model. The paper used is white three-ply bristol upon which is drawn a continuous elevation of each wall in the setting with pictures, draperies, and some furniture in place. All corners of the room are left joined so they can be scored and folded to fit the floor plan. Tabs are left on the top and bottom to stiffen the walls as well as to provide a glueing surface with which to attach the model to the floor plan and ceiling piece.

The scale of the model varies with the designer. Some like to work at the scale of $1''=1'-0''$ while others prefer a smaller scale. The ¼-inch scale model is a convenient size for fast execution, which sometimes is important. Also in the smaller scale it is easier to make changes and experiment than in a larger scale.

The sketch and model are the designer's means of presenting or selling a design concept. Once the director and designer have reached an area of agreement and the idea has been bought, the designer has to prepare another type of presentation; this time to the artisan and craftsmen who will build, paint, and light his design.

Figure 4–8d.   THE FLOOR PLAN for *He Who Must Die*.   An unusually complicated floor plan showing many different levels. The heavy, double-weight lines indicate scenic elements. The single-weight lines define the shapes of the various levels. Note how top levels have been cut away, in some places, to show the shape of walls underneath.

This particular drawing was prepared to aid the director in planning the action of the play. It is, therefore, stripped of dimensions to clean up the drawing. Normally, each change in level is dimensioned by noting its height off the stage floor.

5

DRAFTING THE DESIGN

Although scene design is three-dimensional in final form, most of the presentation of the design idea in preparation for construction is two-dimensional in character. The graphics of presentation is the visual language, or fundamental means of communication between the designer, stage technicians, and director. The planning of a show throughout all its phases relies upon a common knowledge of simple drafting techniques to communicate technical and artistic information. If the designer wants his ideas carried out efficiently and accurately he must give simple, clear, and accurate information.

DRAFTING TECHNIQUES

In the theatre, drafting practices are so numerous and loosely defined that it is difficult to unify them. There are as many ways to draft a show as there are designers. A close inspection, however, reveals that each designer differs only in the amount of information he gives and in the way he organizes his material. All have in common a background of engineering drawing and its basic principle—orthographic projection.

THE ORTHOGRAPHIC PROJECTION. In spite of its academic sound, the orthographic projection is a simple drawing. Orthographic means "straight line." A straight-line projection is a method of representing the exact shape of an object in a line drawing on a plane perpendicular to the lines of projection from the object. It is easier to understand when it is compared to the converging line projection inherent in the foreshortening of a perspective drawing or photograph. A perspective of a three-dimensional object is very descriptive and easy to visualize. The object, however, is not represented in true dimension due to the foreshortening of some surfaces.

For example, it is easy to recognize the familiar three-step unit from a perspective drawing (Figure 5–1a). The carpenter, however, needs more information than a pretty sketch. He wants to know its height, its width, and its depth. An orthographic projection is a draftsman's way of drawing the three steps to give this information. It reveals the object one view at a time and from all angles. The observer is free to move around the object to view it from front to rear and from top to bottom. Each view is seen in true dimension by straight-line projection.

VIEW ALIGNMENT. Obviously, a series of unrelated views of an object are of little value unless they are organized in a connective manner to show the position of the object in space. Hence, there is a conventional arrangement of views that is the basis of all drafting techniques.

To understand the method of transposing the views of the object in space onto the drawing board requires some visual imagination. Using the three-step unit as an example, it is imagined in the center of a transparent cube. Projected on each side of the cube is a line drawing of the object as it appears in each view. With the side containing the front view as the center, the other faces of the cube are unfolded to either side, to the top, and to the bottom (Figure 5–1b).

The front view is always the most recognizable one, showing the main characteristics of the object. It is the key view that gives the carpenter his bearings for visualizing the three-step unit in three dimensions. The top and side views are shown above and to the side of the front view providing the three principle views of the object.

Borrowing from architecture, some views are referred to as elevations, a term that is applied to all views seen in a horizontal direction. The horizontal views include the front elevations, side elevations, and rear elevations.

An academic and a less used expression is to refer to the views as projections. The front, top, and side views become respectively the vertical, horizontal, and profile projections. It is just another way of describing the three principle planes of projection.

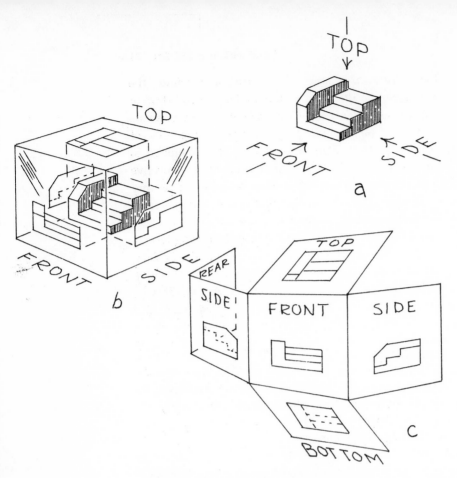

Of course the carpenter does not refer to the drawings as orthographic projections. To him they are working drawings, for with the simple addition of a few dimensions and material specifications to the orthographic projection of the three-step unit, the carpenter is ready to start building (Figure 5–2).

DESIGNER'S WORKING DRAWINGS

The most important part of a set of working drawings is the **dimensions**. Although the carpenter may understand the drawings, he can't begin to build until he has some indication of size. He relies on a scaled drawing or a dimensioned drawing for such information. Most misunderstandings that occur between the drawing board and the finished setting are over dimensions such as the wall that is too small for the side board or the door that is too large for the door opening.

Figure 5–2.   SCALED AND DIMENSIONED DRAWINGS.   Designer's working drawings generally show three views of the object drawn to scale and dimensioned. On occasions, one view may be omitted, or an additional view included, such as a section, depending upon the complexity of the object.

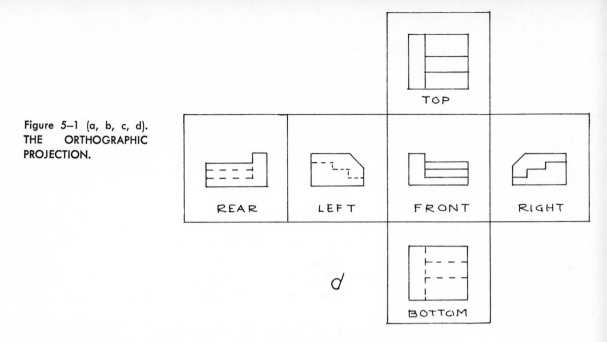

Figure 5–1 (a, b, c, d).
THE ORTHOGRAPHIC
PROJECTION.

TOP

REAR   LEFT   FRONT   RIGHT

d

BOTTOM

SCALED DRAWINGS. Many errors can be avoided if the designer uses a scaled drawing. If it is carefully drawn, it not only provides the carpenter a way to figure sizes, but also gives the designer a fairly accurate basis for studying the proportional relationship of various elements of the set.

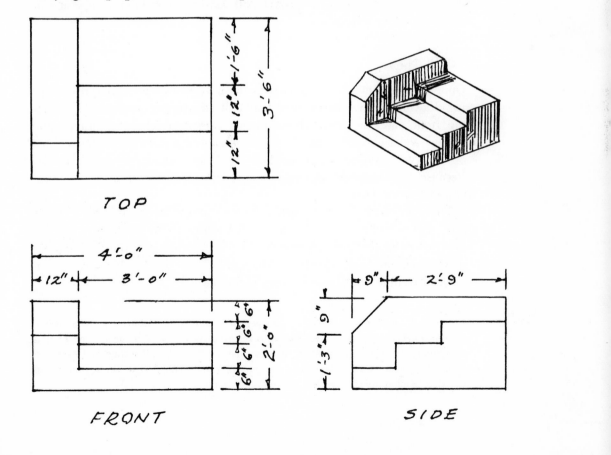

TOP

FRONT

SIDE

The usual scale of a working drawing is ½″ = 1′ − 0″ which means that every half inch on the drawing is equal to one foot at full-scale or actual size. Decorative details which might not be clear at the small scale are frequently increased to the scale of 1″ = 1′ − 0″ or larger. Any important bits of detail that the designer wants accurately reproduced, such as wallpaper patterns, scrolls, brackets, railings, and the like, are presented at full scale.

DIMENSIONS. An unscaled drawing needs some indication of size before the carpenter can begin building. The placing of dimensions opposite a surface is done in a manner to show its exact limit and measure. Dimensions, however, are not reserved strictly for unscaled drawings. It is common practice to place dimensions on a scaled drawing to save time in the shop. A properly given dimension includes the dimension line, figure, and extension lines.

The dimension line is a light-weight line with arrowheads at either end to indicate the extent of the surface being dimensioned. Figures set into the line show the exact distance. If the dimension lines are set too close to the drawing they may become confused with the object's outline. To keep the dimension line away from the object, extension lines are used. They are drawn perpendicular to the surface and, as the name implies, they are an extension of the surface.

SECTIONS

On many occasions the designer feels the need of supplementing the working drawings with another view that will add information to the normal top, front, and side views. The additional view most frequently used is the section. A designer often finds it easier to explain a three-dimensional piece of scenery by cutting it open to show the inner structure or exact contour. Because it is a more descriptive view, the section is sometimes used in place of a side or top view.

There are many types of sectional views and a variety of uses (Figure 5–3), but the two sectional views used consistently in the theatre are the floor plan and the hanging section. Of the two drawings the floor plan is most important to the designer, although he may use the hanging section to check technical details and vertical sightlines.

Figure 5–3.   SECTIONAL VIEWS.   (a) Revolved section, drawn directly on the elevation to indicate contour. (b) Removed section, a revolved section that has been removed and set to one side of the elevation. (c) Cross section B–B is a vertical section and A–A is a horizontal section frequently called a *plan*. (d) Half section, used on a symmetrical object combining the cross-section and elevational views.

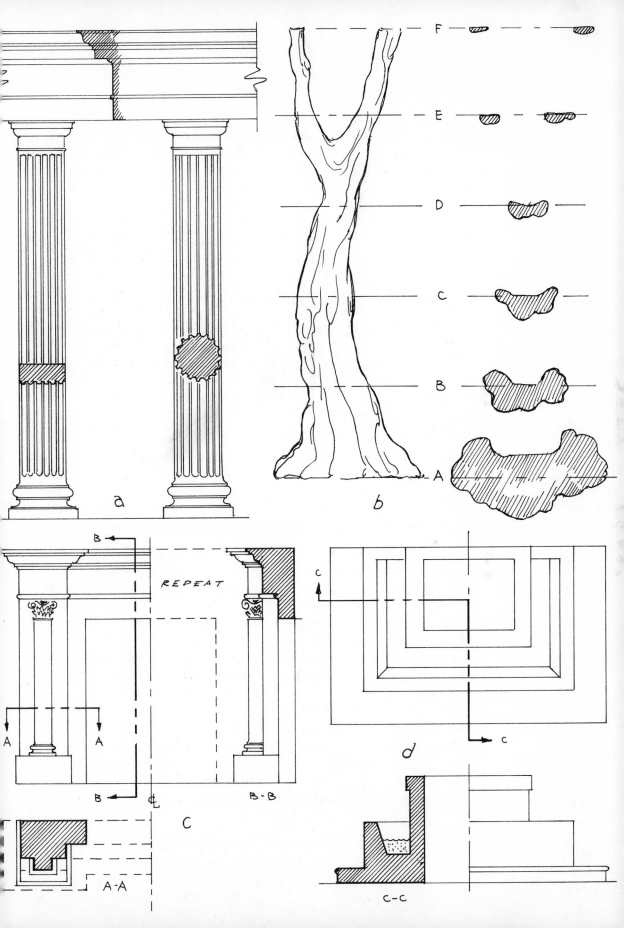

a

b

F

E

D

C

B

A

B

REPEAT

A — A

B

A

A

B

₵L

B-B

C

c

c

d

c

C-C

FLOOR PLAN

Long before starting the working drawings of a set, the importance of the floor plan is realized. A designer continually thinks of the plan while the idea of the setting is being developed. The plan grew with the design, pushed one way for esthetic reasons, altered another way for practical reasons, modified for staging reasons and, finally, solidified into the key working drawing and information center, the floor plan.

All phases of production seek information from the floor plan. To explain the design of his set adequately, the designer finds it necessary to refer often to this plan. The carpenter consults it to lay out the construction. The director and stage manager are unable to map out the staging without understanding and studying it. The setup, rigging, and lighting depend on information in the floor plan to complete the final assembly of the set on the stage.

The floor plan is a horizontal section with the cutting plane passed at a level that shows (when the upper portion of the set is removed) the most characteristic view of the shape of the set. Because a stage set is made up of many small units of scenery, the floor plan is also an assembled view. The floor plan, then, reveals the horizontal shape of the set, locates it on the stage, shows the scenery assembled and identifies with labels the units and pieces that make up the complete setting.

SYMBOLS.   The floor plan is usually drawn at the scale of $\frac{1}{2}'' = 1' - 0'$ or smaller. At this scale, it is necessary to use symbols and conventions to help explain the set with a limited amount of detailed drafting. Most of the symbols shown in Figure 5–4 are familiar ones; their use and meanings are logical enough if it is kept in mind that a plan is a sectional view.

DIMENSIONING THE FLOOR PLAN.   The floor plan is dimensioned from two reference lines, the center line of the proscenium opening and the set line— a dashed line drawn from the right return to the left return of the set to mark the downstage extremity of the set. It is not necessary to dimension the plan in great detail because all the scenery will appear in separate elevational views with complete dimensions. If it is kept in mind that the floor plan is also an assembled view, it will help to determine what dimension the stage carpenter needs to know to locate and assemble the set on the stage.

How wide are tormentors? How deep is the back corner of the set? Distances to the left and right use the center line as a base line while all depth measurements are taken directly or indirectly from the set line. Any point on the stage is located by its distance right or left of the center line and its measurement upstage from the set line. After all important corners and backings are located, a few additional dimensions may be needed, such as, over-all dimensions of a wall or unit of scenery, and radius dimensions of circles or arcs that may be in the floor plan.

LABELING.   Part of the function of an assembled view is to identify and label the parts that make up the whole. The floor plan gives this information in varying degrees of completeness depending upon the working conditions and the nature of the show. In designing for summer stock or university and community theatres, where the bulk of the structural planning falls on the designer's shoulders, he may want to be more specific in his labeling of each piece of scenery in the show. The label becomes an easy, accurate means of identification for a single piece of scenery or assembled units of a setting.

As in the theatre, the floor plan of a television show contains a careful notation of each piece of scenery. Television scenery is almost entirely of stock units and standard sizes. The designer's labels and notes on the plan are a catalog, or index guide, for assembling the set in the studio.

DESIGNER'S ELEVATIONS

Of almost equal importance to the floor plan, as a working drawing, are the designer's elevations. Compared to the floor plan which is an assembled section showing the relationship of many parts, the elevational drawings are, in a sense, a disassembled or dismantled view of the individual parts. Because the elevation of an assembled set as it would appear in a normal front view has little value as a working drawing, the scene designer uses another technique. The set is taken apart, flattened out, and each piece of scenery is shown in front view at a scale of $\frac{1}{2}'' = 1' - 0''$. Starting with the right return, the setting is drafted to show all pieces of scenery laid out in order, piece by piece, to the left return. All pieces are represented at $\frac{1}{2}$-inch scale in true size and shape.

Each flat wall surface or unit of scenery is outlined. A solid line or space between units marks an open joint. For special reasons, it may be necessary to indicate a covered joint, or the line where two or more wings are hinged together to make up a flat wall surface. The covered joint is indicated with a dotted line and a note to hinge and to dutchman, or cover the joint. Normally, this isn't necessary as the carpenter decides just how an oversized surface will be subdivided. His decision as to how it is to be made is guided by such technical considerations as the size of the stage, the method of handling the sets, and, if the scenery has to be transported, the nature of the transportation. The standard maximum wing width of 5 feet 9 inches is based on the height of a baggage-car door through which all the scenery of a road show must be able to pass if it is traveling by train. If the

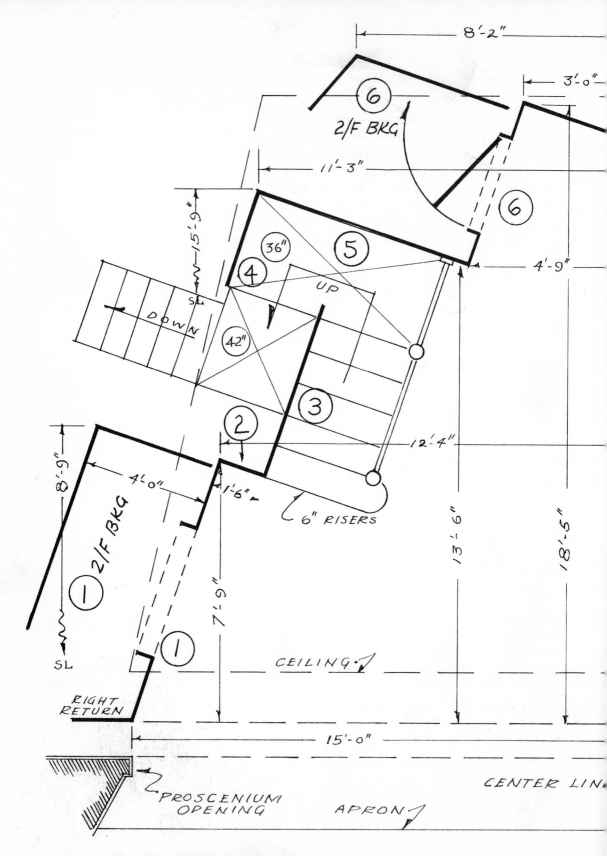

Figure 5–4. THE DESIGNER'S FLOOR PLAN. A horizontal section taken through all wall openings and above all steps and levels wherever it is feasible. The dark solid lines represent a cross section of

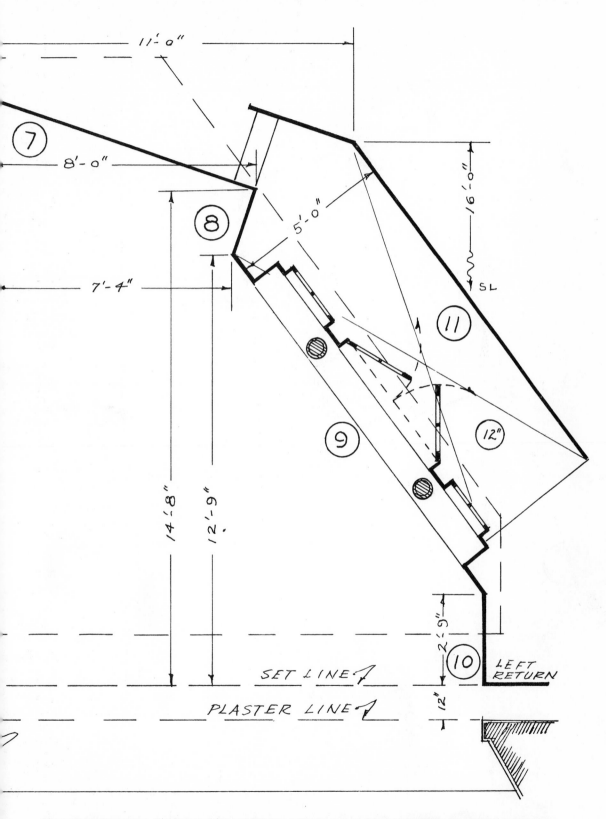

the walls of the setting. The lightweight solid lines outline the steps and levels which are seen in a top view. The dotted lines within the wall openings indicate a "header" or presence of wall above the opening.

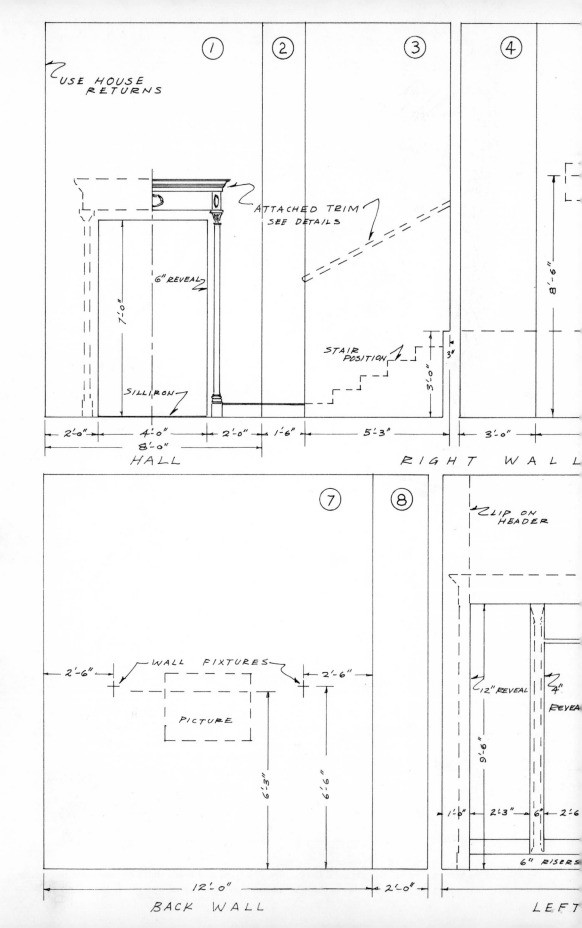

USE HOUSE
RETURNS

ATTACHED TRIM
SEE DETAILS

6" REVEAL

7'-0"

STAIR
POSITION

3"

3'-0"

SILL IRON

2'-0"   4'-0"   2'-0"   1'-6"   5'-3"   3'-0"

8'-0"

HALL

8'-6"

RIGHT   WALL

7   8

LIP ON
HEADER

WALL   FIXTURES

2'-6"   2'-6"

PICTURE

6'-3"   6'-6"

12" REVEAL   4"

REVEAL

9'-6"

1'-0"   2'-3"   6"   2'-6

6" RISERS

12'-0"   2'-0"

BACK   WALL

LEFT

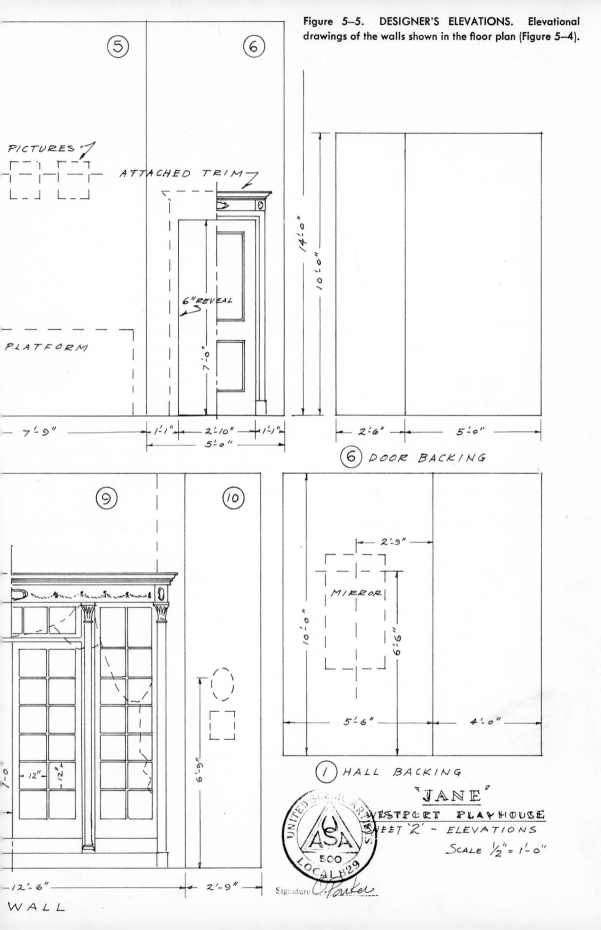

Figure 5–5. DESIGNER'S ELEVATIONS. Elevational drawings of the walls shown in the floor plan (Figure 5–4).

scenery is moving by truck, or not traveling at all, the maximum standard width can vary accordingly. The designer will do well, however, to keep in mind these technical considerations as he plans his scenery, for they are the limiting features that control the size and shape of his design.

APPLIED DETAIL. Designers vary in the amount of detail they show at ½-inch scale. Although the decorative trim and other details are better shown at a larger scale, it is sometimes wise to at least sketch a portion of the detail on the ½-inch elevations. It not only shows the trim in assembled view but also gives the carpenter some idea of any special construction that may be needed. Because of the light wood frame and canvas construction of scenery, pictures, valance boxes, or lighting fixtures can't be placed in the middle of a wall without providing extra structural support from behind. If the applied details are partially sketched in the elevation, or indicated with the dashed-line symbol of an adjacent part, the carpenter will know where to supply the additional construction (Figure 5–5).

Obviously, the labels of the elevation must agree with the labels of the corresponding units in the floor plan. The accuracy of cross-labeling is especially important when stock scenery is being used, for unless the set is extremely simple, it is the carpenter's only guide as to how the pieces assemble. On occasions, for clarification, a portion of a floor plan may be repeated near the elevation drawings of a complicated unit of scenery. If there is still a possibility of misunderstanding, a pictorial drawing can be included.

COMPOSITIONAL ELEVATIONS. Borrowing a trick from the interior decorator, the scene designer sometimes uses a compositional elevation. It is most useful on an interior setting, for it is an assembled view of each wall with all the set dressings related to that wall in place. Jogs or breaks in the wall are not flattened out but are shown in position. In this manner, the scene designer can study the composition of the furniture, pictures, and window draperies at small scale.

A compositional elevation is usually drawn at ¼-inch scale, or smaller. If it is drawn on graph paper, the necessity of using dimensions is eliminated as sizes and proportions can be calculated by counting the squares (Figure 5–6b).

It can be seen that the compositional elevations are in no way a working drawing for the carpenter. They are of value to the designer himself as an aid in making decisions on furniture and picture sizes during the hectic stages of collecting properties.

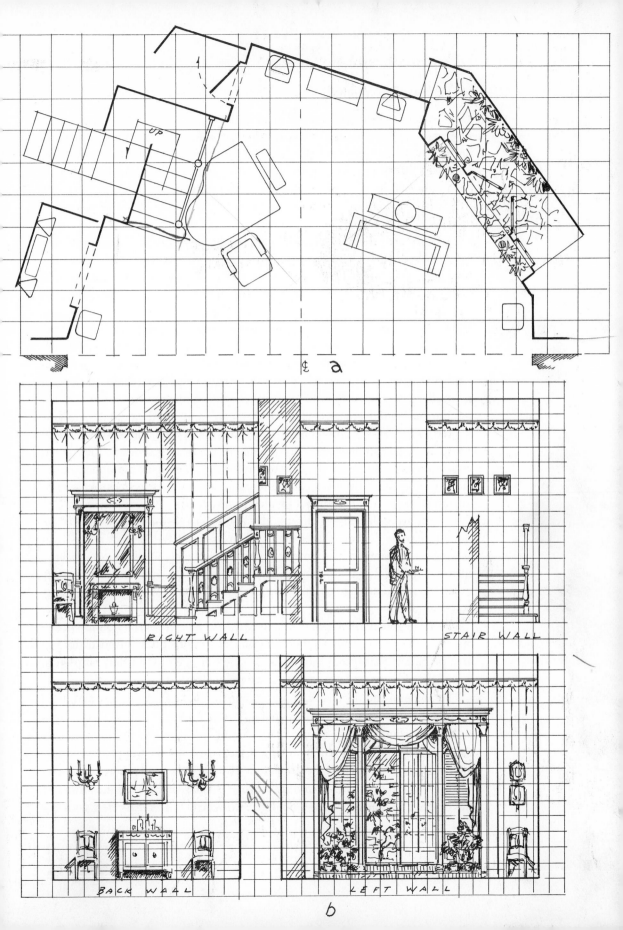

a

RIGHT WALL

STAIR WALL

BACK WALL

LEFT WALL

b

PICTORIAL DRAWINGS

The designer's sketch is a type of pictorial drawing, but because of the fore-shortening it can't be used as a working drawing. By imagining a pictorial drawing with the edges of the receding surfaces not converging and sides not foreshortened, a type of drawing is represented that can be drawn to scale and used as a supplementary view to the working drawings. The lack of perspective makes it possible to draw to scale, although the view may have a distorted mechanical appearance.

The two basic kinds of pictorials are the isometric and oblique drawings. Their difference is dependent upon the angle of the view. The isometric drawing represents an object seen from one corner and slightly above (Figure 5–7a). An oblique drawing shows the object as seen opposite one face with the side angled off to the right or left (Figure 5–7c).

The term, isometric, meaning equal measure as compared to the fore-shortened distances or unequal measure of perspective, accurately describes its appearance. An isometric drawing has three axes to represent the principal planes of the object. The first is a vertical line to indicate all the up-right edges; second, a slanted line to the right, 30 degrees to the horizontal, for the horizontal edges of the right plane, and third, a 30-degree line slanted to the left to represent the horizontal edges of the planes to the left. These lines, and all lines parallel to them, are known as isometric lines. Conversely, lines that are not parallel to any of the three axes are nonisometric lines. Heights and distances can be measured on isometric lines but a non-isometric line cannot be drawn to scale (Figure 5–8).

Because irregular edges, curves, and angles are distorted in an isometric view, it may be desirable to change the direction of the view to show them at a better advantage. By moving around the object until the complicated surface is parallel to the plane of the paper, or frontal position, it is possible to see the irregular edge or curve without distortion. A view from this direction is an oblique drawing.

The same general pictorial characteristics are present in the oblique drawing as in the isometric with the exception of a more pronounced distortion in appearance. Because of the frontal position of one of the principal planes, two of the oblique axes are at right angles to each other.

The angle of the third axis, representing the plane of the sides, may vary from 30 to 45 degrees to the horizontal. It can be drawn either to the right or left, and slanted either up or down (Figure 5–9). By placing the side that contains the irregular outlines, angles, or curves in the frontal position drafting time can be saved and the appearance of the view made more attractive.

To reduce the distortion and improve the looks of the oblique drawing, the draftsman sometimes uses a cabinet drawing. It is constructed with the

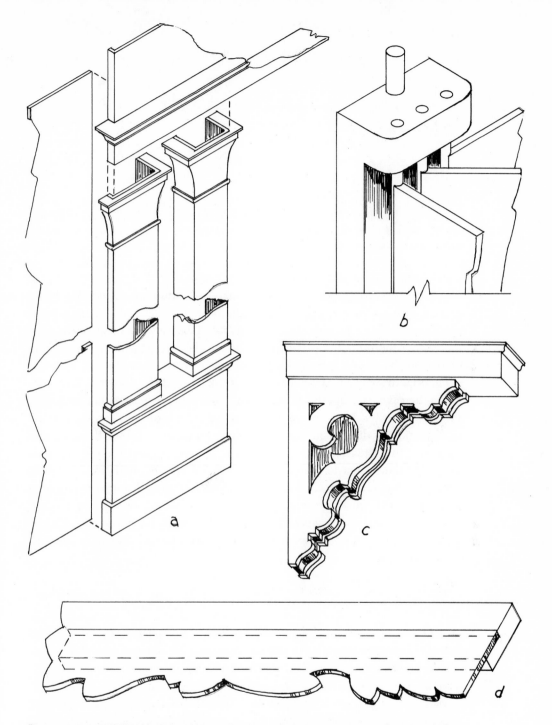

Figure 5–7. PICTORIAL DRAWINGS.   (a) An exploded isometric drawing to show how
certain pieces of scenery fit together. (b) Isometric drawing used to explain a complicated
pivoting movement. (c) An oblique drawing of a decorative bracket. (d) An Isometric
drawing using a horizontal axis instead of the usual vertical axis.

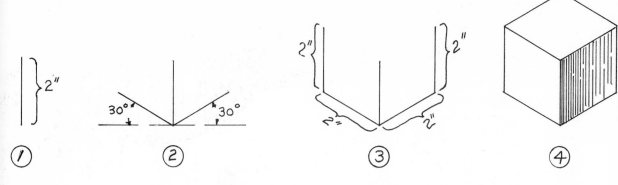

Figure 5–8. CONSTRUCTION OF THE ISOMETRIC DRAWING. The object is a two-inch cube. (1) Vertical axis, the nearest corner of the cube. (2) Slanted axes, right and left. (3) Slanted lines and uprights drawn to scale. (4) The completed isometric drawing of the cube.

complicated face parallel to the picture plane—like the oblique—but distances measured parallel to the angled axis are reduced in scale. A ratio of two to three, or three to four between the frontal planes and the angled axis produces a pleasing proportion. By always labeling the cabinet drawing and giving the ratio of the measurements on the angled axis, the possibility of it being mistaken for an oblique drawing is avoided (Figure 5–9[4]).

Pictorial drawings may be dimensioned like a working drawing. The technique, however, is slightly different. Instead of being perpendicular to the surface, the extension lines are drawn as extensions of one of the isometric planes, and the dimension line is parallel to the object rather than perpendicular to the extension line. To help give the feeling that the dimension is in one of the isometric planes, the figures are slanted with the extension lines. If the object is not too complicated a dimensioned pictorial drawing can be used as a working drawing.

Besides their use as a working drawing, pictorials are frequently used as a supplementary view to explain a bit of complicated assembly, or mechanical detail.

Figure 5–9. CONSTRUCTION OF THE OBLIQUE DRAWING. (1) The principal face with slant line drawn to right, or left. All the lines are drawn to a scale. (2) The completed oblique drawing. (3) An oblique drawing of a circular disk. The center of the circle of the thickness is set to the right on an oblique line. (4) A cabinet drawing. All slanted lines are drawn at a reduced scale to minimize the distorted look of a regular oblique drawing.

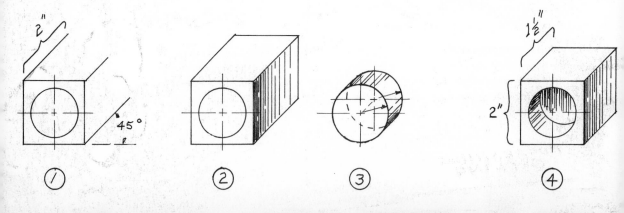

TECHNICAL PLANNING

The designer is normally not concerned with the details of technical planning. If the scenery, however, is going to be built with unskilled hands, as is the case in most community and university theatres, the designer finds himself the chief guardian of construction. Unless he wants to be tied up to shop supervision at the time when he is busiest selecting properties, designing the lighting and countless details, it pays to make a set of construction drawings.

The simplest way to lay out the framed construction of scenery is to use rear elevations. A view from this direction looks at the scenery as it appears under construction in the shop. A rear elevation shows the framing and profiling, explains the assembly, locates the hinges, and indicates bracing and stiffening. The detail and completeness of the rear elevations can be gauged by the aptitude of the shop help. An experienced carpenter might need a construction drawing for the occasional unusual piece of scenery while inexperienced help would need every piece of scenery detailed (Figure 5–10).

The construction of three-dimensional pieces, such as fireplaces, doors, steps, and rocks are not clearly explained in a rear elevation. How they are built can be shown by combining sectional views with designer's front and side elevations. The sectional view not only shows the internal structure but helps to explain the contour of the object. Irregular forms, of course, may require many sections. Very special shapes or profiles many times are drawn at full scale to serve as a pattern.

THE HANGING SECTION AND PLAN.   The hanging section, mentioned earlier, is another important part of the technical planning. It becomes a very necessary drawing to the designer in planning a multiscene production, or heavy hanging show. The designer soon discovers that the flying space is filled very quickly with lighting equipment, traveler tracks, masking curtains, and the like. To avoid a hopeless tangle in the flies, the hanging plot of a heavy show is carefully studied first in plan and section.

The hanging section, which is a sectional view taken vertically through the stage on the center line, is not a working drawing in itself. It provides information that can be used in the floor plan and elevations as working drawings. Besides taking the guesswork out of vertical masking by checking the extreme vertical sightlines, the hanging section gives an accurate picture of floor space problems. It shows the up- and downstage space requirements more clearly than the floor plan which becomes the working drawing.

If the show is extremely heavy it may require a separate hanging plan to indicate the disposition of all the scenery that is to be flown. To keep the plan from becoming confusing, most of the scenery on the floor is not shown. The hanging plan may be very general and schematic, or quite detailed, depending on the proportion of the rigging, the theatre, and the type of show. For a wing and backdrop type of production, for example, it is little more than a listing of drops in the order they will hang and the numbering of the act and scene in which they will work. A more complicated hanging plan would indicate the exact positions of spot lines and extra rigging.

Recent engineering developments in a more flexible flying system and gridiron design than the existing pin and rail and counterweight methods indicate a time in the future when the hanging plan will be a required drawing for every show.

PLANNING OF PROPERTIES

The designer is responsible for the selection of properties, for the design of specially built pieces of furniture, and for the furniture plot or general arrangement of properties in the setting.

In planning the properties, the designer's chief concern is to correlate the needs of the director with his own ideas. A meeting of minds can be achieved easily if the designer can show by sketches, clippings, or photographs what he plans and indicate in a scale furniture plot the size and position of set properties as they appear in the setting plan.

The furniture plot is a schematic plan locating the position of the set properties in each scene. It is generally drawn at ¼-inch scale with all furniture in position. The furniture plot is not dimensioned unless there is need to call attention to a certain measurement. It is drawn on a grid of one-foot or two-foot squares, so anyone can figure distances by counting squares. Such a plan is useful to the director and stage manager for laying out rehearsal space and studying the staging. It is valuable to the property man as a visual reference list of his set props. And the designer will find he can use it in planning the lighting of the production (Figure 5–6a).

The floor plan of a television show is handled in essentially the same way. It is drawn at ¼-inch scale over a grid of 1-foot squares showing the set props in place as well as noting and numbering each piece of scenery.

The construction of a special prop, like any three-dimensional piece of scenery, would require some sort of working drawing. The usual plan, front and side views, can be used or, if the piece is not too complicated, a

Figure 5–10.   REAR ELEVATIONS.   Detailed construction drawings show the framing of each piece of scenery and indicate how each is assembled. Note the use of vertical and horizontal sections as assembled views.

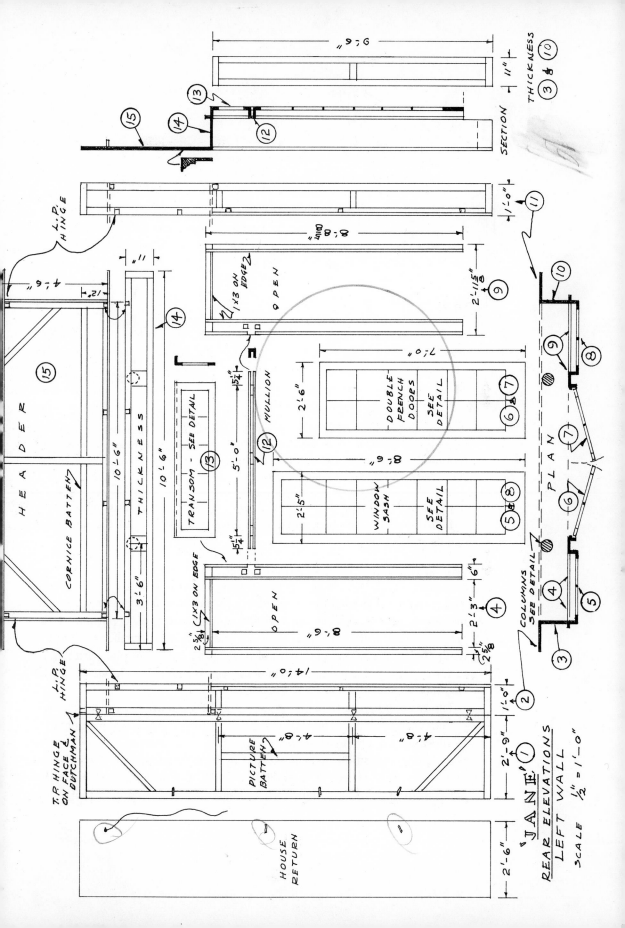

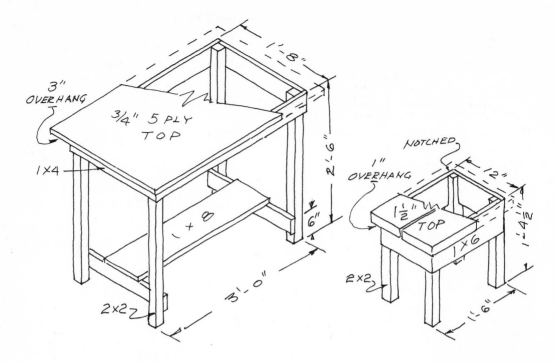

Figure 5–11. FREE-HAND PICTORIAL DRAWINGS. Dimensioned free-hand isometric drawings of simple furniture. If an object is simple in form, a pictorial drawing with dimensions can serve as a working drawing. There is enough information provided in this type of drawing to allow the carpenter to begin building immediately. A more complicated object would need additional views.

dimensioned pictorial drawing will serve as a working drawing (Figure 5–11). Again, the designer will find it wise to study out all the important details at full scale.

THE PLANNING OF LIGHTING

The planning of the lighting is set down in the form of a lighting plot and instrument schedule. They are mentioned here chiefly as a portion of the graphics of presentation expected of a scene designer to further explain the design of a setting. The mechanics of developing a lighting plot with regard to instrument performance and dimming control are fully discussed in the Lighting section, Chapter 20.

The basic design of the lighting, or "ideal," is established in the designer's sketch (Chapter 4, pages 60–61). The action of the play is frozen momentarily to illustrate the atmosphere and composition of a dramatic moment. Any change of composition by a movement of lights is often shown in a series of sketches. It is, of course, impossible to make an atmospheric sketch without considering the light sources. The beginning of the lighting plot, then, is in the designer's sketch. But, like the carpenter, the electrician needs more than a pretty sketch before he can start to hang lighting instruments.

The lighting plot is comparable to the working drawing which expresses the design of the set in terms of feet and inches, materials, and shows how it works. The plot translates the designer's ideas of atmosphere, composition, and color into lighting areas, types of instruments; designates their position, use, and color medium.

The lighting plot is usually drawn on a ¼-inch scale floor plan showing the set props in position, as in the furniture plot. The plan is divided into acting areas, and symbols of instruments are drawn in their approximate hanging position. They are assigned to light a certain area. The division and number of areas may be arbitrary to cover the entire acting area systematically or may be motivated by the action and mood of the play.

Because the lighting plot is so schematic, most of the specific information is presented on an accompanying instrument schedule. The combined lighting plot and instrument schedule tell the electrician the number and type of instrument, the wattage, color, use and hanging position.

PART 2

EXECUTING

THE DESIGN

6

SCENE DESIGN AND
TECHNICAL PRODUCTION

Before the ideas of the designer can reach the stage, his designs, in the form of working drawings, have to go through a preparation or construction period. The scaled model is transformed into full-scale elements of scenery, the graded wash in the sketch becomes a carefully painted backdrop, the insignificant spot on the elevation is fashioned into a pointed bit of detail, and so on, moving towards the moment when all the scenery is fitted together on the stage under lights and in final form.

Although the study of technical production is placed here in the logical order of the development of a stage setting, it also, paradoxically, represents knowledge a scene designer should possess before beginning to design in the theatre. For this reason a study of technical production is a necessary part of a scene designer's training and background. As the architect is familiar with building techniques and materials, so should the scene designer be acquainted with methods of constructing and handling scenery as well as the uses of theatrical materials and techniques. A logical place to begin is with a survey of the tools and materials that are used to make scenery and an examination of the working procedures of a scenery shop.

THE SCENERY SHOP

Scenery is frequently built and painted under the adverse condition of an inadequate shop. The designer soon learns that an ill-equipped shop with sparse working space places a limit on the kind and amount of scenery that can be built and painted. Occasionally he finds himself in the enviable position of being able to plan his own shop, or at least asked to specify the space requirements of the ideal scenery shop. In preparation for such an occasion the designer should have some knowledge of the space requirements and layout of a good scenery shop.

SPACE REQUIREMENTS.　The over-all area of a scenery shop depends upon four things: the size of the stage the shop is to serve, the location of the shop in relation to the stage and storage areas, the number and kinds of

Figure 6–1.　SCENERY SHOP LAYOUT.　A bird's-eye view of a scenery shop for a community or university theatre. Although housed in a separate wing to isolate operational noises, it is, at the same time, attached to the left side of the stage it serves. (S) Stage—left side. (A) Assembly area—serves three functions: (a) Provides an area equal to the playing area of the stage for trial assembly of part or all of the setting. (b) Becomes space to store the offstage wagon of a transverse-wagon scheme for moving scenery. (c) Also serves as a painting area; the last stage of scenery construction before moving it onto the stage. The split paint frame (top) often can be used as two separately operated small frames or be locked together as a single large frame. The available floor space can be used for horizontal painting and full-scale lofting. Although the assembly is closed off from the stage by a pair of sound-deadening doors, the work in this area still has to be essentially quiet work, such as painting and lofting, when the stage is in use. (C) Construction area—where the cutting and working of materials as well as small-unit assembly takes place. This area is further isolated from the stage by sound-deadening doors. (T) Technician's or shopman's office. (B) Balcony over a portion of the shop—provides extra storage space for materials and supplies. Could also have long cutting table and sewing machine for making stage draperies. (M) Metal-working area—removes welding and metal-working tools from main shop area. (P) Property shop —area for building, rebuilding, upholstering, and finishing furniture and special properties. (D) Drafting room above metal and property shop on the same level as the balcony. (1) Space between shop building and stage house to reduce the amount of structure-borne sound. (2) Vertical painting area with movable palette table. (3) Paint supplies, sink, and burners. (4) Storage bins for scenery waiting to be painted or to be assembled after painting. (5) Drop storage racks on this wall above doors. (6) Lift—serves basement scenery and property storage rooms and balcony storage above. (7) Movable template tables which can be used together or separately. Space beneath top can serve as storage space for plywood and upson board. (8) Lumber storage racks and pullover saw tables. (9) Small tool and hardware storage. (10) Power tools in woodworking area under the balcony. (11) Canvas and muslin storage.

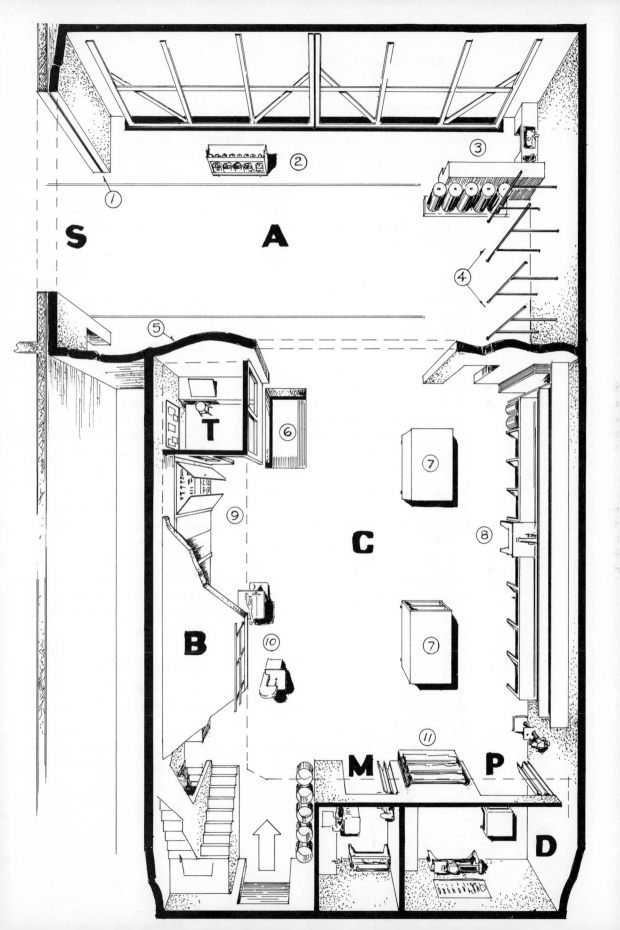

productions to be produced in an average season, and the nature of the shop's working procedure and personnel.

The size of the stage, or, in some cases, several stages, which the shop is to serve, has a direct bearing on the size of the shop itself. A large stage requires large elements of scenery. A shop serving a large stage, of course, needs the space to execute the expansive proportions of such scenery. In a similar manner, the large amounts of scenery necessary to supply more than one stage would influence the size of the shop. Although the scale of the scenery might be smaller, a shop serving several stages would have to be arranged to handle quantities of scenery.

The location of the scenery shop also affects its size. For example, a shop near the stage could utilize stage space for the construction of scenery and thereby supplement the shop area. On the other hand, a shop in a remote location needs additional space for the storage of scenery and properties as well as the necessary construction and painting areas. Although a distant shop has the disadvantage of causing the additional handling of scenery from the shop to the stage and back again, it does have the decided advantage of being able to operate free of preperformance uses of the stage. A shop adjacent to the stage is doomed to conflict with rehearsals and performances which render it inoperative a major portion of the time.

Besides the size of the stage and location of the shop, it is apparent that the number and kinds of productions also help to determine the space requirements of a scenery shop. A repertory company, for example, would require enormous storage space to retain the scenery of numerous productions intact, while perhaps only building one or two new productions a year. An opera or musical comedy production group would have a greater demand for scenery than a season of more intimately scaled productions, and so on.

The final consideration that has some prevalence on the over-all size of the shop is the shop procedure and personnel. The nature of the shop's personnel and working hours may vary from a staff of full-time professionals to scattered groups of part-time student apprentices or volunteers. A small highly skilled staff working steadily can use building space more efficiently than large sporadic groups requiring sufficient area to do many separate jobs at once to fully utilize the workers' time. A further evaluation of the space requirements resulting from shop procedure includes an analysis of the areas of work, tools and equipment, and materials of the average scenery shop.

AREAS OF WORK.   The shop is divided into areas related to the various steps in the process of building and painting. Organization is: (1) storage of materials and tools, (2) the cutting and working of lumber (boring, planing, and so on), (3) the framing and covering of basic units of scenery, (4) the trial assembly of basic units into portions or all of the complete setting, (5) the painting of scenery and properties, (6) the building of properties which although listed last would be in process along with scenery construction.

(1) The first necessary space in a scenery shop is for the storage of materials and tools. This means lumber racks, paint bins, and hardware cabinets located near their area of use yet convenient to the loading door. Provisions must also be made for the storage of brushes near the painting area and for small tools near the woodworking area.

(2) The second area, related to the next step in building scenery, is the woodworking area. Here the lumber is cut and worked (bored, planed, jig-sawed, and so on). Convenient to this area is the lumber supply, hardware storage, and the hand tools. Within the area there should be space for the large power tools such as table saws, band saws, drill presses, and the neces-sary work benches for working wood.

Careful consideration should be given to the lighting of the woodworking area and the other work areas, as well as the placing of power outlets con-venient to the working position of the power tools associated with each area.

(3 and 4) The third space is the assembly area, which ideally should be as large as the playing area of the stage to allow a trial assembly of the setting. The space can also be used for the framing and canvassing of basic units of scenery. Regular-shaped flats are framed and canvassed on a tem-plate bench (Figure 6–2), while irregular-shaped units are laid out or

Figure 6–2. TEMPLATE BENCH. The type shown is adaptable to a shop with limited working space where the same area may be needed for other operations. The template is a waist-high work bench with movable planks in the center (1) to provide support for framing the various widths of regular-shaped flats. The casters on one side (2) enable it to be tipped onto that side and pushed out of the way for storage. The casters on the base (3) provide easy movement when the bench is in working position. Although not equipped with built-in square corners and clinch plates, the template can also be used for such tasks as saber-saw cutting and small assembly work.

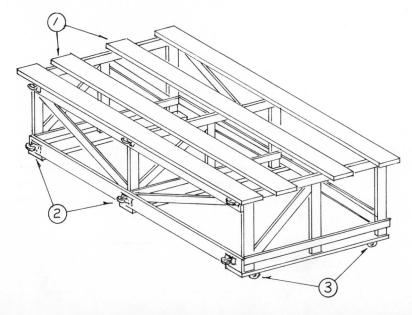

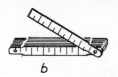 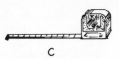

a

b

c

"lofted" and then assembled on the floor. The assembly area can also serve as a temporary storage space for completed scenery waiting to be "loaded out."

(5) The painting area is another important space in the shop. It should be convenient to a sink, gas or electric burners, and the paint bins. Vertical painting, which occupies the least amount of floor space, requires overhead clearance, or sufficient height to stand the scenery upright. The simplest vertical painting method is to mount the scenery on a fixed frame against a wall and paint from a rolling platform or "boomerang." The most convenient method is the use of a counterweighted vertical paint frame which lowers into a well, or raises off the floor. The painting is done from different levels or "decks" (see Methods of Painting, Chapter 8).

A more precarious method is to raise and lower a painting scaffolding in front of a fixed frame. Besides being laborious and dangerous, the scaffolding has the added inconvenience of usually being some distance from a sink, burner, and paint supplies.

With even the best equipment for vertical painting, it is sometimes necessary to paint horizontally on the floor. Certain painting techniques require horizontal painting. The floor of the assembly area, or stage floor, often serves this purpose if it can be worked into the production schedule.

(6) The most frequently neglected area, in shop planning, is a space to build properties. The altering, repairing, upholstering, and finishing of furniture is a specialized operation which requires different tools, materials, and paints than those found in the scenery shop. A property shop does not need a lot of space. It should, however, be an area near but separated from the dust and confusion of the scenery shop and the splatter of flying paint from the painting area.

d

TOOLS AND EQUIPMENT

The tools of a scenery shop are primarily for woodworking with limited provisions for the working of metal. To build scenery it is necessary to cut, pare or shape, bore and join the wood. The tools to work the wood are either hand tools for limited and special work, or power tools for mass production and precision work. The working and joining of wood, however, is always preceded by careful measuring and marking.

MEASURING AND MARKING TOOLS.   (Figure 6–3) Tools for measuring and marking are not only used with each technique of working wood but also in every step in the construction and assembly of the completed setting. Almost all mistakes in building are directly traceable to wrong measurements, or a misinterpreted mark. The importance of accurate measurements cannot be overstressed.

e

f

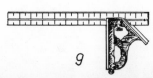

g

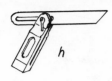

A list of the essential measuring and marking tools for a scenery shop should include (Figure 6–3 a-o):

Measuring	Marking
(a) Framing square	(h) Bevel gauge
(b) 6-ft. folding rule	(i) Scribe
(c) 6-ft., 8-ft., and 12-ft. steel tape	(j) Tri-square
(d) Marking gauge	(k) Spline or spring curve
(e) 50-ft. steel tape	(l) Trammel points and bar
(f) Protractor square	(m) Chalk line
(g) Combination square	(n) Centering square
	(o) Spirit level

Some of the tools are obviously for measuring only (6-foot rule and 50-foot tape) and others are made specifically for marking (Tri-square, bevel gauge, scribe, spirit level, spline and center square). There are, however, a few tools designed for both measuring and marking.

The *protractor square* is able to measure an angle in degrees and provide a marking guide.

The *combination square,* with its adjustable sliding bar, is calibrated for measuring as well as establishing a marking guide for the 90-degree and 45-degree angles.

The *framing square* with calibrated edges is a useful tool in marking the angle cut of a stair carriage, and for establishing a right angle for framing.

The *marking gauge* is calibrated to mark for a rip cut, an operation that can be duplicated by the combination square.

Within the group of marking tools, the *tri-square* is calibrated for limited measuring although its chief function is as a marking guide for a 90-degree angle cut. The *bar* or *beam* holding the trammel points is sometimes calibrated to measure the radius of the circle or arc it is to swing. The other tools in this group serve as marking guides only.

The *bevel gauge* is designed for transferring or saving a predetermined angle or bevel.

The *scribe* can follow an irregular surface with one point and scratch or mark the outline of the surface at a fixed distance with the other point.

The *spline and spring curve* are used to mark an irregular curve, or to plot a curved edge in full-scale lofting.

The *spirit level* establishes a true vertical or horizontal, and the *center square* locates the unmarked center of a circle or round stock.

The *chalk line* is for snapping an extremely long straight line that may be used as a framing guide, as a reference line for full-scale lofting, or as guide line for painting.

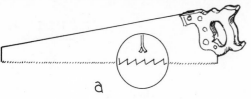

a

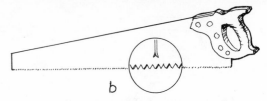

b

CUTTING TOOLS. (Figure 6–4 a-m.) The chief cutting tool is the saw. A list of saws for a scenery shop is as follows:

Hand Saws	*Power Saws*
(a) Ripsaw	(g) Saber saw
(b) Crosscut saw	(h) Pullover saw
(c) Keyhole saw	(i) Cut-awl
(d) Scroll saw	(j) Jigsaw
(e) Miter box and backsaw	(k) Skilsaw
(f) Hack saw	(l) Table saw
	(m) Band saw

The specific work a saw can do depends upon the shape of the tooth (pointed or chisel), the set of the tooth (flare of every other tooth in the opposite direction), and the tooth count (number of teeth per inch). Because wood has a grain, which is the alternating density of the fibers within its structure, it requires a different kind of saw to cut across the grain than to cut with the grain. The teeth of a crosscut saw are sharp and straight to cut through the wood fibers while the teeth of the ripsaw are angled and flat edged like a chisel to chip the wood with the grain. The ripsaw has the widest set and the lowest tooth count (6 to 8 teeth per inch). The crosscut saw has a tooth count of 8, 10, to 12 teeth per inch.

The ripsaw and crosscut saw are for straight-line cutting as is the hack saw, which is used to cut metal. A hack saw, with a tempered-steel blade of 18 tooth count, will cut strap iron, bolts, and pipe that are frequently used in scenery construction.

An angled cut or miter can be cut freehand with a crosscut saw, or it can be accurately cut in a miter box with a backsaw. The backsaw, with a high tooth count (10 to 12 teeth per inch) is a stiff-bladed saw with a straight back which serves as a guide in the miter box (Fig. 6–4 e). It is extremely useful in mitering moldings for a cornice, picture frame, or panel.

9

Power Saw. Power tools made for straight-line cutting are the table saw, pullover saw and Skilsaw. Each may be fitted with a rip or crosscut, or combination blade for specific work.

A 10-inch, tilting-arbor, 1-horsepower table saw, with miter gauge and rip fence is a basic piece of equipment. It is a heavy enough tool to do precision work in quantity. It miters and rips with ease and accuracy.

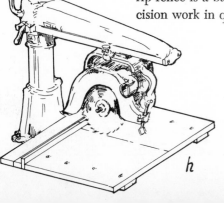

h

i

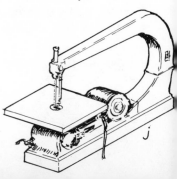

j

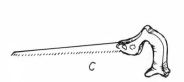

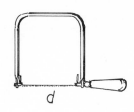

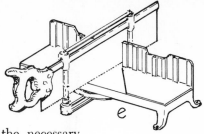

c

d

e

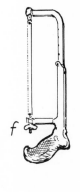

A 10- to 12-inch one-horsepower pullover saw provides the necessary power for cutting heavy lumber. Its pullover action above the wood and long table make it an accurate crosscut and limited mitering tool. Because the guide fence becomes inaccurate from repeated crosscutting, it is not a very accurate ripping tool.

The Skilsaw, which is a portable circular saw, is designed to be brought to the work rather than for bringing the work to the saw. It can be used to an advantage as a rip or crosscut saw on partially completed units of scenery. Because of its light weight and small blade it is limited as to depth of cut and accuracy. It is, however, a useful tool to have in a busy shop.

f

IRREGULAR CUTTING. Not all cutting in the making of scenery is straight-line cutting. As a matter of fact a high percentage of the cutting is irregular or "scroll" work. Cutouts and profile edges require the greatest amount of scroll work.

A hand saw to cut on an irregular line must necessarily have a small blade to be able to turn and follow the irregular line. The scroll saw has a high tooth count of 12 per inch to produce a smoothly cut edge. It has a removable blade for inside cuts. The deep throat of the frame that holds the blade allows the saw to reach well into the work.

The keyhole saw with a tooth count of 8 to 10 is made for heavy, coarse, and fast work. The small blade, although not as small as the scroll saw, allows irregular cutting beyond the limits a scroll saw can reach.

POWER TOOLS FOR IRREGULAR CUTTING. Power tools that speed up the production of scroll work are the band saw, jigsaw, saber saw, and cut-awl. The *band saw* with its continuous blade is limited to outside cutting and to work as large as the depth of its throat. A band saw with a 20-inch throat will serve the average need of a scenery shop if it is supplemented with other equipment to do inside cutting.

The *jigsaw* with its removable straight blade and deep throat is made for both inside and outside scroll cutting. The saber saw, which is a portable jigsaw, does not limit the size of the work. It is a very versatile tool for scroll cutting at any stage of assembly.

The *cut-awl*, which is designed for light, detailed cutting, works best on profile and composition board. It also requires a padded bench or table for satisfactory results.

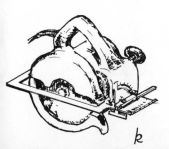

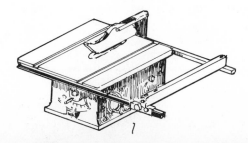

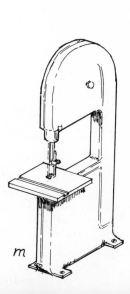

k

l

m

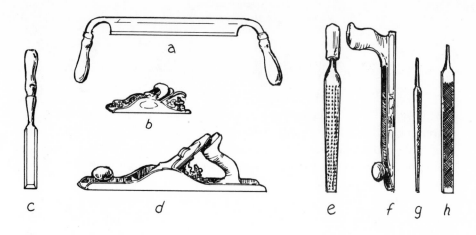

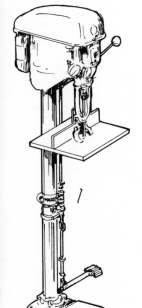

PARING TOOLS (Figure 6–5 a-o). Chisel or knifelike tools made to smooth or shape the wood are paring tools. A list of the most useful follows:

Hand Tools		Power Tools	
(a)	Drawknife	(i)	Rotary planer (joiner)
(b)	Block plane	(j)	Disk and belt sander
(c)	Chisel	(k)	Router
(d)	Smoothing plane	(l)	Mortise machine
(e)	Rasp	(m)	Rotary shaper
(f)	Rasp blade in holder	(n)	Emery wheel
		(o)	Lathe
(g)	Triangular metal file		
(h)	Flat metal file		

The simplest tool for freehand shaping of wood is the chisel. Although the hand chisel can not compare in speed and accuracy to power tools, it can be used to do a limited amount of shaping and notching of wood. It is an excellent tool to clean up a power-cut dado, rabbet, mortise or routed area. With skilled handling it can, if necessary, make any of these cuts itself. A set of chisels would include a variety of widths from ¼ inch to 1¼ inch.

The drawknife is not a precision tool. It is useful to pare away waste, or roughly shape a surface before planing.

The smoothing plane can pare a surface to an accurate dimension. It is

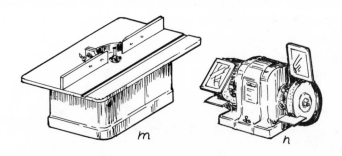

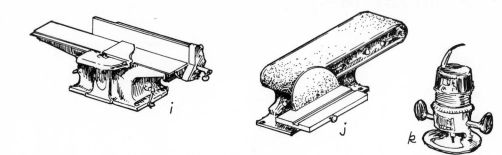

made to smooth with the grain of the wood while the small block plane is designed to work across the grain and to smooth or shape the end of a board.

The rasp is also used for cross-grain smoothing or shaping. Its sharp teeth tear the fibers so that unless a rough finish is desired the surface has to be smoothed with a fine rasp or sandpaper.

Power tools designed to do various shaping and smoothing operations are limited mostly to special cuts. The rotary planer or joiner, for example, can smooth a board, size a board by changing the depth of cut, bevel the edge by angling the fence, as well as cutting a rabbet on one side of the board.

Likewise the rotary shaper is designed especially to cut moldings. It can cut a variety of molding by changing or combining different blades.

The mortising machine, or mortising attachment for a drill press, with its square chisel, is limited to cutting the deep square hole of a mortise. It is a time-saving tool in a professional scenery shop where there is a lot of mortise and tenon joining.

Probably the most useful small power tool for shaping is the router. Besides routing to countersink hinges, it can cut tenons, dados, and rabbets. With special bits it can also do a limited amount of molding cutting.

Some of these shaping operations can be performed on the table and pullover saw. The circular table saw can be equipped with a dado head which is a set of special blades to cut a groove. Molding cutters can also be attached to the circular saw for simple molding cutting. The pullover saw can also be rigged to dado, shape, and rout. Any change over, of course, takes time and ties up the saw for other uses.

For finished smoothing, a power sander, both belt and disk, quickly and accurately smooths the end, edge, or face of a board. In this same category, the emery wheel is used to smooth and shape metal as well as sharpen hand tools.

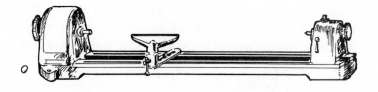

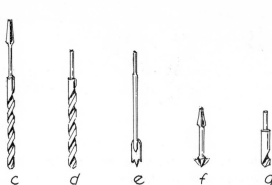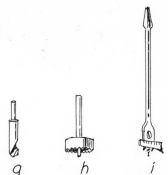

BORING TOOLS (Figure 6–6 a-m).   Tools with a cutting edge that revolves about a central axis to cut a circular hole are boring tools. The tool is comprised of two basic parts: the bit, which is the cutting part of the tool, and the brace or some similar mechanism to rotate the bit.

There is, of course, great variation in the types of bit depending upon the size and depth of hole, kind of hole (clean bore, taper, ream . . .), and the nature of the material (hardness, thickness . . .). Likewise the power-providing part of the tool will vary with type of bit used and the speed of rotation necessary to do the work. The types of bit and means of rotation found in the average scenery shop are:

Bits	*Rotating Tools*
(a) Auger bit (square shank)	(j) Brace
(b) Twist drill (round shank)	(k) Hand drill
(c) Twist drill (square shank)	(l) Power hand drill
(d) Twist drill (¼ in. round shank)	(m) Drill press
(e) Power bit (¼ in. round shank)	
(f) Countersink, wood	
(g) Countersink, metal	
(h) Hole cutter	
(i) Expansive bit	

The auger bit has a screw lead which, when rotated, pulls the cutting edges of the bit into contact with the wood. The auger bit does not need to rotate at a high speed. It is usually driven with the brace made to receive its square shank. The brace is a cranklike form designed to give the carpenter a mechanical advantage rather than to increase the speed of rotation. Augers are manufactured in size differences of one-sixteenth of an inch. They are numbered by sixteenths, thus a ½-inch auger would be a No. 8 bit.

Twist drills have no screw lead and depend upon speed of rotation and pressure to advance into the material. The hand drill is designed to increase the speed of rotation as well as provide some mechanical advantage. The high speed, portable, powered hand drill is excellent for this type of work.

The power bit is a wood-cutting bit made for high-speed rotation with a small round shank (¼ inch) for the small power drill.

Also in the auger-bit class are the gimlet and expansive bit. The gimlet is made to bore a small hole in an inaccessible place; and the expansive bit, which is adjustable, can bore a hole as large as 1¼ inch to 2½ inches in diameter.

The hole-cutter is made to cut oversized holes (1½ inch and up) at high speed. Although faster and cleaner than the expansive bit, it is limited in its depth of cut.

The drill press, which is a stationary power drill has the added advantages of such controls as depth of bore and speed variation for precision

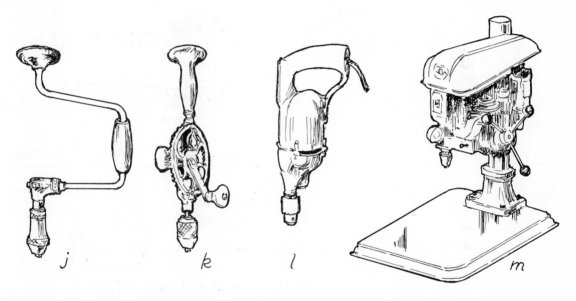

j   *k*   *l*   *m*

work. The drill press with a mortising attachment makes a very useful tool in the scenery shop (Figure 6–6 m).

WOOD-JOINING TOOLS. The joining of wood is the last stage of carpentry. The tools that are used are designed to drive or set the joining hardware (nails, screws, or staples) in such manner as to hold the pieces of wood together. The hammer and hammerlike tools (staple gun) drive a nail or staple; the screw driver sets a screw into wood; the wrench and pliers tighten a bolted joint; and the clamps hold a glued joint together until the glue has set.

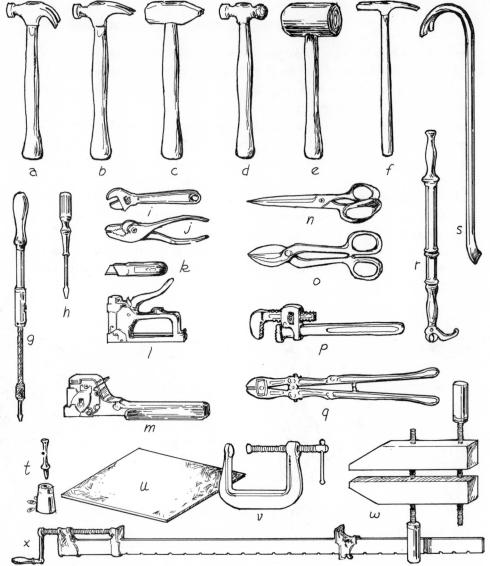

Wood Joining and Other Tools (Figure 6–7 a-x)

(a) Claw hammer

(b) Straight claw hammer

(c) Blacksmith's hand hammer

(d) Ball peen hammer

(e) Mallet

(f) Magnetic tack hammer

(g) Ratchet screw driver

(h) Screw driver

(i) Crescent wrench

(j) Pliers

(k) Mat knife

(l) Staple gun

(m) Staple hammer

(n) Scissors

(o) Tin shears

(p) Stillson wrench

(q) Bolt cutter

(r) Nail puller

(s) Pinch bar

(t) Grommet setting die

(u) Clinch plate

(v) C-clamp

(w) Jorgensen, hand screw clamp

(x) Bar clamp

The bolt cutter, tin shears, scissors, and mat knife are cutting tools that are used in the covering and assembly process of scenery construction.

MATERIALS

Although some materials will be mentioned relative to the construction of certain types of scenery, it may be wise to consider briefly all the materials that are used for making scenery. To compile a conclusive list is, of course, next to impossible, for designers and technicians are constantly bringing new materials into the theatre every day as well as discovering new uses for old materials.

Materials can be divided and classified into four groups of similar functions: (1) structural (lumber and metal), (2) cover stock (fabric and hard surfaces), (3) hardware (joining and stage hardware), (4) paints and related supplies.

STRUCTURAL MATERIALS.   Lumber is the principal framing and structural material, supplemented and reinforced on occasions by structural steel, pipe, and aluminum. As supplies and prices change, aluminum may become the framing material and wood the supplementary or decorative material. Until this is an actuality, lumber remains the chief structural element.

LUMBER.   To fill the needs of scenic construction, lumber must be lightweight, strong, straight, and inexpensive. The best combination of weight and strength is found in white pine. Although woods such as redwood and spruce are lighter, they do not have the strength and tend to splinter and split. The hard woods are stronger, of course, but weigh and cost too much.

Lumber is classified at the yard into quality groups. The straightness of grain and freedom from knots determine the quality. Hence, clear-white pine is of the highest quality. It is further classified as to its expected use. A board that is to become trim or a finished surface is of a higher quality than a structural member hidden from view.

The finishing lumber, or, "select" grades are designated by the letters A, B, C, and D. Hence B—select or better—is a high-grade pine. C-select is the usual quality of lumber used in professional scenery.

The "common" grades are numbered 1 to 5. They are not intended for a finished surface although many times 1 and 2-common are used as knotty-pine paneling. No. 2-common is the usual framing material for amateur scenery unless the theatre is in an area of the country where the better grades of pine are available at reasonable prices.

Lumber Sizes.   The stock sizes of lumber refer to the rough cut size and not to the finished dimension after the wood has been dressed (planed or smoothed on all sides). Thus 1 x 3 is really ¾" x 2⅝". The longest stock

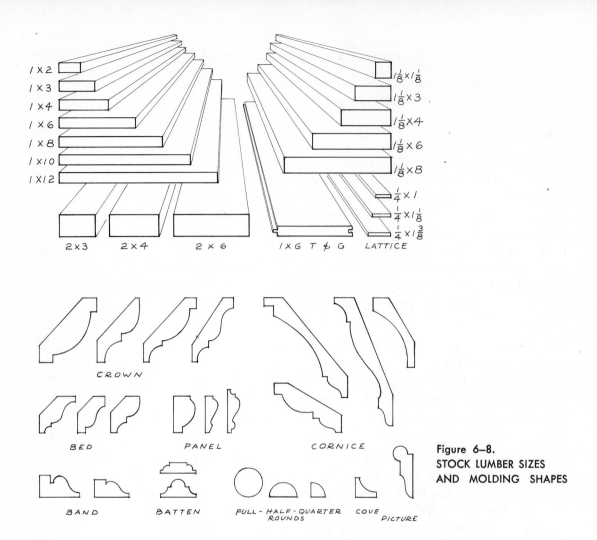

Figure 6-8.
STOCK LUMBER SIZES
AND MOLDING SHAPES

length is sixteen feet, although longer lengths can be obtained on special order.

Because lumber is cut in a variety of widths and thicknesses it has a unit of measurement, the board-foot, common to all sizes. A board-foot is a one-foot-square unit measuring one inch in thickness. A piece of lumber of any size can be reduced from its linear dimensions into board-feet. A 16-foot length of 1 x 3, for example, contains 4 board-feet. All lumber prices are based on the board-foot measurement.

Special shapes like "rounds" are stocked in diameter from ¾ inch to 1½ inch and sometimes as large as 3 inches in diameter. Dowel is available in ⅛- to 1-inch diameter and 3-foot lengths made of maple and birch.

Other special shapes are stock moldings which are made in a great variety of sizes and contours. A few of the most frequently used moldings are illustrated in Figure 6–8 along with the stock lumber sizes.

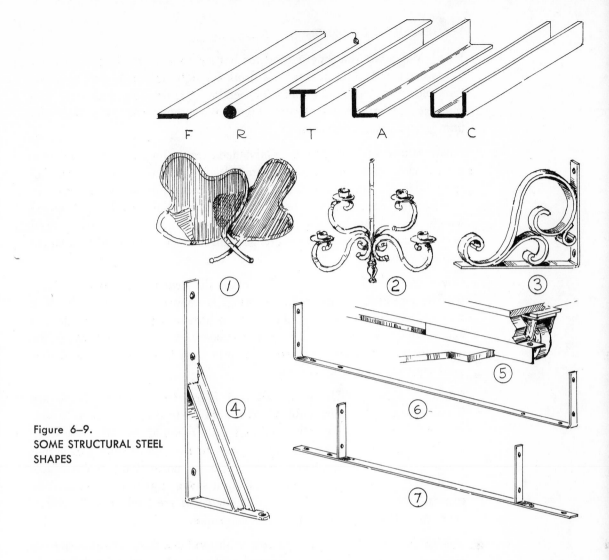

Figure 6–9.
SOME STRUCTURAL STEEL
SHAPES

Shown are a few of the basic lightweight structural steel shapes and their uses in scenery construction: (F) Flats or strap iron. (R) Rounds or rod. (T) Tees. (A) Angle. (C) Channel. DECORATIVE USES OF ROD AND STRAP IRON: (1) Stylized leaf forms. (2) Chandelier or candelabra shapes. (3) Decorative bracket. A FEW FAMILIAR USES OF STEEL IN SCENERY CONSTRUCTION: (4) Special jack or over-sized footiron. (5) "Knife" guide in the track of a guided wagon. (6) Sill iron used under door opening in a flat. (7) Saddle-shaped sill iron.

METAL. Structural steel has many special uses in scenery construction. The sizes and shapes in relation to their uses are illustrated in Figure 6–9.

Uni-strut and its fittings are a method of knockdown framing in special channel-shaped steel that is adaptable to platforming and trussing in the theatre. It eliminates the necessity of welding and cutting, and is available in different forms.

111

PIPE.   Malleable iron pipe is used for battens to support hanging scenery; as a weight or bottom batten for a drop; for lighting booms; and as structural elements. Pipe fitting and pipe bending increase the number of uses pipe can perform in the theatre. Figure 6–10 shows the stock sizes and fittings, and some of the uses.

SHEET METAL AND SCREENING.   Galvanized iron, aluminum, tin, and zinc are the most frequently used sheet metals. Light pans, shadow boxes and special effects are a few of the uses of sheet metal in scenery construction.

The metal screening such as hardware cloth (¼-inch mesh), galvanized screen (¹⁄₁₆-inch mesh) and chicken wire (1-inch mesh) are primarily used as structural materials. Occasionally, galvanized screening is used to simulate window glass.

COVER STOCK.   The material used to cover the structural frame of scenery, thereby providing a surface for painting, is known as "cover stock." The frame can be covered with a fabric or hard surface depending upon the use and handling of the particular piece of scenery. A translucent backing, for example, is framed and covered differently than is a section of wall that must support the weight of an actor.

COVERING FABRICS.   The usual covering fabrics for framed scenery are 8-ounce canvas duck and unbleached muslin (5 to 6 oz.). Muslin, as was mentioned, is more frequently used as a drop material than as cover stock for framed scenery. However, almost any fabric can become a covering material to serve as a special effect, or as an unusual painting surface. Burlap, velour, scrim, terry cloth, and even string rugs have been used as covering fabrics. The thin, translucent, materials are backed with canvas, of course, if the surface is supposed to be opaque.

HARD SURFACES.   If the surface has to withstand active handling during the action of a play, the frame is covered with a harder surface than canvas. The most frequently used hard-surface material is ⅛-inch plywood board called EZ curve or profile board. It is lightweight, but still strong enough to supply a hard surface with a minimum of framing. Tek board, ⅛-inch laminated wood and paper, is a close substitute for profile board although not quite as strong.

Other hard surface materials are: ⅛-inch, ³⁄₁₆-inch Upson Board, an inexpensive but weaker substitute for profile board made of laminated paper; ¼-inch fir 3 ply, a very sturdy but heavy board (also used for keystone and corner blocks); ½-inch Homosote, a paper-pulp board with very little strength but thick enough to be carved or textured; and ³⁄₁₆-inch Masonite, a very heavy, hard surface of compressed wood pulp. The tempered Masonite is an extremely hard surface that is occasionally used as a floor covering.

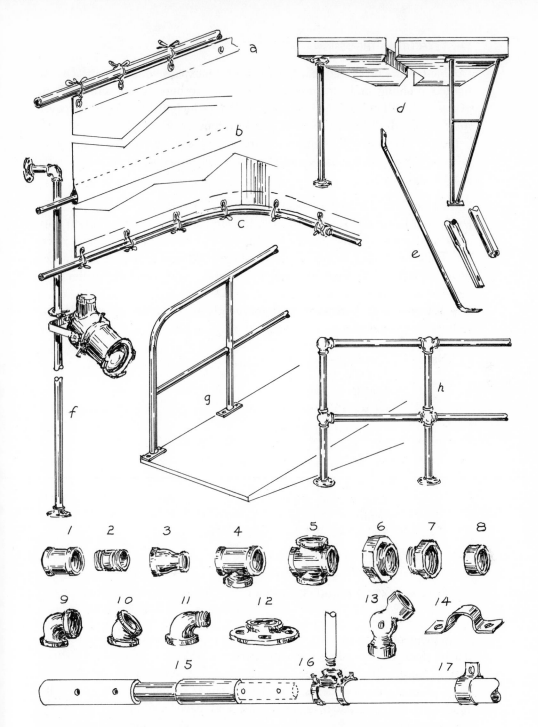

Figure 6–10.   VARIOUS USES OF IRON PIPE.   **(a)** Top batten for drop, cyc, or stage drapery. **(b)** Bottom batten for a drop in pipe sleeve. **(c)** Curved bottom batten using tie-lines. **(d)** Free-standing platform legs. **(e)** Special bracing. **(f)** Lighting booms and battens. **(g)** Bent pipe and welded railing. **(h)** Cut pipe and fitted railing. SOME OF THE SCREW FITTINGS USED TO JOIN SECTION OF PIPE: (1) Coupling. (2) Nipple. (3) Reducing coupling. (4) Tee. (5) Cross. (6) Union, ring end. (7) Union, screw end. (8) Cap. (9) 90-degree elbow. (10) 45-degree elbow. (11) Street ells. (12) Floor flange. (13) Adjustable elbow (railing fitting). (14) Pipe strap. (15) Batten inside sleeve splice. (16) Saddle tee, double strap. (17) Pipe hanger.

Double-faced corrugated cardboard is an inexpensive hard surface for limited profiling and covering providing the scenery is not subjected to excessive handling. Some shops also include ¾-inch, 1-inch 5 ply as cover stock, although its chief use is for platform tops.

Most of the cover-stock materials are available at the local lumber yard in stock 4′ x 8′ sheets. Occasional oversize sheets are stocked such as 5′ x 9′, 4′ x 10′ and 4′ x 12′.

HARDWARE.   In the scenery shop, hardware is divided into two categories: joining hardware and stage hardware. Joining hardware is an important part of normal scenery construction. It includes all the necessary nails, screws, and bolts for joining wood or metal. Stage hardware is a part of "knock-down" construction methods, stage assembly, and handling techniques peculiar to scenery.

A list of joining hardware most frequently used in the construction of scenery would include:

Nails:	Common— 8d, 10d
	Box—3d, 6d
	Finish—4d, 6d, 8d
	Clout—1¼″ (or 3d box nail)
Screws:	Flat head bright steel:
	No. 8—¾″, ⅞″, 1¼″
	No. 10—2″, 3″
Tacks and Staples:	
	Carpet—#6, #10
	Gimp—½″
	Staples—⅜″, ½″
Bolts:	3⁄16″ stove—2″, 3″
	⅜″ carriage—3″, 4″, 6″
Washers:	¼″ ID (Inside Diameter)
	7⁄16″ ID

Supplementary to this list are many special items which might or might not be stocked, depending upon the personal whims of the shop carpenter and his construction techniques. Such items as lag screws and machine bolts are sometimes used under special conditions. Corrugated fasteners, wire brads and nails, screw eyes, eye bolts, and decorative-headed tacks are often needed.

STAGE HARDWARE.   The necessary portability of scenery leads to the use of many pieces of hardware made especially for the stage. Most of it is designed to brace, stiffen, and temporarily join units of scenery as well as

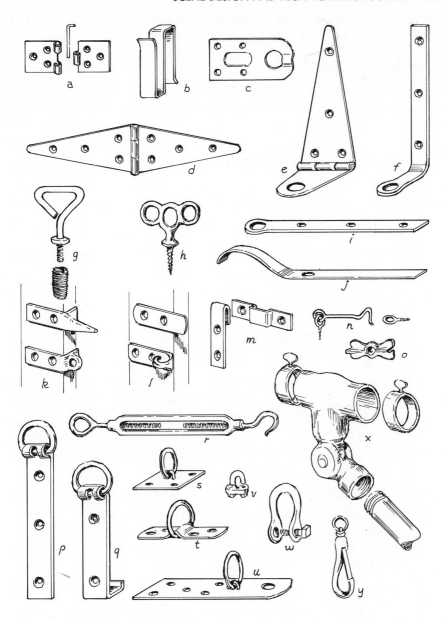

Figure 6–11.   STAGE HARDWARE. (a) Loose-pin back-flap hinge. (b) Batten hook. (c) Brace cleat. (d) Strap hinge. (e) Hinged footiron. (f) Bent footiron. (g) Stage screw and plug. (h) Stage screw. (i) Straight footiron. (j) Floor stay. (k) Lash cleat and lash eye. (l) Stop cleat and lash hook. (m) Picture-frame hanger. (n) Hook and eye. (o) Turn button. (p) Hanger iron, straight. (q) Hanger iron, hooked. (r) Turnbuckle. (s) Square plate and ring. (t) Oblong plate and D-ring. (u) Ceiling plate. (v) Cable clamp. (w) Shakle bolt. (x) Cyc knuckle. (y) Swivel-eye snap hook.

provide rigging hardware for the flying of scenery (Figure 6–11). A list of essential stage hardware would be:

Stiffening : Batten hooks
Loose-pin hinge (back flap)

Bracing : Footirons (straight, bent, and hinged)
Stage brace
Stage peg
Stage screw and plug
Brace cleat

Joining : Lash cleat and eye
Stop cleat
Loose-pin hinge (strap, butt, and back flap)
Hook and eye

Rigging : Hanger irons (straight and hooked)
Ceiling plate
Wire clamps
Rope clamps
Shackle bolts
Turn buckles

ROPE, CABLE, AND CHAINS.   Pertaining to rigging and joining of scenery are some specific types of rope, chain, and cable. A listing of their specification and uses on the stage is as follows:

Rope used in the theatre is of two general types: cotton braid or stranded manila. The cotton braided rope is softer (easier to handle), more flexible, but of course not as strong as the stranded manila rope.

Rope (*cotton braid*). No. 8 Sash cord is used as lash line, lightweight rigging, and as an occasional drawline on a lightweight traveler.

No. 10 Braided rope—drawline for heavy traveler track.

⅛″ Awning cord—lightweight curtain rigging and "trick line" to trigger a mechanical effect from an offstage position.

Manila rope.

¾″ three-strand manilas—purchase line of counterweight system (see Chapter 7) and heavy rigging line.

½″, ⅝″ manila—Lightweight rigging, breasting, and bridling.

Wire rope or cable is used to hang scenery when the supporting wires will be in view. The wire rope is very strong for its small diameter and can inconspicuously support a fairly large unit of scenery. The types of wire rope used most frequently in the theatre are: airplane strand, tiller rope, and hoisting rope.

Airplane strand:

1/32-, 1/16-, 1/8-inch—Nearly invisible at a distance, very strong for size, flexible but expensive.

Tiller Rope: (6 x 42)

1/8-in. (smallest diameter) strong, flexible and less expensive.

Hoisting Rope: (6 x 19)

1/4"-in. (smallest diameter) extremely strong, less flexible and not too expensive for its weight.

Chain, outside of instances of special rigging, is used primarily as weight for stage draperies.

Jack chain:

1/2-, 3/4-in. (single or double) curtain weight.

7

THE CONSTRUCTION
OF SCENERY

The scene designer is interested in the construction of scenery not only to become familiar with building techniques but also to become aware of the uses of various materials and their limitations. The more he knows about present-day theatrical materials and techniques the better able he is to introduce new materials and original methods into his designs as well as develop a knowledgeable use of contemporary types of scenery.

TYPES OF SCENERY

Scenery construction may seem at first glance to be unduly flimsy and unnecessarily complicated. This is due, chiefly, to the unique demands placed upon scenery by the theatre. The demands are: first, that it be portable and lightweight in structure so as to move easily on the stage and from theatre to theatre; second, scenery has to be able to assume large-scale proportions for either decorative or masking reasons, therefore large areas of scenery

118

must be furnished with the minimum of structure and the maximum of portability; and last, because scenery is here today and gone tomorrow, its construction must be economical. To be economical does not necessarily apply to the buying of the cheapest materials. It is the balancing of costs against the weight and structural demands of a material. It also means the economical use of scenery. Higher material costs can be afforded if a scenic element has more than one use, or can be reused at a later date.

For the purpose of discussing construction techniques, the various types of scenery are divided into groups which are similar in construction and alike in function as well as related in handling methods. Scenery is broadly divided first, into two general classifications: two-dimensional and three-dimensional scenery.

Two-dimensional scenery, under this broad division, is meant to include all flat scenery with reference to its basic shape rather than to the way it is used on the stage. Although units of flat scenery, for example, may be assembled together to make a three-dimensional form on the stage, the individual pieces are still classified as two-dimensional scenery.

Two-dimensional scenery is further subdivided into two groups: framed and unframed, or "soft," scenery. Within these two groupings falls the bulk of the scenery that is used on the stage either in the form of stage draperies and drops or wings and flats.

Three-dimensional scenery obviously refers to the pieces that are built in three dimensions to be handled and used as solid forms. Some three-dimensional units, particularly platforms, knock down into smaller, nearly flat, pieces for ease of handling, but, because of their weight and use, they are still classified as three-dimensional scenery.

Three-dimensional scenery is also separated into two basic groups: weight-bearing solids, meaning the weight of the actor, and nonweight-bearing forms. Steps and platforms are examples of weight-bearing scenery as compared to such nonweight-bearing examples as tree trunks, logs, and the like.

SOFT-SCENERY CONSTRUCTION

Numbered under soft scenery are such large unframed pieces as stage draperies, the drop, and the cyclorama, or "cyc." They all have the same function, to provide a large area of scenery with a minimum of construction and a maximum of portability. Being soft, they are dependent upon hanging from a batten or pipe for support. As a result they can be easily folded or rolled for transportation or storage.

STAGE DRAPERIES. The large panels of stage draperies are made by combining small widths of materials sewn together with vertical seams. There are three sound reasons for using vertical seams. First, because the direction of the weave or decoration is with the length of the fabric, it hangs and looks better in a vertical position. Second, a vertical seam is less conspicuous as it is lost in the folds of the drapery. Third, there is less strain on a vertical than on a horizontal seam which carries the accumulative weight of each width of material from the bottom seam to the top.

The seams are face to face to present a smooth front surface. The top is reinforced with a 3- to 4-inch webbing through which are set the grommet rings at 1-foot intervals for the tie-lines. The bottom has a generous hem containing a chain which functions as a weight for the curtain. Occasionally, the chain is encased in a separate sound-deadening pocket which is sewn on the backside of the drapery instead of being enclosed directly in the hem.

Drapery fabrics may be sewn on the top webbing, or may be gathered or pleated onto the webbing to give a fixed fullness to the curtain. Fixed fullness is an advantage for a front curtain or traveler curtain. However, it is not as flexible as a flat curtain panel, as the latter can be hung either flat or with varying degrees of fullness in a greater variety of uses (Figure 7–1).

DRAPERY MATERIALS. Stage draperies can be made of a variety of fabrics depending upon the specific use they are to perform and the limitations of the budget. Are the draperies to be opaque, translucent, or transparent? Are they to be pictorial, decorative, or just masking? Are they to be stock draperies or a one-shot special effect? Answering such questions as these helps to decide the kind of material to choose in relationship to its cost and use.

Velour, although expensive, is the favored drapery material. Its pile weave has a rich texture under the stage lights that cannot be duplicated with cheaper substitutes. It hangs and drapes beautifully and is also easy to maintain, handle, and store. Among the more economical velour substitutes which bear mentioning are duvetyn and flannel.

Duvetyn is almost as opaque as velour but drapes poorly and lacks as rich a surface quality. Flannel drapes a little better than duvetyn, and it has almost the same opacity. Its woolly-nap surface is a fair texture under stage lights.

Stage draperies are made of other materials not with the intention of imitating velour but to create their own effect. Cotton rep and monks cloth have enough texture to make an interesting inexpensive curtain when hung in fullness. Wide-ribbed corduroy is another drapery texture which, though semi-opaque, drapes and hangs well.

Sometimes draperies are expected to be translucent or on occasions, transparent. Dyed muslin is the least-expensive translucent fabric. It has a further advantage of coming in wider widths than such materials as satin or nylon crepe in the translucent class.

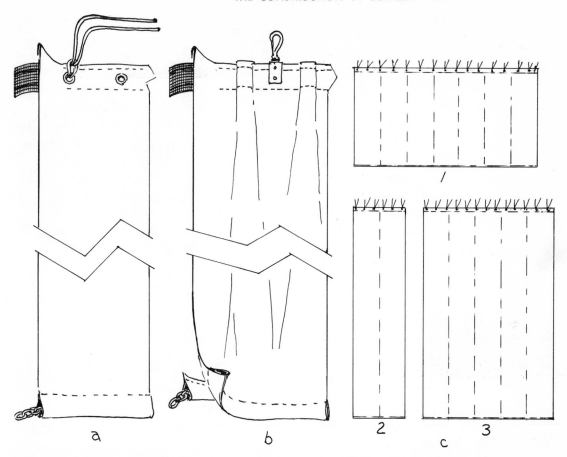

Figure 7–1. STAGE DRAPERIES. (a) Flat drapery construction. Webbing with grommets and tie-lines at top; hem enclosing chain weight at bottom. (b) Gathered drapery. Fullness gathered on top webbing; chain pocket attached above hem at the bottom. (c) Types of stage draperies: (1) border, (2) leg, (3) panel.

Gauze, the general term applied to all transparent materials, is available in a variety of fabrics such as cotton or nylon net, chiffon, and organdy to name a few familiar commercial textiles. Although these fabrics are available at the local dry-goods store, their chief disadvantage is their narrow width which increases the number of seams in a curtain. The seams become visible when the transparent curtain is back-lighted. There are gauzes, as well as muslin, that are woven on wide looms especially for theatre use. Bobbinet and shark's-tooth scrim, two transparent materials are made in 30-foot widths. Bobbinet is a hexagonal net that is more sheer but weaker than shark's-tooth scrim, which has a rectangular or ladder pattern. The shark's-tooth, besides draping well, is dense enough to provide a dye-painting surface and still become transparent when back-lighted.

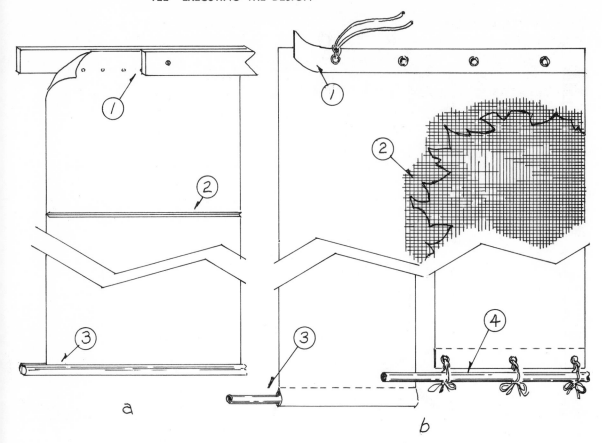

a

b

DROPS. Another large-area piece of scenery is the drop, taking its name from the fact that it hangs on a batten and is "dropped" in, as opposed to the older method of the shutter that slid on stage from opposite sides. The drop is made with horizontal face-to-face seams to create a smooth surface. The horizontal seams, when the drop is hanging, are under enough tension from the weight of the material and bottom batten to stretch into a smooth surface. A drop can be made to fold or roll depending upon whether it is to be translucent or opaque.

A translucent drop is dye painted and can be equipped with tie-lines at the top and tie-lines or a pipe-pocket at the bottom. The position of the seams of a translucent drop become important because if they are not care-fully hidden in the design they produce a distracting shadow line. For this reason, translucent drops are sometimes made with vertical seams and with irregular spacing, or, if the budget permits, they are made seamless by using 30-foot-width muslin.

As opaque scene paint is used on a regular opaque drop or a drop with opaque areas, it cannot be folded and therefore is rolled on the bottom batten. The opaque drop has a top and a bottom batten. Its construction and shape variations are shown in Figure 7–2.

Drops are commonly made of muslin because it is available in wide widths and is an excellent inexpensive translucent material. Drops are sometimes made of other materials frequently for an unusual textural quality, such as, burlap, velour, and terrycloth. And, of course, drops can be made of the gauze materials. Shark's-tooth and bobbinet are used more often than other sheer fabrics because they come in wider widths.

The cut-drop in Figure 7–2c is often backed with bobbinet or scrim more for a lighting effect than for strength. The cut edges of a drop or border are better supported with a special lightweight net which has a 1-inch-square mesh. When the net is dyed to match the background it becomes nearly invisible.

Figure 7–2.   DROP CONSTRUCTION.   Left. (a) Rear view of a roll drop. (1) Top batten, doubled 1 x 4. (2) Face-to-face horizontal seam. (3) Bottom batten, doubles 2 inches half round. (b) Rear view of a folding drop. (1) Top webbing with grommets and tie-lines. (2) Netting glued over openings or cut edges to support loose ends. (3) Drop bottom with pipe sleeve for the removal of bottom batten. (4) Drop bottom made with grommets and tie-lines.   Below. (c) Types of drops: (1) Plain back drop. (2) Cut border. (3) Cut drop, netted. (4) Leg drop. (5) Also referred to as leg drop or leg.

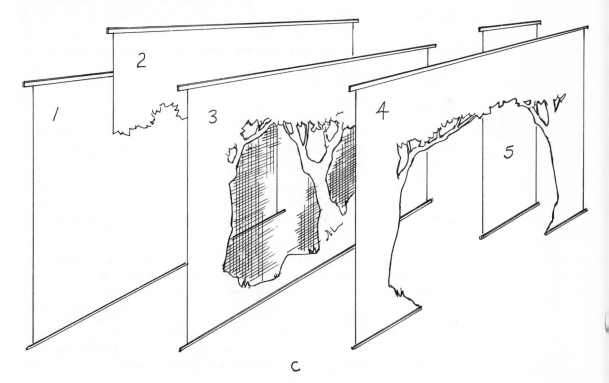

C

THE CYCLORAMA.   The largest single piece of scenery in the theatre is the cyclorama or "cyc." As the name implies, it encircles or partially encloses the scene to form the background. The cyclorama's most familiar use is as a sky or void backing a setting or elements of scenery placed in the foreground. Because the flat center of the cyclorama is blended into the sides with a gentle arc it can't be made on ridged battens like the drop. It is kept soft by using dyed material which is fastened by the tie-lines to a curved top and bottom batten of pipe.

A cyclorama is not always a sky or void. Occasionally it is painted with a decorative or pictorial scene to fit a specific show. Sometimes, stage draperies are hung in the same position to form a drapery cyclorama.

The sky cyclorama presents the greatest problem in its necessity to create a large, uninterrupted, smooth surface. Because the "cyc" material, dyed or dye-painted canvas, is hung flat without fullness from a curved batten, the direction of the seams become important. If the seams are horizontal the tension on the seams draws the surface smooth, but the resulting strain distorts the shape of the curve as the seams turn the corner.

Vertical seams round the corners better than the horizontal seams, but they do not present as smooth a finished surface. In both cases the seams are sure to show under a high level of illumination. This can be corrected by hanging a large flat panel of dyed (very light blue) shark's-tooth scrim directly in front of the canvas cyclorama using the same batten. Because it is a wide-width material the number of vertical seams can be reduced to two on the normal cyclorama. The scrim becomes the reflecting surface and the canvas acts as a backing (Figure 7–3).

FRAMED SCENERY

The structure of framed scenery is planned to support itself in a standing position. Although a framed piece may be aided by hanging support, or may be flown altogether, the basic framing principle remains the same. Framed scenery, as a construction technique, does not lend itself easily to the framing of a large area. It is possible to develop the framing for a large area, but to do this, it has to be hinged to fold into a smaller size or be dismantled into

Figure 7–3.   THE CYCLORAMA.   (1) Cyc backing, white vertical-seamed canvas. (2) Cyc face, shark's-tooth scrim dyed pale blue. (3) Bottom pipe, made up of various curved sections that can be joined to match the contour of the top. (4) Top batten, a combination of shallow and deep curves to provide a variety of contours. (5) Spot-sheaves, spotted on gridiron over the general shape of the top batten. (6) Mulling blocks, a change-of-direction pulley to direct the liftlines towards the headblock. (7) Headblocks. (8), (9), (10) Some of the cyc contours achieved by selecting various curve combinations in the top batten. (11) A drapery cyc hung from the same top batten.

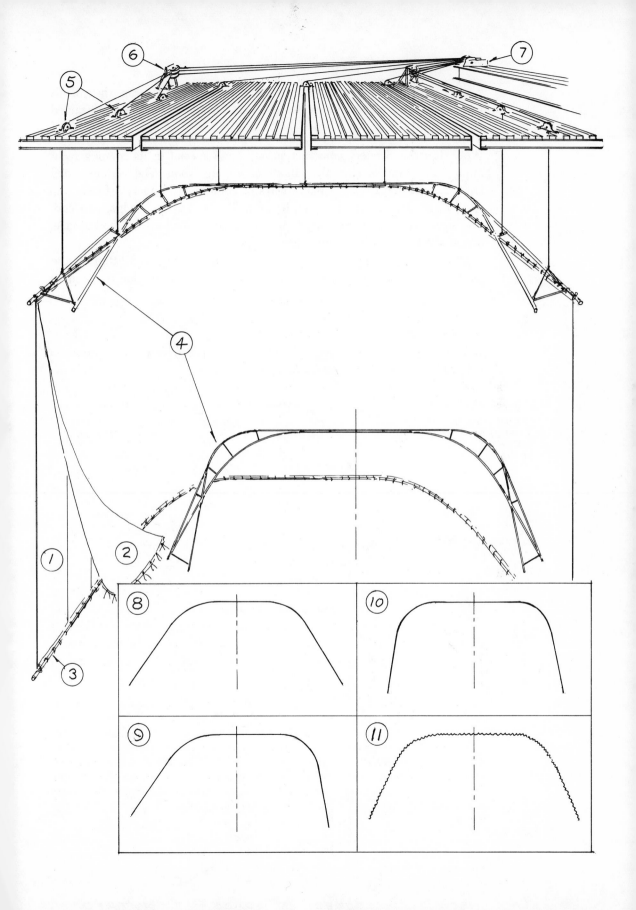

smaller parts to move in and out of the theatre. Most framing, then, deals with relatively small modules when compared to the large sizes of unframed scenery.

WOOD JOINTS.   Scenery construction, although special in its framing techniques, employs the normal methods of joining wood. The various wood joints are derived from the many ways of combining lumber surfaces. The surfaces of lumber are described as its face (flat surface), edge, and end. The surface-joining combinations are classified as: end-to-end, end-to-face, edge-to-end, edge-to-face, and edge-to-edge.

The making of a joint has two steps: first, the cutting and fitting of the joint; second, the securing of the joint with hardware or glue. In scenery

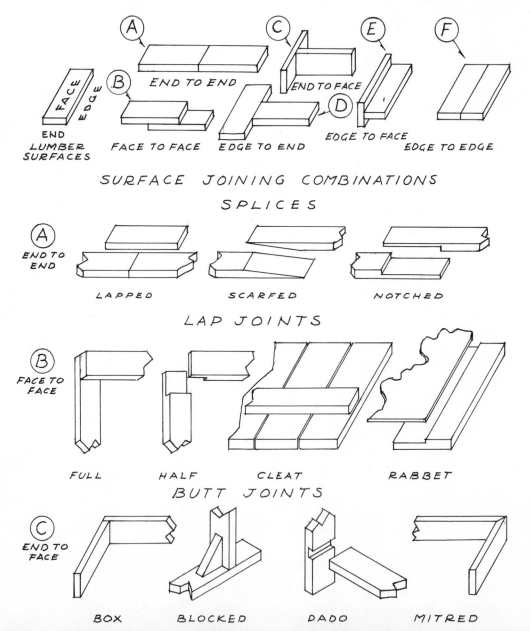

construction the joint is not always fixed but is many times temporarily secured or hinged. The fixed or permanent joint is used on standard-sized units of scenery, or smaller. The knockdown or temporary joints are used on oversized pieces that must be dismantled to get in and out of the theatre.

Figure 7–4 illustrates the numerous joints used in scenery construction classified in groups that combine the same surfaces. Fixed joints are secured with nails, clout nails (soft nails that clinch on the opposite side of the joint), screws, and glue. Knockdown or temporary joints are held with bolts, loose-pin hinges, keeper hooks, pegs, and turn buttons.

Figure 7–4. Left and below. TYPICAL WOOD JOINTS USED IN SCENERY CON-STRUCTION.

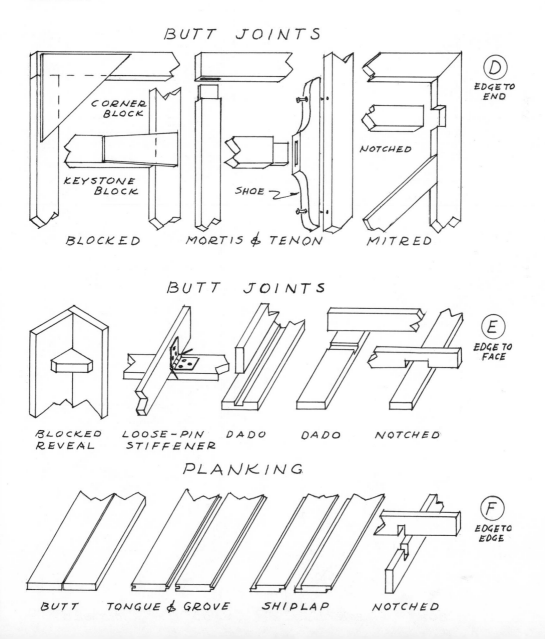

BUTT JOINTS

CORNER BLOCK

KEYSTONE BLOCK

SHOE

NOTCHED

D
EDGE TO END

BLOCKED   MORTIS & TENON   MITRED

BUTT JOINTS

E
EDGE TO FACE

BLOCKED REVEAL   LOOSE-PIN STIFFENER   DADO   DADO   NOTCHED

PLANKING

F
EDGE TO EDGE

BUTT   TONGUE & GROVE   SHIPLAP   NOTCHED

Figure 7–5.   FRAMED SCENERY.   Basic framing techniques for the single unit of framed scenery, the flat. (1) Style, vertical member. (2) Top rail. (3) Bottom rail. (4) Toggle rail. (5) Brace. (6) Corner block. (7) Keystone block. (8) Split-keystone block. (9) Canvas, 8-ounce duck. (10) Brace cleat. (11) Lash cleat. (12) Lash-line eye. (13) Lash line. (**14**) Toggle rail and shoe. (15) Profile edge. Style rabbeted for profile board. (16) **Profile** edge. Cut profile board attached over style. (17) Method of setting curved sweep **into** flat. Note that the sweep butts to the toggle and is notched into the style. Sweep can **be** cut into any shaped curve.

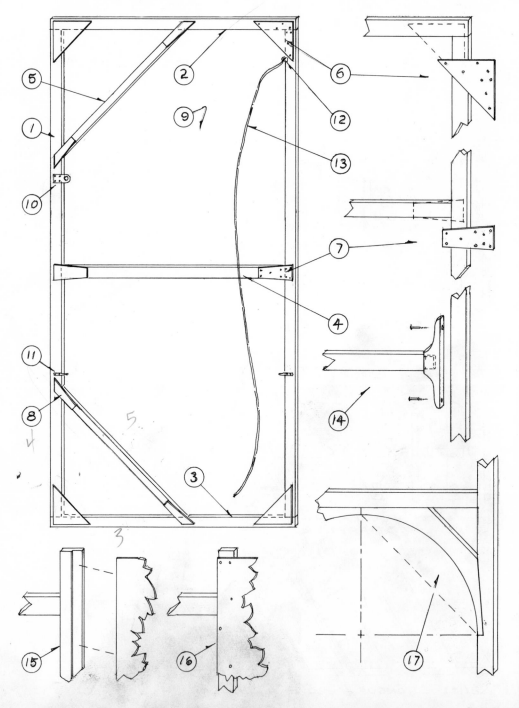

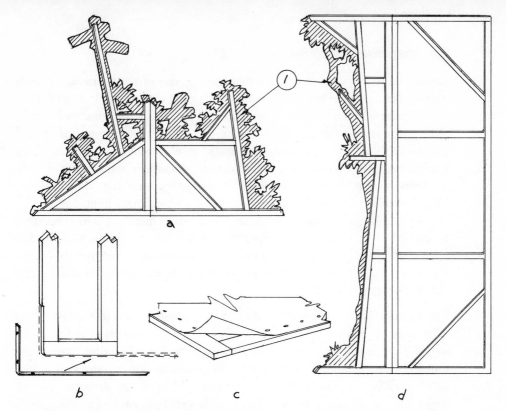

Figure 7–6. TYPES OF FRAMED SCENERY. (a) The framing of a set-piece with profile edges of three ply (1). (b) Detail of a sill iron used across the bottom of a door opening in a flat. (c) Detail of canvas-covering technique. (d) Flat with profile edge. (1) Three ply. Below. (e) Door flat. (f) Window flat. (g) Two-fold flat with double-door opening. Note hinged sill iron.

The framing of a simple flat illustrates the basic technique that is applied to any size or irregular shape (Figure 7–5). The area is enclosed with a lightweight frame of 1 x 3 white-pine lumber. The face of the lumber is kept flat in one plane causing edge-to-end butt joints at the corners. In this way, the wide surfaces of the framing boards are in position to support the canvas which is tacked to the inside edge of the outer frame and then pasted

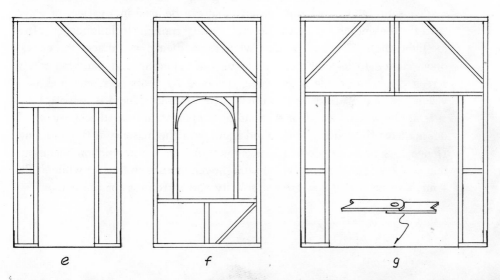

down. The end-to-edge joint is strengthened by one of two methods, or both. The joint can be mortised and tenoned with glue, or a simple butt joint reinforced with a three-ply plate or corner block. The mortise and tenon, although a stronger joint, takes longer to cut because it requires special power machinery or special attachments. It also reduces the amount of lumber that can be salvaged if the scenery undergoes remodeling. Unless the scenery is going to be subjected to excessive handling, the butt-joint keystone and corner-block method provides a simple, sturdy joint.

Toggle rails and diagonal braces are the internal members which function to strengthen and hold square the shape of the outside framing. If the flat has an opening, they also help to frame the opening. Any irregular shape involving profile edges or elaborate openings is framed in fundamentally the same manner (Figure 7–6).

THE FRAMED DROP.   As was mentioned, it is possible to frame a large area of scenery. The framed drop and ceiling piece are examples of this technique. They use a drop-like construction except that the battens are single instead of double and therefore are made of heavier lumber stock (1 x 4 or 1⅛″ x 4). The top and bottom battens are held apart by stretcher bars at about six to eight-foot intervals. They are bolted by means of ceiling plates to the battens. The loose ends of the drop are laced around the two end stretchers (Figure 7–7). A ceiling piece is made in the same manner, but will of course hang flat instead of vertically like the drop. Both the drop and ceiling fold and roll on their battens when the stretchers are removed.

DOORS AND WINDOWS.   Doors and windows are those important details that are often neglected in the haste of preparing a set. A door, in a sense, is a moving piece of scenery that is used by the actor. In a split second, its malfunction can not only give away the scenic illusion but can also break the carefully built-up mood of a scene.

The building and hanging of a door is a skilled and time-consuming job. For these reasons, the average amateur group is better off to make or have made a set of good stock door casings that can be used in a variety of ways.

In the making of a door the normal scenery-framing techniques are often too lightweight. There was a time when the audience would accept a canvas door painted to look like oak planking but sounding and handling like a screen door. The modern audience, schooled by years of movie and television realism, is jarred by this obvious theatricality. There is a limit, however, to the weight of a door that can be supported in framed scenery which doesn't have the solidity of the stud framing or the masonry it is simulating. Hence it is necessary to reach a compromise in a construction technique that will keep the door portable and lightweight enough to shift while at the same time achieving a degree of solidity and sturdiness for the action.

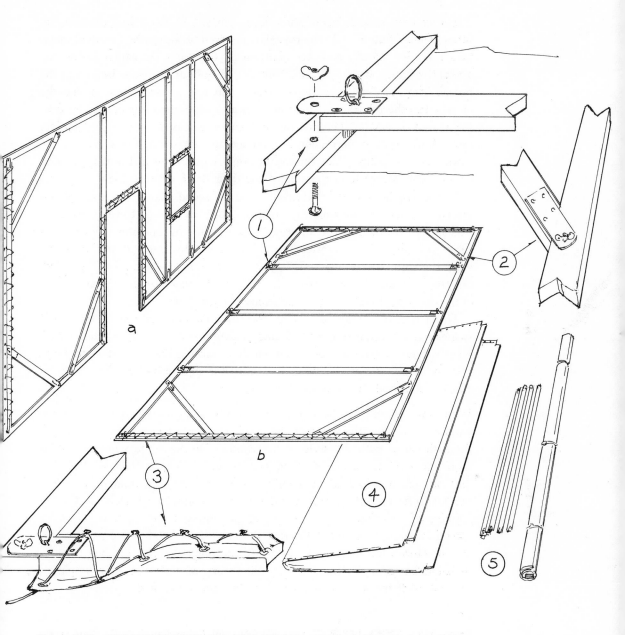

Figure 7–7.   **THE FRAMED DROP AND ROLL CEILING.   (a)** Rear view of a framed drop. Notice how the canvas is laced around the ends and through the openings. The canvas is permanently attached to the top and bottom battens. The vertical stretchers and braces are removable. **(b)** Rear view of a roll ceiling which is very similar to the framed drop in construction. (1) Detail of ceiling plate on the end of the stretcher. The stretcher is bolted to the two battens. (2) Same technique used on the diagonal brace. (3) Detail of lacing. (4) To roll, stretchers are removed and battens are brought together, face to face. (5) Ceiling rolled on battens.

A door unit is made up of three basic parts: (1) the actual door, sometimes called "shutter"; (2) the reveal, comprised of the jambs (vertical members), header (top), and sill (bottom); (3) the trim which forms the decorative frame around the door opening. The door is always hinged to the reveal. The trim, however, is constructed in one of two ways: it may be attached to the reveal, or it may be kept as a separate member and applied to the face of the flat. The first method, called a "cased door," is a complete unit. With the trim permanently attached to the reveal, the reveal of the cased door assembly slides through a prepared opening in the flat which is considerably larger than the size of the door itself (Figure 7–8a).

In the second method, referred to as a "scene door," the trim is not attached to the reveal which is built to the exact size of the flat opening. The reveal, containing the shutter, "butt fits" to the opening from behind (Figure 7–8b). The scene door provides a great deal more flexibility in the ways the trim can be handled. It can, for example, be completely painted, or attached and set away from the opening to increase the apparent size of the doorway, to name a few variations (Figure 7–9a).

The action of a door affects its construction. For example, a door that swings onstage requires double facing; a double-action door (kitchen door) takes special hinging as does a Dutch door; sliding doors involve tracking; and additional rigging becomes necessary for the trick door that, as if by magic, opens and closes by itself.

WINDOWS.   Similar to the door, a window has a reveal and trim, but the window sash takes the place of the door. The arrangement of panes within the sash varies with the style of the window. Because the window sash is more open than a door, it is difficult to build. The pattern of the thin mullions often becomes too fragile for normal stage framing unless the window is far enough upstage to fake them in profile board. Delicate tracery is frequently reinforced by a backing of galvanized screening that passes for glass and strengthens the mullions at the same time. To simulate glass, panes are sometimes left clear or backed with netting. The net, although nearly invisible, has enough density to give the feeling of glass. It is more apparent by contrast if the window is opened during the action of the play.

Figure 7–8.   STOCK DOOR CONSTRUCTION.   (a) Cased-door unit: (1) Door reveal and trim built as one unit. (2) Flat with a standard door opening. (3) Detail of door construction. (4) Angled strap hinge on jamb to hold door unit in the opening. (5) Blocks to hold trim in place. (6) Cross section of door unit through the header. (7) Plan of the cased-door unit showing the hinging. (8) Butt hinge on door. (b) Scene-door unit: (1) Separate trim. (2) Flat with a standard door opening. (3) Door and reveal. (4) Corner blocks to hold reveal frame square. (5) Rim lock. Attached on back side of door. (6) Tubular latch. Sets into edge of door.

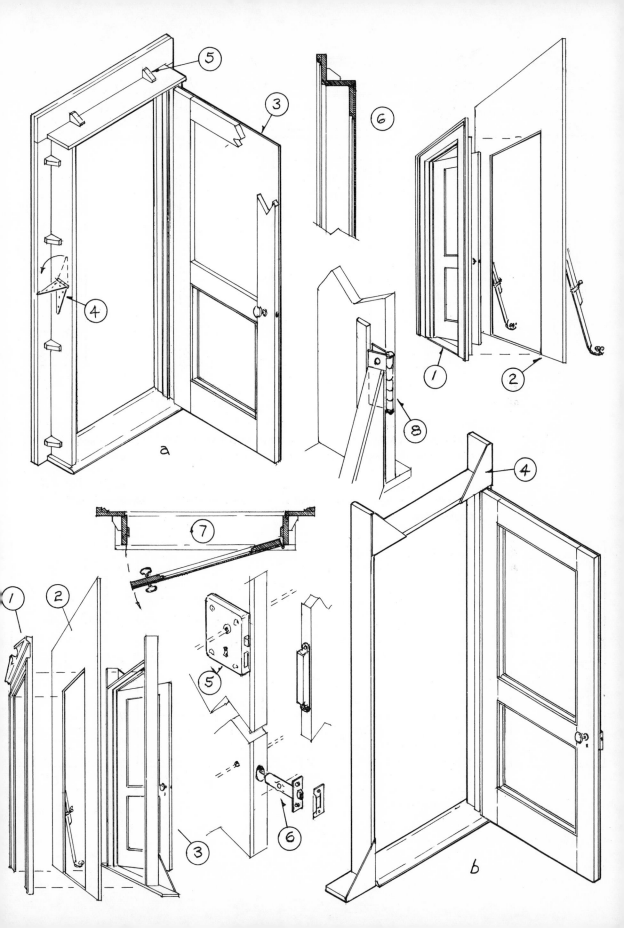

a

b

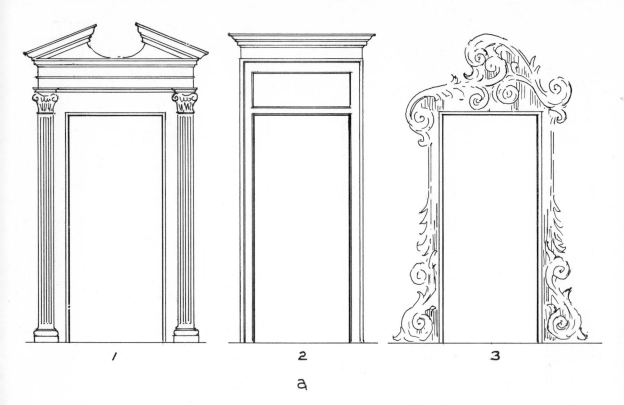

Figure 7–9. VARIATIONS IN DOOR TRIM AND PANELING. (a) Various methods of handling the trim around the same-size door opening, possible with a scene-door unit: (1) Wide-set trim. (2) Close-set and high trim with transom. (3) Painted trim. (b) Door paneling: The paneling of (2), (3), and (4) are all constructed within the basic paneling of a stock door (1). (5) The flush side of a stock door painted and cleated to look like a planked door.

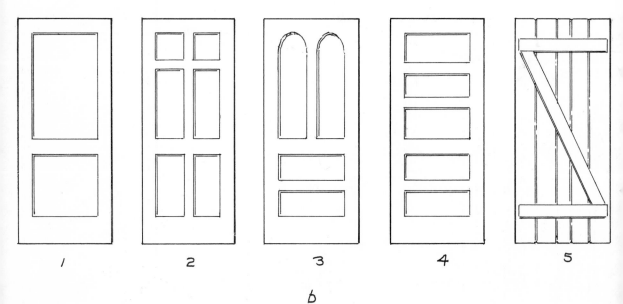

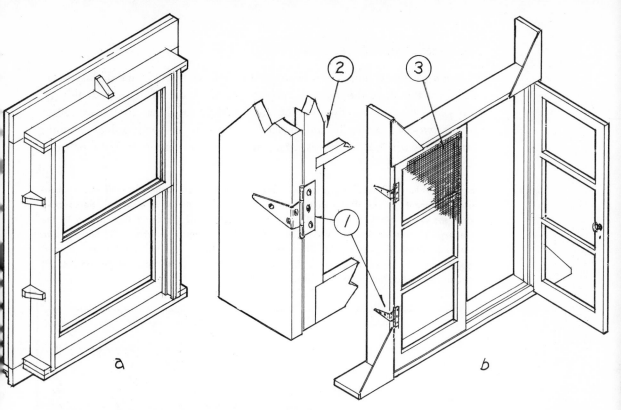

Figure 7–10. WINDOW CONSTRUCTION. (a) Double-hung window. Trim is attached to reveal in the same manner as the cased door. (b) Casement window. The reveal is constructed in the same way as the scene door with hinged sashes. (1) A bent T-strap hinge in place of the butt hinge. (2) Notched mullions. (3) Galvanized screening to strengthen the sash and simulate glass.

Window action, like that of the door, involves sliding or swinging on hinges. A window may have the vertical sliding action of a double-hung window, or slide horizontally. It may have the vertical hinging of a casement window, or the horizontal hinging of the awning-type window.

It is a little more difficult to plan a set of stock windows than doors because of the greater variation in sash styles. Certain often-used conventionally styled windows can be standardized and put into stock. Also the casing (reveal and trim) may be kept in stock to be used with interchangeable or new sashes for each show (Figure 7–10).

TRIM. Decorative trim appears in a set in other places than around door and window openings. Some additional areas of trim, painted or practical, are baseboards, chair rails, wainscoting, cornices, and overmantel decoration. Trim that is attached in these areas must be removable so the flat scenery will fold easily.

The attached trim requires additional framing within the flat for support. Chair rails and baseboards are easy to attach but the construction and hanging of a cornice is more complicated. Although trim details are slightly over-sized for the stage the average cornice can be made up of stock moldings. To keep the framing lightweight, the molding is nailed to blocks set at about two-foot intervals and backed with 3-ply or longitudinal framing strips. The whole assembly is attached to the wall flats with bolts or turn-buttons (Figure 7–11).

Figure 7–11. CORNICE CONSTRUCTION. A cornice is a lightly framed three-dimensional element of trim designed to attach along the length of a wall. The perspective view shows the block-framing technique and a method of attaching the cornice to the scenery. (1) An elevation of the cornice showing the amount of overhang. (2) Stock crown molding. (3) Nailing block. (4) Three-ply face. (5) Linear support for blocks. (6) Bed molding, stock. (7) Carriage bolt. (8) 1 x 2 stiffener along the back of the blocks. (9) Added support at the top of the flats.

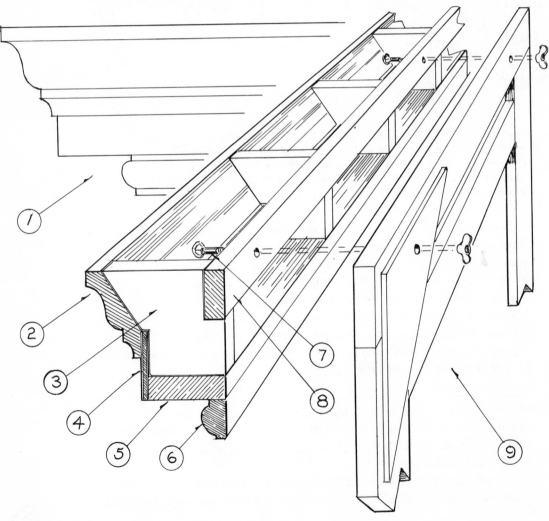

THREE-DIMENSIONAL SCENERY

WEIGHT-BEARING STRUCTURES. Certain elements of scenery cannot be reduced to flat planes or, because they are so small, it is more practical to build them as a three-dimensional form. This is especially important if the form is to bear the weight of a sitting or standing actor. Weight-bearing structures are present in such architectural forms as steps, ramps, and raised levels; in the irregular forms of rocks; and in the free form of an abstract design. The raising of a large portion of the stage floor and the use of steps and ramps brings excitement to the design composition, variation to the staging, and headaches to the stage technician. In the absence of any mechanical means of raising sections of the stage floor, the problem becomes one of creating a second floor at a specific distance above the stage floor. The level must be structurally sound enough to support actors and furniture with a minimum of deflection and, at the same time, be portable and economical. A large expanse of platforming is subdivided into smaller units for ease of handling. A single unit is made to "knockdown" into even smaller parts.

The Parallel.   The familiar way of providing a raised level for the stage is the parallel method. The parallel is a hinged trestle structure that opens to support a top and folds into a flat pack when not in use (Figure 7–12).

As a stock platforming method, the parallel has the advantage, of being lightweight, easy to assemble and transport, and fairly sturdy. It also can be adapted to irregular shapes as well as the conventional rectangle. Its chief disadvantage is a storage problem. To maintain any variation in levels, duplicate sets of parallels of different heights have to be kept in storage.

A convenient stock size for regular-shaped parallels depends upon: first, general handling and storage conditions; second, the construction of the top; and last, the riser heights of stock steps which work with the platforms.

If the top is to be made of ¾-inch 5 ply a 4- by 8-foot top is the most economical size. Planked tops, however, can be made smaller or larger without material waste if space permits the storage of larger parallels.

Stock parallel heights, obviously, should be at intervals related to riser heights of the steps, 6 inch or 7 inch being normal. Parallel heights usually vary at double-riser intervals such as, 12, 24, and 36 inch, or 14, 28, and 42-inch intervals.

There have been various attempts to standardize platforming construction with the aim, first, to cut down the size of stored parts; second, to reduce the amount of internal framing (by using material other than wood) and at the same time to provide a sound structure. The post-and-rail and scaffolding methods (Figure 7–13) are ventures in this direction. Both succeed in reducing the storage space of spare parts and provide a very sturdy platform with a minimum of framing. The techniques, although very practicable for regular shapes do not lend themselves readily to irregular shapes. The limits placed upon design, however, are minor in restrictions when compared to the stage space and sightline limitations imposed upon scene design by some theatre buildings.

Regardless of whichever type of platforming is favored, the parallel method is, like the framing of a plane flat, an example of basic structural framing. With this basic knowledge the carpenter can modify or embellish the technique to fit his special needs.

Platform Construction.   Any platforming technique can be resolved into its three structural members which are always present in some form or other, they are the top, rail, and post. The top, which is the actual bearing surface is directly supported by the rails. Crossrails run parallel to the shortest dimension of the level. Their interval is linked to the material and thickness of the top. The average top, made of 1 x 6 tongue-and-groove planking or ¾-inch 5-ply board, should be supported at 30-inch intervals. The span, however, can be increased by use of cleats or stiffeners on the underside and thereby, in effect, increasing the thickness of the top material.

The rail is, in turn, supported by the post. The interval of posting is dependent upon the size of the rail. A 1 x 3 rail (on edge) should be posted at not more than three-foot intervals and at four-foot intervals for a 1 x 4 rail.

The framing of a single trestle or "gate" of a parallel employs the post-and-rail technique. In Figure 7–12a note that the top rail is borne by the two vertical members, or posts, which carry through to the floor. The bottom rail is merely a tie-rail that completes the rectangle. The diagonals are necessary to hold the gate square and eliminate side sway or "rack" in the finished platform. The single gate, though lightweight, gathers strength when it is hinged to the other members of the parallel. The parallel to fold flat must hinge as shown.

Any irregular shape that can be reduced to flat planes may be constructed by the parallel method. The gates can be loose-pin-hinged together rather than folding, for many times the pattern of the supports is so irregular the parallel cannot fold flat (Figure 7–14).

Figure 7–12.   THE PARALLEL PLATFORM.   (a) Basic parallel construction with open-corner hinging. (1) Top, ¾ inch 5-ply with cleats. Typical trestle framing includes (2) top rail bearing on (3) the post, tied by (4) the bottom rail, and strengthened by (5) the diagonal brace. The framing may be joined either by (6) corner blocks, or (7) by mortise and tenon joints. (b) The parallel technique used on a slanted platform or ramp.

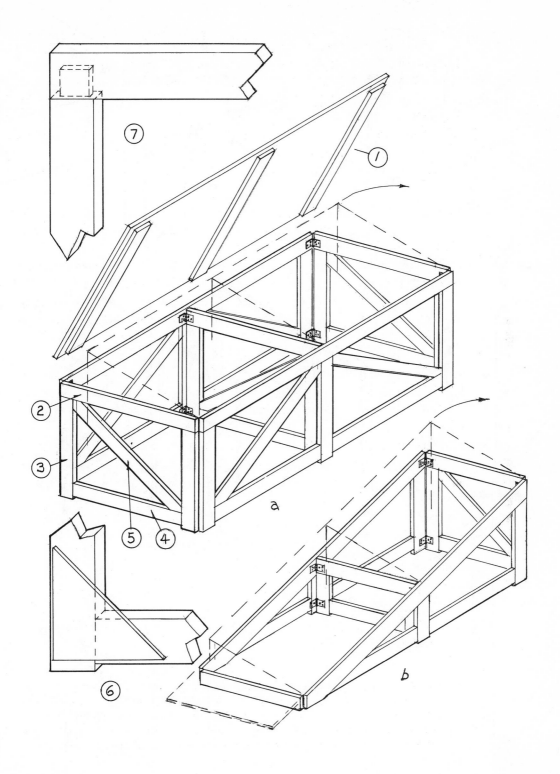

a

b

① ② ③ ④ ⑤ ⑥ ⑦

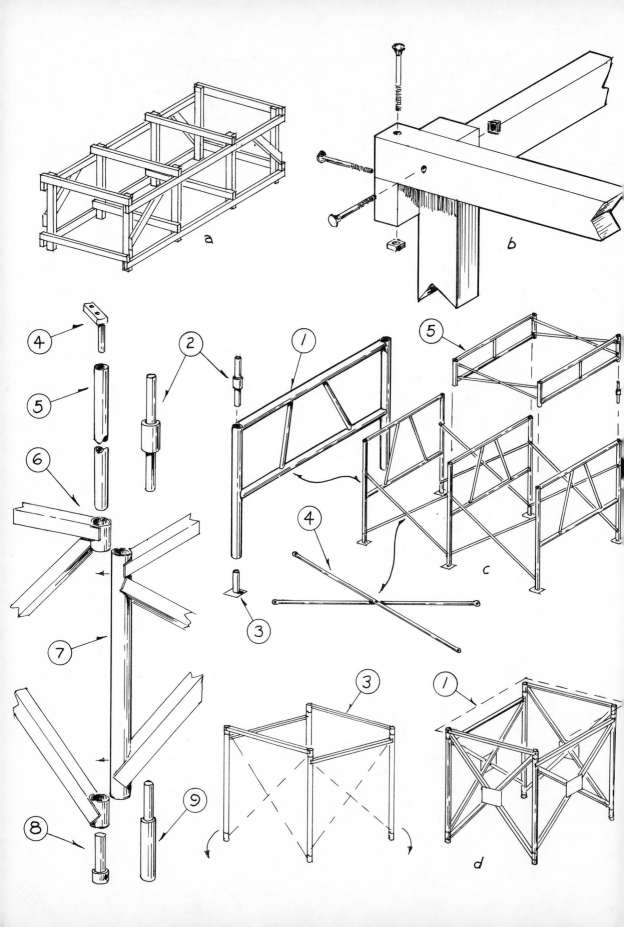

Figure 7–13. OTHER PLATFORMING TECHNIQUES. Left. **(a)** Post-and-rail method which knocks down into individual 2 x 3 units. **(b)** Detail of post-and-rail corner bolting. **(c)** Scaffold method. (1) Tubular steel or aluminum scaffold unit. (2) Spacer to interlock scaffold units. (3) Foot. (4) Cross braces to space and stabilize scaffold units. (5) The stacking of one scaffold unit upon another to gain height. **(d)** Steel parallel method. A smaller moduled tubular steel and angle iron-framed parallel. (1) Top overhangs unit to allow for facing flat. (2) Spacer to interlock and stack units. (3) Corners become hinges. (4) Pin attached to top to lock it in place. (5) Internal pin of hinge corner made up of (6) and (7). (6) Opened-end trestle. (7) Closed-end trestle. (8) Foot. (9) Extended foot.

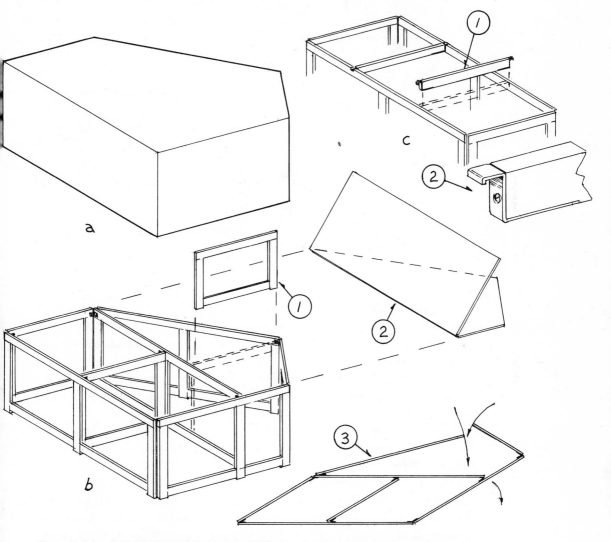

Figure 7–14. THE IRREGULAR-SHAPED PLATFORM. **(a)** The hinging and assembly problems of an irregular-shaped platform are solved individually. **(b)** To fold: (1) loose-pin-hinged internal trestle is detached after top (2) has been removed. (3) By unpinning the hinges of one corner, the parallel will fold into a flat pack. **(c)** The use of a "spanner" allows the removal of internal trestles in cases where it is necessary to keep the area under the top clear. (1) Spanner is of heavy enough stock, usually 2 x 4 or 2 x 6, to make strong span. (2) Detail of keeper-hook on end of spanner.

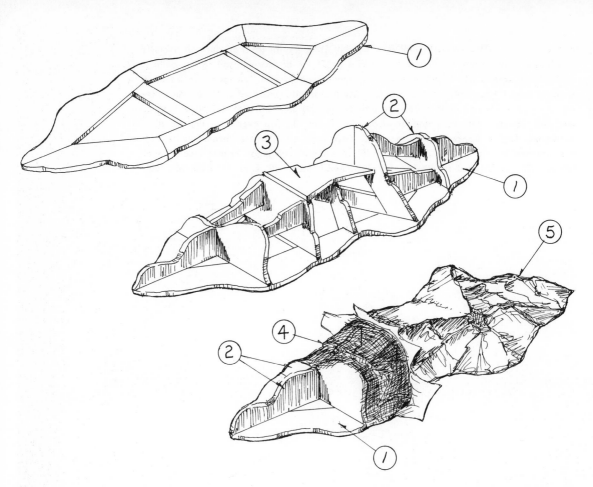

Free Forms. The irregular surfaces that cannot be reduced to a series of flat planes have to be constructed as a three-dimensional unit. Rock pieces and abstract forms that have to bear weight are examples of this type of irregular surface.

The framing of an irregular surface is, of course, more or less extemporaneous and dependent upon some final sculptural touches by the designer to complete the form. For this reason the design drawings of a free-form should be accompanied with a scaled model. The form usually suggests the manner of construction, nevertheless there is a basic method that can be adapted to most irregular shapes.

The method of construction of a rock piece demonstrated in Figure 7–15 goes through the following steps: (1) The exact shape of the base of the rock is framed in the conventional flat-scenery technique. (2) Across the shortest dimension of the base is set a series of contour pieces that follow the contour of a section taken at that point (see Sections, Chapter 5 page 74). (3) The contour pieces are stiffened with cross bracing and all bearing surfaces are reinforced. (4) Over the contour pieces is placed 1-inch chicken wire or ½-inch screen wire, which is pinched or stretched in the desired shape. (5) The final surface is applied to the screen wire. The kind of

Figure 7–15. CONSTRUCTION OF ROCK FORMS. (1) Shape of form on floor. Conventional framing. (2) Contour pieces. (3) Cross bracing. (4) Wire screening. (5) Burlap. Photos: (a) Three-dimensional shape before covering. (b) Same shape covered with burlap.

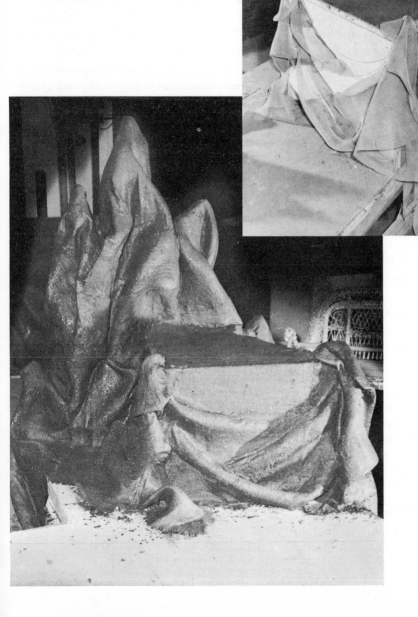

covering material depends upon the nature of the texture that is desired. The best results are usually obtained with burlap. It is applied by first dipping it into a mixture of strong glue size and base color. The burlap is then draped over and tacked to the framework, and allowed to harden. A form made in this manner is lightweight, inexpensive, and surprisingly sturdy.

A harder exterior surface is sometimes built up by using asbestos pulp applied on a ¼-inch wire-screening undersurface.

Ramps. The parallel as a platforming technique can also be adapted to a ramped surface (Figure 7–12b). The side trestles are built to the angle of the incline. Gates of varying heights connect the outside trestles and are hinged to fold like a regular parallel.

Steps. Whereas the ramp is a gradual change of level, the step is more direct, dividing the change into a series of intermediate levels. A flight of steps is made up of risers and treads. The tread is the bearing surface and the riser is the interval of change in level. The rule of thumb guiding the size relationship of the tread to the riser is based upon the ease of movement up and down the steps. The sum of the riser and tread in a continuous flight of steps is kept about 18 inches. Hence a 6-inch riser would require a 12-inch tread; an 8-inch riser a 10-inch tread and so forth. Obviously the low riser and wide-tread combination is more desirable for the onstage steps, permitting the actor to move easily and gracefully up and down.

A flight of steps can be built for the stage in one of two ways. One method is a modified platform trestle construction with each tread supported by a complicated post-and-rail framework (Figure 7–16a). This way the steps are a part of a bulky three-dimensional platform which is difficult to store and move.

Steps can be made to knockdown into more easily handled parts by the use of the carriage method of construction (Figure 7–16b). The pattern of the riser and tread is cut from a wide board running parallel to a line drawn through the nosing of each step. The nosing is at the intersection of the top of the riser and the outside edge of the tread.

A carriage is cut from a wide enough board to retain at least 3 inches

Figure 7–16.   STAIR CONSTRUCTION TECHNIQUES.   (a) Trestle method. (1) Trestle with the top edge framed to riser-tread pattern. (2) Three ply used as riser stock. (b) Cut-carriage method. (1) Carriage cut to riser-tread pattern. Step unit leans on platform for support. (c) Closed-carriage method. (1) Closed carriage can only be used on the outside of stair unit. Hence this type of construction limits the width of the stairs. (2) Cleat to hold tread. Note that no riser is used. (d) Cut-carriage method used on an irregular-shaped flight of steps. (1) Carriages with same riser height but varying tread dimensions. (e) Stair facing, framed out of 1 ⅛ inch-baluster stock (1) which is pin-hinged to steps (2). If both faces are covered with 3 ply (3), the facing unit becomes reversible with minimum alterations.

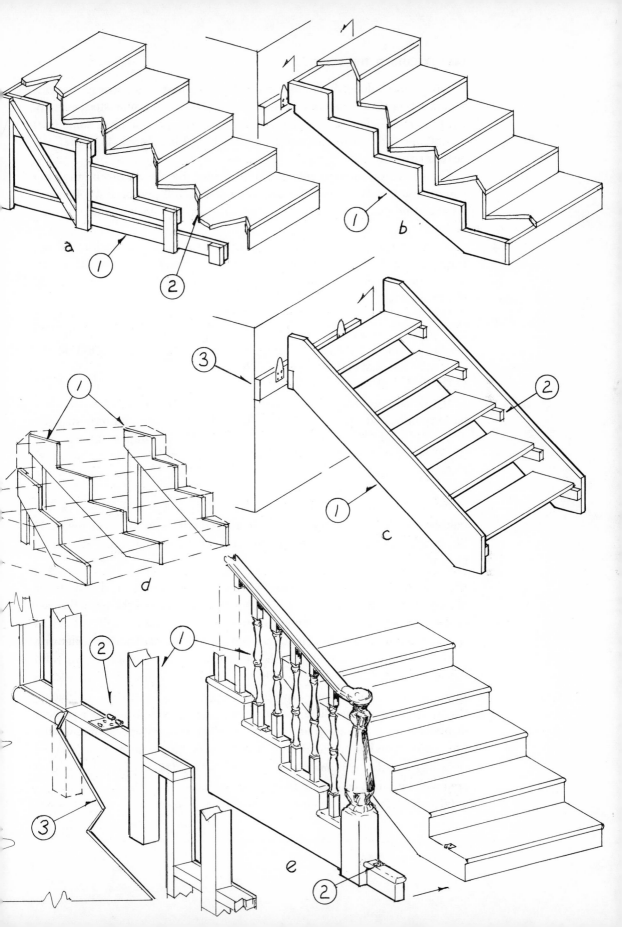

of uncut board along the bottom edge. The thickness of a carriage depends somewhat on its unsupported length. Frequently 1⅛-inch pine stock is used, chiefly for its lightness as well as strength. 1-inch pine stock is sometimes substituted for lightweight construction while 2-inch stock is used for a heavier structure.

The choice of carriage stock is also affected by the nature of the riser material. Is the riser made of 1-inch pine or ¼-inch 3 ply, or is it left open? As the riser material becomes lighter, the carriage stock should increase in thickness.

A flight of steps would have, of course, two carriages. Additional carriages would depend upon the thickness of the tread and the width of the steps. For example, a tread ¾-inch thick would need a carriage every 30 inches of width.

The lower step of the carriage sits on the floor and the top step rests on a prepared cleat fastened on the front of a platform, thus eliminating the need of a post underneath. The steps, or carriage unit, can be lifted off the cleat to be handled and stored separately.

The facing of stairs (also levels) is a separate piece of scenery attached to the downstage edge of the step or platform. The facing of a stair is a more complicated unit because it includes the stair rail, balusters, stringer, and newel post (Figure 7–16e). The stringer, which parallels the carriage, supports the bottom ends of the balusters. It can be an "open stringer" revealing the tread and risers or it may be a "closed stringer" masking the ends of the steps with an uncut surface.

The railing completes the stair facing. It spaces the top ends of the balusters while being supported by them. The whole assembly of the stair-facing flat and steps must be kept to a practical size or it can become too large to handle.

NONWEIGHT-BEARING STRUCTURES. Columns, tree trunks, and any other objects that have to have dimension but do not bear weight form the last type of scenery. Since the structure need only be strong enough to hold its shape, the framing is lightweight in comparison to weight-bearing structures.

An irregular shape is built in three dimensions by the use of two structural elements: the basic silhouette of the object and numerous contour pieces. In a tree trunk, for example, the basic silhouette is the vertical outline of the trunk and branches. The contour pieces are spaced at intervals perpendicular to the silhouette frame. After sufficient bracing and stiffening, the form of the trunk is rounded into shape by attaching chicken wire or wire screening over the contour pieces (Figure 7–17). The chicken wire is covered with burlap or canvas for the finished surface.

In a rock, the basic silhouette is horizontal and the contour pieces are

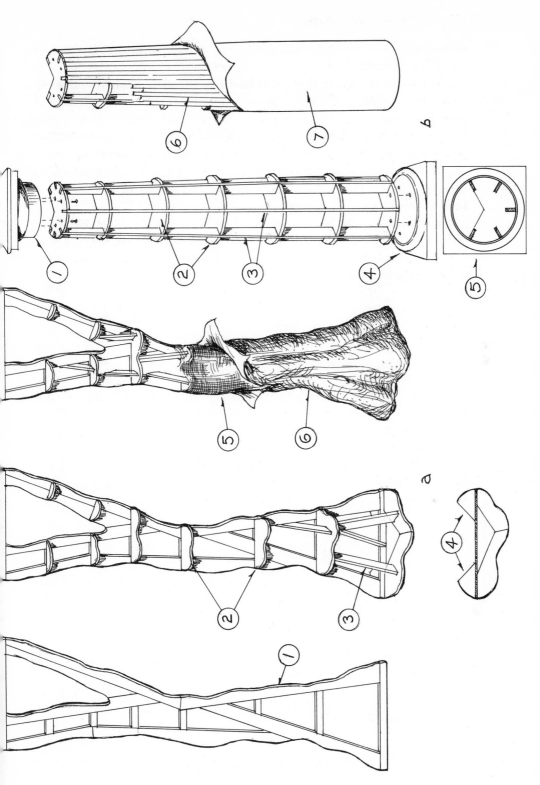

Figure 7-17. COLUMNS AND TREE TRUNKS. (a) Construction of a tree trunk. (1) Framing of basic silhouette. (2) Contour pieces set at intervals. (3) Cross bracing. (4) Pie-shaped contours to fill out base of tree where it meets the floor. (6) Wire screening or chicken wire. (6) Burlap. (b) Stock column construction. (1) Removable cap. (2) Contour pieces. (3) Vertical stiffeners. (4) Removable base. (5) Top view showing stiffener spacing. (6) Lattice slats. (7) Canvas cover.

vertical which, as has been mentioned, can become structural if the rock has to bear weight.

Columns are a regular shape and lend themselves to a slightly different construction method. It is not necessary to use a silhouette piece. The circular or semi-circular contour pieces can either be attached to a central core or be held at intervals by slats on the outer surface (Figure 7–17b).

The exterior surface of the column can be handled in two different ways. The surface can be made up of thin vertical slats (best for a column with a taper or entasis) that are covered with canvas after all of the slats have been rounded with a plane or rasp.

The column can also be covered with a flexible paperlike ⅛-inch EZ curve, or for a temporary column, heavy building paper can be used. When a light exterior covering is used, the amount of bracing between contour pieces has to be increased to stiffen the column.

8

THE PAINTING
OF SCENERY

The painting of scenery is a highly skilled and specialized portion of creating a setting. It is also a very interesting and fascinating part of scene design and technical production. Most of the methods and techniques of handling scene paint are familiar to one with visual-arts training. The main difference between painting scenery and easel painting is that of scale. Instead of painting at a small drawing-board size, the scenic artist paints at life size or larger.

Because scene painting is large in scale, the scenic artist uses a broad technique; sometimes so broad that what appears to be slaps and dashes up close does not take form until viewed at a distance. Learning to paint on a large scale and in a broad technique is an easy adjustment for the visual artist. The uninitiated, however, should first become accomplished in handling water colors in sketch form before attempting large-scale painting. Sketching and painting from still life or landscape not only improve the student designer's drawing and painting ability but also increase his per-

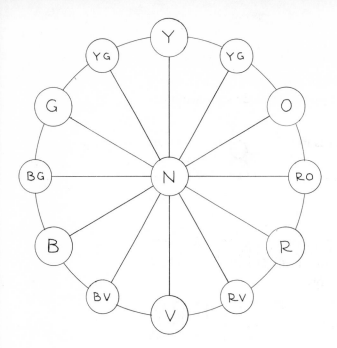

Figure 8–1. THE COLOR WHEEL. The six basic colors of the spectrum—red, orange, yellow, green, blue, and violet, and their intermediate hues—make up the twelve principal **hues** of the color wheel.

ception of light and color in nature. These processes serve to point up the significance of color as an element of design.

PAINT AND COLOR

The design of a setting can succeed or fail in the strength of the painting. Hence, the designer should carefully plan how the scenery is to be painted. The most important part of the planning and actual painting is the use of color. A scene designer must be familiar not only with the mixing and use of pigments, but also with the use of colored lights.

The prominence and forcefulness of color as an element of design was mentioned in Chapter 3. A color, it was pointed out, has three variants: hue, value, and intensity.

HUE. The spectrum notation of a color is its hue. The spectrum is formed by the prismatic refraction of sunlight which breaks up the normally white light of the sun into several visible hues. The number of clearly defined steps or hues varies with the different color theories. The Munsell color theory, for example, is based upon ten principal colors: Ostwald has twenty-four different hues, and Pope begins with twelve principal colors. Due to the nature of scene paint and the inability of present pigments to approach the brilliance of the colors in light, a six- to twelve-principal-color system works the best for scenery painting.

The six basic colors of the spectrum—red, orange, yellow, green, blue and violet—and their intermediate hues make up the twelve principal colors.

The relationship of hues to each other is best shown by placing them in a circle referred to as a color wheel (Figure 8–1). The center of the wheel is neutral and colors opposite each other through the center are hue opposites or complementary colors. Their mixture in equal parts produces a neutral or "grey."

VALUE. The light to dark variant of a color is its value. A hue as it appears on the spectrum is lighter or darker than another hue. Yellow, for example, is lighter than blue, red is also lighter than blue but darker than yellow, and so on. In Figure 8–2b the twelve hues of the color wheel are rearranged next to the value scale to show the natural value of the unaltered hue. Besides its natural value alignment, a hue can be raised in value by the addition of white, or lowered in value by adding black.

The greatest number of separate steps between black and white that the eye can detect is about seven. The point halfway between black and white is a medium value. Halfway between medium and white is the light value with high light above and low light below. The intermediate point between medium and black is the dark value with high dark above and low dark below (Figure 8–2a).

INTENSITY. The degree of hue pureness is its intensity or chroma. As was mentioned, complementary colors neutralize each other. The neutralization is a change of the intensity of the color. This can be measured in an arbitrary number of steps, usually from four to six. The intensity of a hue is also changed if it is raised or lowered in value. The addition of black or white to a hue lowers its chromatic content and greys the hue. It is interesting to note that, although it is not possible to raise or lower the value of a hue without changing its intensity, it *is* possible to alter the intensity of a color without changing its value.

For example, in Figure 8–2c complementary hues orange and blue are shown in an intensity–value relationship. If mixed directly in equal proportions, they would theoretically produce a grey of medium (M) value. However, each can be neutralized without raising or lowering its value if the opposite color is raised or lowered respectively in value before mixing. The blue, for example is raised from its natural value of high dark (HD) to a low light (LL) value before it is mixed with the orange, and vice versa.

A color theory beside explaining all colors, tints, and shades provides a means of describing a color in semi-scientific terms instead of such description as DuBarry pink or robin's-egg blue. A particular shade of pink, for example, can be identified as red-violet at three-quarters intensity and low light value.

A thorough understanding of the nature of color has a further significance to the scene designer. As he spends so much time mixing new and matching old colors in both pigment and light, the knowledge of a color theory can

W   WHITE

HL   HIGH LIGHT

L   LIGHT

LL   LOW LIGHT

M   MEDIUM

HD   HIGH DARK

D   DARK

LD   LOW DARK

B   BLACK

a   b

help him analyze the content of the color he is matching as well as aid in the mixing of new and unusual tones.

COLOR MIXING. Colors are mixed by two different methods: subtraction and addition. Both methods are related to the aspects of color in light. Each hue in the spectrum is of a different wavelength in the visible portion of the electromagnetic spectrum; red is the longest and violet the shortest. (The electromagnetic spectrum is discussed in detail in Chapter 13). A particular hue is visible because light is either reflected off an opaque surface such as paint or is transmitted through a transparent surface such as stained glass or a translucent drop. The two surfaces appear colored because some of the light's wavelengths are absorbed while reflecting or transmitting the wavelength of the actual surface color. Hence, blue paint, for example, appears as a blue hue because the other hues (red, green, yellow . . .) have been absorbed and only the blue wavelength is reflected.

The physicist, to explain color mixing in light, picks three primaries from the spectrum produced by prismatic refraction of sunlight. These primaries—red, green, and blue—when mixed by addition produce the secondary hues—yellow, blue-green and red-blue. The secondaries and primaries approach in theory the six basic hues of the spectrum.

Although the theory of light primaries helps to explain the phenomenon of color mixing, it is not too useful as a paint-mixing guide because light primaries cannot be reproduced accurately in pigments or dyes. Hence the scenic painter thinks of color in terms of the six basic hues or twelve principal hues (or more if he wishes) rather than in terms of the primaries.

SUBTRACTIVE MIXING.   Mixing by subtraction is the direct combining of hues. The painter generally mixes his pigments together before they are applied. When colors are mixed in this manner the second color cannot add but can only subtract its wavelength from light. For example, if blue paint is poured into and mixed with a pot of yellow paint, the resulting green hue is visible because of the subtraction of the red, yellow, and orange wavelengths. The blue and yellow wavelengths are reflected as a single green hue. The mixing

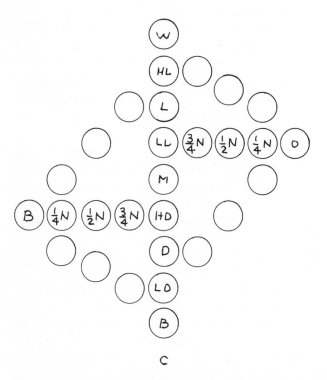

C

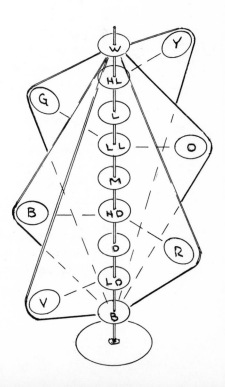

Figure 8–2.   THE VALUE AND INTENSITY OF COLOR.   (a) The value scale. Seven steps between white and black. (b) The natural-value relationship of the twelve principal hues. (c) The intensity-value steps of two complementary colors, blue and orange. (d) The color tree, a visualization of the color wheel in three dimensions.

of hues by the subtractive method, however, tends to neutralize or grey the colors which is especially apparent if the two colors are complementary. For this reason, the painter avoids mixing at least the intense hues by working from a large palette of principal colors. Neutral shades and pastel tints are, of course, the result of subtractive mixing involving the use of black and white pigments as well as other hues.

ADDITIVE MIXING.   Mixing by addition on the other hand is the indirect mixing of color. It is the mixing of colored light, either reflected or transmitted, thereby adding rather than subtracting the hue wavelengths. The light primaries are mixed in this manner to produce the secondary hues. For example: if the light primaries red and blue are mixed in the air they form the secondary color, red-blue or magenta. Magenta is a shade of violet lifted slightly in value, for the mixing of hues by addition tends to raise the value of the resulting color.

Although additive color mixing in stage lighting is used chiefly in the border lights and cyclorama lights, it can also be used as a painting technique. The painter knows that large areas of color in juxtaposition influence each other because of the phenomenon of additive mixing. That is to say that the reflected colors from each area tend to mix in the air before they reach the eye. If the areas of color are made much smaller (dots), their reflected colors mix in the air and appear at a distance as a single hue. A more controlled use of additive mixing known as pointillage was used as a painting technique by such artists as Seurat and Manet, with great mastery.

The use of additive mixing in scene painting is rather limited when compared to the highly effective results of pointillage in halftone color printing. Additive mixing does, however, lead to painting techniques and uses of color to bring life and vibrance into the colors of a setting. The type of paint used on scenery is by necessity flat so as to avoid any reflection of the stage lights. Life and vibrance have to be introduced by painting techniques and choice of colors even if the background shades are neutral. The additive mixing of colors used in a spattering or scumbling technique can give depth to a neutral tone, especially if the shades are coordinated with the colors of the stage lighting.

COLOR MODIFICATION.   The use of color in the theatre has a further variation that seldom occurs in other visual-art forms, the modification of a painted color by colored light. The scene designer not only has to consider the colors of the painted background, draperies, costumes, and other materials of the set, but also the colors of the lights that will reveal them. This is especially true if the lighting for the scene is unusual, such as a romantic moonlight scene or the arbitrary flooding of the stage with a red or green hue as an unnatural effect.

Fortunately, color modification is not quite as complicated as it seems. The effect of colored light on a colored surface is that of subtractive mixing. The modification of the painted color is the same as adding pigment of the same color as the light to the original paint color. In other words, if a red light is thrown on a yellow surface, the yellow is modified into orange shades.

An easy way to judge color modification in advance is to view the proposed color scheme through a sample of the gelatine or color medium that is to be in the lights. Some scene designers use a miniature duplication of the planned lighting setup to check their color schemes and plan their color effects. The greatest complication comes in the selection of light colors that are most favorable to both costumes and the setting. This requires close cooperation of the scene designer and costume designer at the formative stages.

THE COMPONENTS OF SCENE PAINT

The three basic components of scene paint are: pigment ('color), binder, and medium. The pigment and binder are suspended in a liquid medium which allows the paint to be brushed or sprayed onto a surface. The medium then evaporates and the binder holds the pigment to the surface.

The dry colors used for scene paint are the pigments which are suspended in a water medium with a water-soluble glue as a binder. A fourth ingredient is frequently added to scene paint as a filler. Whiting, which is an inexpensive chalk and not a pigment, is often added to the mixture to give the paint body and opacity. As whiting affects the intensity of the color it is not used in pure or full-intensity colors.

MIXING PROCEDURES

The mixing of scene paint begins with the preparation of the binder and medium or "size." The mixing proportions of a working size depend upon the kind of glue that is being used. Ordinary flake or ground glues are strong and usually have to be cut about 16 to 1 to make a size. Rubber and gelatine glues, although more flexible and easier to handle (dry slower) make into about a 10-to-1 size. Both types require advance preparation. They have to be soaked and cooked in a double boiler to soften them into a liquid state. Once the glue has been made into size, it stays in a liquid state. The size will deteriorate, however, if it is allowed to stand for too long a period. A small quantity of carbolic acid or formaldehyde added to the size acts as a preservative.

Because scene paint dries about two to three values lighter than it appears when wet, it is easier to mix the dry colors together first to acquire the desired tone. The size is then added to the premixed pigment, thereby saving repeated testings and sometimes the mixing of twice as much paint as is needed in the attempt to match an elusive shade. The size is added slowly, first making a pulp or paste. If the paste is vigorously stirred to make sure all the dry color is thoroughly moistened before thinning it to a painting consistency, there is no need to break up the unmixed lumps by hand. If the dry paint refuses to go into suspension (some colors such as Van Dyke brown and Prussian blue are poor mixers), a little alcohol added to the paste helps to wet the troublesome color.

READY-MIXED PAINTS

The question may be raised as to whether or not it wouldn't be wiser to use ready-mixed paints and thereby avoid all the bothersome procedure of mixing the dry scenic colors. Casein and latex based paints are two water-color paints that are sometimes used in the theatre. Casein (a milk deriva-tive) is the binder in a casein-based paint which is available in prepared mixtures of dry or pulp form. The dry colors, however, have a very limited color choice and the pulp mixtures are expensive when compared to the cost per area of coverage of dry scenic colors. Texolite and Luminal Fresco Colors are the two brands of casein paints most frequently used in the theatre.

One important thing to remember in using casein paints is that, when they "setup" or dry they are water repellent. This can play havoc with uncleaned brushes or buckets. It also means that scenery painted with casein paint cannot be washed down for repainting. Casein paint, however, covers very well, one coat usually being sufficient. The water-repellent quality of casein is, of course, an advantage for scenery that is to be used outdoors.

Latex-based paints have limited use in the theatre. For one thing, although called a flat paint, they reflect more light than regular scene paint. Besides being expensive the latex-paint color range is smaller than casein. It can, however, be used to advantage on properties and wood surfaces that might receive excessive handling for a latex-painted surface is washable after the paint is thoroughly dry.

There are other dry-color mixtures on the market which claim to have a binder included. The binder never seems strong enough for scenery use. Additional binder should be added to prevent the color from dusting off.

The dry-pigments and size method when compared to ready-mixed paints, requires more skill and time to mix and prepare, but is less expensive in the long run, has a greater color range, as well as being more flexible to handle.

SCENE-PAINTING PALETTE

Dry pigments are ground for theatrical use and, therefore, the spectral hues at least are available only at supply houses specializing in scenic paints and supplies. Earth colors can be found in local paint shops, although many times they are of inferior quality for painting scenery.

In preparing a list of stock scenic colors it is natural to compare the quality of the pigment's hue to the twelve principal colors of the color wheel. A good scene-painting palette would include them as well as some special colors and the earth colors.

Yellow

Light Chrome Yellow— A straight yellow, close to a primary hue. It is important to have a yellow with a sharp cut-off (minimum green or orange content).

Yellow Orange

Medium Chrome Yellow—Excellent yellow-orange hue. Not necessary to stock with light chrome yellow. Some painters, however, prefer stocking two yellows, warm (slight red content), and cool (slight blue content).

Orange

French Orange Mineral—Excellent spectrum hue. Heavy, therefore a little expensive.

Red Orange

American Vermilion— Brilliant red orange.

Red

Turkey Red Lake— Good red, slight yellow content.

Alizeran Crimson— Excellent red, close to spectrum red but is not always available.

Red Violet

Magenta Lake— A brilliant bluish red, makes rich violets with blue. Expensive but goes a long way.

Violet and Blue Violet

Purple Lake— A rich, brilliant violet. Very expensive. Special, not necessary to stock with magenta lake at hand.

Blue

Cobalt Blue— A pure primary blue although a little high in value.

Ultramarine Blue— A rich blue with a touch of red content. Mixes well to make purples, but poorly for greens.

Blue Green

Italian Blue—
A brilliant turquoise, although not a true blue green (high in value), it is a very useful color. Mixed with primrose yellow, it makes vibrant yellow greens and greens.

Prussian Blue—
Dark, rich blue green. Difficult mixer, good for near-black tones.

Green

Emerald Green—
Intense green, slight yellow content.

Medium Chrome Green—
A straight green but a little low in value.

Yellow Green

Primrose Yellow—
A cold yellow. Not necessary to stock with light chrome yellow, except as a special color.

Earth Colors

The earth colors are inexpensive neutral shades that can be used in place of the expensive method of neutralizing the more intense colors.

French Yellow Ochre—
Rich ochre or neutral yellow shade, extends into good cream shades.

Raw Italian Sienna—
Warmer and richer than ochre.

Burnt Italian Sienna—
Terra cotta and brick color.

Raw Turkey—
A cold brown, has greenish cast. Not too useful by itself. It is used to neutralize other colors.

Burnt Turkey Umber—
Rich brown, good wood-graining color.

Van Dyke Brown—
Very rich brown, but hard mixer. Excellent wood color.

Ivory Drop Black—
A bone black (avoid using lampblack which is commonly mistaken for bone black. Lampblack is greasy and therefore a hard mixer).

Zinc White—
A white pigment not whiting. Sometimes called Permanent White.

Danish Whiting—
Pure whiting, doesn't settle out. Excellent filler.

PAINTER'S ELEVATIONS

The designer must prepare for scene painting even if he is going to do his own painting. His painting ideas are expressed in the painter's elevations, which, unlike his sketch, remove all the atmosphere of stage lighting to show the true colors and exact form. The painter's elevation is a scaled drawing showing in detail the cartooning, or line drawing, a notation of actual color, and a clear indication of the painting technique. The scale of the drawing

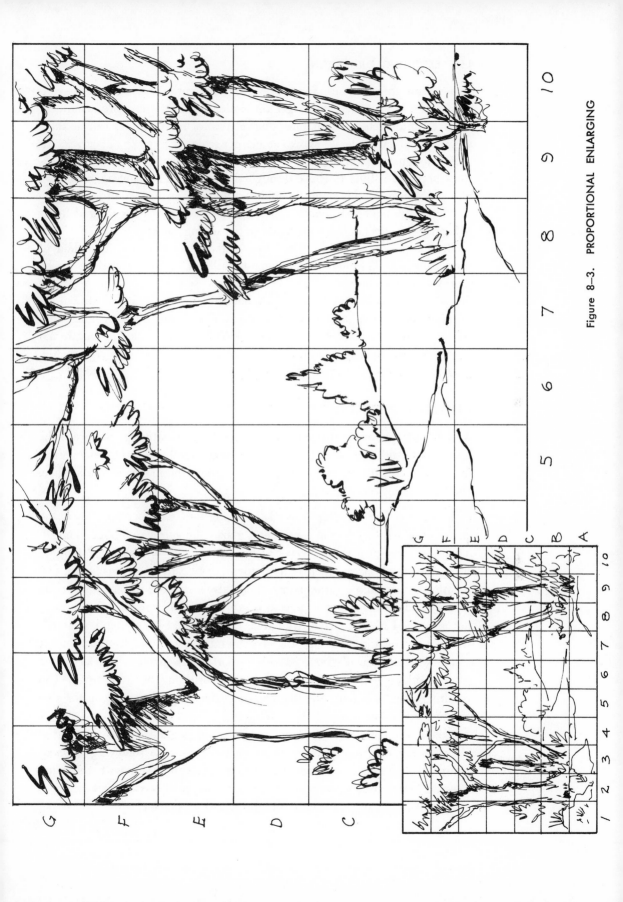

Figure 8–3. PROPORTIONAL ENLARGING

varies with the designer, some preferring to work at a small scale and others in a large scale. The larger the scale, however, the more accurately it can be interpreted. The painter's elevations for most settings can be done at ½-inch scale, with details shown at a larger scale.

If a designer is painting his own scenery, the preparing of painter's elevations becomes a time to think through the appropriate painting technique and procedure. At this point, if lights are to play an important part of the design, the designer can check the painter's elevations under colored lights to foresee the effect of the stage lights on the setting colors.

The painter, as he works from the painter's elevation, has a method of proportionally enlarging the drawing to full scale. Over the drawing he places a grid of horizontal and vertical lines, spaced, in the scale of the drawing, at two-foot intervals. A similar grid, at full scale, is drawn on priming coat of the surface to be painted. The spaces (not the lines) are lettered or numbered along the edges to facilitate the location of an internal square within the area (Figure 8–3). Proceeding square by square, the painter transposes the small-scale elevation into a full-scale drawing.

PAINTING PROCEDURE

The three steps toward preparing a surface for decorative painting are the size, prime, and base coats of paint. Their individual use or omission varies in accordance with the complexity of the design, the nature of the surface, and the painting technique.

Size Coats. The first step toward preparing new canvas or muslin is the size coat which shrinks the canvas and glazes the surface without filling it. There are several uses and ways to mix size coats that bear mentioning. First, the starch size, which is used to prepare canvas or muslin for dye painting or very thin opaque paints. It can also serve as a surface for opaque paints, especially if the opaque coat is not completely covering the surface, but is applied so as to leave large areas of unpainted background. A starch size is made by adding a cup of cooked laundry starch to a 16-quart bucket of hot working size of about 20-to-1 proportion. A touch of dye or scenic color is added to make it more visible for brushing on the canvas. The resulting coat is a taut, slightly glazed surface that is excellent for dye painting.

Second, the alum size which is used over old painted canvas to stop the old coat of paint from picking up or bleeding through following coats of paint. Formaldehyde is sometimes used in place of alum with the same effect. A small quantity of powdered alum (½ cup to a 16-quart bucket) is mixed into working size of about a 10- or 16-to-1 proportion.

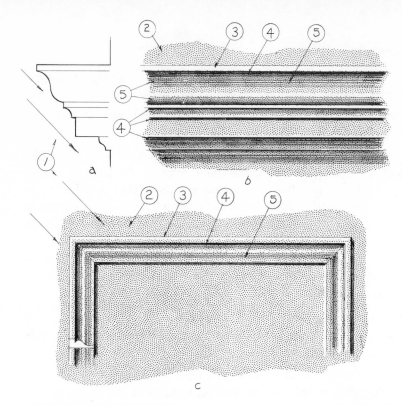

Figure 8–4. LINING TECH-NIQUES. (a) Profile of cornice to be painted. (1) Assumed direction of light. (b) Lining of cornice molding. (2) Local color. (3) Highlight. (4) Shade, darkest tone. (5) Shadow. (c) Lining of a raised panel molding.

A third use of a size coat is as a glaze. A glaze is a thin, transparent coat that is more of a painting technique than a preparation step. It gives the surface a slight gloss without covering up the undercoat. A glaze mix is prepared by weakening or strengthening the working size, depending upon the degree of gloss that is desired. The stronger the size, the higher the gloss. The technique can vary from a filmy, transparent wash to a fairly glossy finish. A glaze technique is tricky and difficult for a beginner. It has to be applied quickly and lightly to avoid moving the painted detail underneath.

PRIME COAT. The second step in preparing new canvas is the prime coat, which has the function of filling the canvas. When painting on new canvas it is necessary to have it filled or the colors will "strike in" and lose brilliance. This is very noticeable when old canvas is used beside the new canvas on a flat.

A prime coat is made of working size and whiting with a touch of color to facilitate the application. It is kept thin so as not to overload the canvas. Because the prime coat fills the canvas it tends to be an opaque coat and therefore cannot be used over areas of the canvas that are to be translucent or dye painted. If there are no translucent areas on the flats, the size and prime coats are sometimes combined into one operation, shrinking and filling the canvas at the same time.

All cartooning or layout drawing is done in charcoal on the prime coat. After the drawing is completed, key points or portions of the cartoons are "inked" in a fine line of dye or indelible pencil. The rest of the charcoal is "flogged" or dusted off the surface in preparation for the base coat. The inked-in portions of the design will bleed through the base coat and serve as a guide for later detailed painting.

BASE COAT.   The base coat is the under painting for the final decorative painting and texturing. The application and color of the base coat, then depends upon what is to follow. For example, a base coat may be of one tone as a basis for a slick, modern paneled wall; it may be a scumbling of two or three tones in preparation for an antiqued, weather-beaten surface, or it may become a graded wash under a stenciled wallpaper design.

As a mixture, the base coat is kept thin so as not to overload the canvas. Because it is more intense in color than the prime coat, it will have less whiting and more pigment.

DETAIL AND DECORATIVE PAINTING.   The final step of scene painting is the definition of form or the illusion of form through the various painting techniques of lining, texturing, and stenciling.

Lining.   The technique of lining, with straight edge or free hand, is to represent in two dimensions the complicated surfaces of the moldings in a cornice, chair rail, panel, or door trim.

Careful lining, in addition to "local color," is done with a minimum of three tones: high light, shade, and shadow. Sometimes in showing a large cast shadow two shadow tones are used consisting of a light and dark shadow. The high light is cooler and, of course, lighter in value than the "local color," while the shade and shadow are in warmer and darker tones.

The order of lining for a panel or cornice is determined after first studying a cross section of the molding and the direction of the light that would

Figure 8–5.   TEXTURING TECHNIQUES.   (1) Wet blending or scumble. (2) Dry scumble. (3) Spattering. (4) Combing or dry brushing. (5) Rag rolling. (6) Spraying.

1

2

3

reveal the molding if it were real. The position of a window or artificial-light sources are clues for fixing the general direction of light for each wall in the set. If the paneling is for a stock set that will be used in many positions, the light source is standardized as if it were coming from above and left of the surface (Figure 8–4).

Texturing. To avoid the starkness of a single tone and to bring more depth to a flat surface, the painter uses various texturing techniques. Because the stage lighting is from many sources compared to the limited sources found in nature, most of the natural shadows and reflected-light tonalities are eliminated. Much of this natural variation of tonality has to be painted into the set through the use of texturing techniques.

One of the simplest texturing techniques is to wet-blend or scumble three or more tones of a color on a surface. Using three brushes, one in each bucket, the three tones are brushed or blended together on the canvas while the paints are still wet. The result is an impression of one color with more depth and quality than is found in a single flat tone. This technique is usually handled on a broad scale with subtlety or obviousness depending upon the contrast or harmony of the tones.

A scumbling technique can also be done over a dry surface by blending the tones together with a dry brushing or feathering. Dry brushing, as the name implies, is done with the tip of a relatively dry brush so as to cover the under surface only partially and let it show through. Feathering refers to the direction of the brush stroke. The brush is drawn from the wet surface toward the dry so that the stroke ends in a featherlike pattern.

Other techniques that do basically the same texturing function at a smaller scale are: sponging, stippling, spattering, combing, and spraying. Each technique creates an individual feeling of texture as well as blending the tones into a vibrant surface (Figure 8–5).

All these techniques can be used to simulate the textural qualities of a

4

5

6

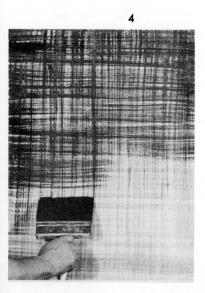

specific material such as stone, plaster, wallpaper, and the like. Some materials, however, require texturing techniques that border on decorative painting, wood and wood graining being a prime example (Figure 8–6).

The painting of wood graining employs the same movement of color found in the other techniques. The grain pattern, of course, will vary with the type and use of the make-believe wood. Is it to be matched-grain walnut veneer on a late Empire break-front secretary, or knotty-pine vertical paneling? Any attempt at realistic representation of wood graining on the stage should be preceded by a careful study of the real wood's color and grain characteristic.

If the wood is a door or door trim and should appear as a varnished finish, the graining can be glazed. Glazing, however, not only reduces the contrast between colors, but also lowers their value. This must be taken into consideration in the preparation of the grain colors.

The glazing of grain that has a varnished finish can be accomplished in two different ways. The first method has been mentioned, which is to grain the surface first then apply a glue, shellac, or flat-varnish glaze. Of the three glazes, flat varnish is the easiest to handle and gives the best results. The results, however, are hard to predict especially if there is a change of surface materials, such as from wood to canvas or vice versa.

A safer and easier approach is to put something with the paint (dry color) that will give a gloss and eliminate the necessity of glazing the surface at all. Scenic paint can be mixed directly with a flat varnish, which serves as a binder as well as giving the paint a slight sheen. Liquid wax mixed with scene paint produces the same effect and is even easier to handle. Either method can be brought into a higher luster by polishing with paste wax later. Glazed surfaces must be handled with caution, however, for there is always the danger of creating a surface that is too reflective; it then becomes annoying to actors and audience.

Stenciling.   The chief use of the stenciling techniques is for a painted wallpaper or similar condition in which a design motif is repeated in an interlocking over-all pattern. The cutting and printing of a stenciled design is the fastest and most effective method of repeating a small motif. After the means of interlocking the motif has been carefully figured out in relation to the size of the wall area, the motif is traced upon a sheet of stencil paper. Stencil paper is a tough, oil-impregnated paper prepared especially for stencils. It is readily available in art shops or paint and wallpaper stores, or can be made by applying a half-and-half mixture of linseed oil and turpentine to a heavy wrapping paper.

A well-planned stencil has at least one full motif with portions of adjacent

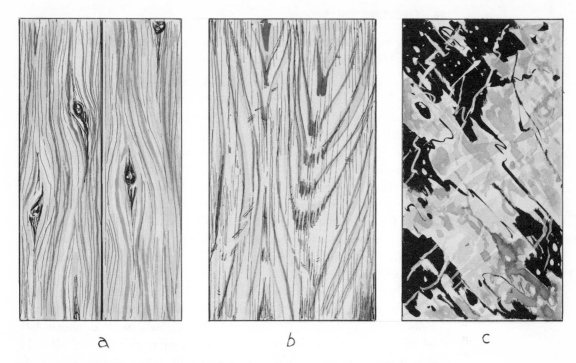

a   b   c

Figure 8–6. WOOD-GRAIN AND MARBLE TEXTURING. **(a)** Pine grain. **(b)** Oak grain. **(c)** Marble.

motifs to key the stencil into an interlocking scheme. The size of the motif and the amount needed for interlocking the design more or less determines the size of the stencil sheet. Care should be taken not to create too large a stencil that might become too awkward to handle. The motif is cut out of the paper with a sharp knife, razor blade, or exacto knife, being sure to leave some tabs within the open parts to support the loose ends and strengthen the stencil as a whole. Two or more stencils can be cut at one time for it is wise to have more than one stencil, especially if there is a large area to cover. They can be alternated in use so as to minimize the tendency of a stencil to become damp and misshapen from hard use.

After the stencil is cut, it is framed at the outside edges with 1 x 2 on edge to further strengthen it and at the same time to provide a shield to the spray if the paint is being applied with a spray gun. The stencil is coated with clear shellac or any water-repellent plastic spray as an additional protection from the water-soaking effect of scene paint.

The stencil print can be made by three different methods: by spray gun, by brush, or by sponge. The spray gun is fast but sometimes messy. Stenciling with a brush is slower. The brush should be kept fairly dry and stroked toward the center of the openings to avoid dribbles. The use of a sponge or soft cloth to apply the paint works best on an open stencil for the print is purposely textured and not clean cut (Figure 8–7).

Pouncing. Pouncing is another method of transferring and repeating a design motif. It is generally used when the motif is either too large for a stencil, doesn't repeat enough times for one to bother cutting a stencil, or is repeated in reverse. Pouncing differs from stenciling in that only the outline or cartoon of the motif instead of a painted print is transferred as in the stencil.

The pounce pattern is made by first drawing the design on a piece of wrapping paper and then perforating the outline with a "pounce wheel." The best type of pounce wheel (Figure 8–7c) has a small swivel-mounted perforating wheel. It works better on a padded surface, such as a blanket or fold of canvas, than by trying to perforate the wrapping paper on a hard table top or floor.

After the design is perforated and the back-side rough edges are lightly sanded, the paper is laid on the canvas in the desired position. The pattern is rubbed with a pounce bag made of a thin material such as cheesecloth filled with a dry color or charcoal dust. The outline is strengthened after the pouncing with charcoal, paint, or dye, depending upon the painting technique to follow.

TEXTURED SURFACES

Although their value on the stage is debatable, textured surfaces are sometimes desirable. Important points to consider before texturing a surface are: (1) A textured surface cannot be reclaimed for a different use without re-covering the piece of scenery. (2) Deeply textured surfaces will not stand excessive handling or wear. (3) Unless the texturing is in the position on the stage to get the proper lighting (preferably side lighting), it may as well be painted.

SPACKEL. The use of a prepared mixture of plaster and whiting called spackel is the most familiar method of texturing. Because of the tendency of any texture coat to crack and flake off, spackel is applied on a base of the same color unless, as an aging technique, some areas are purposely knocked off to reveal an undercoat of a contrasting color. The spackel, which can be obtained at local paint shops, is mixed in cold water, colored with dye, and

Figure 8–7. STENCILING TECHNIQUES. (a) Unframed stencil for dry-brush application. (b) Framed stencil for spray-gun application. Note how the stencil is keyed at the top and bottom. As this stencil follows a vertical line it is not necessary to key it horizontally. (c) Pouncing: (1) Pounce, or perforated design. (2) Pounce wheel. (3) Pounce bag. (4) The pounced design transferred onto the canvas.

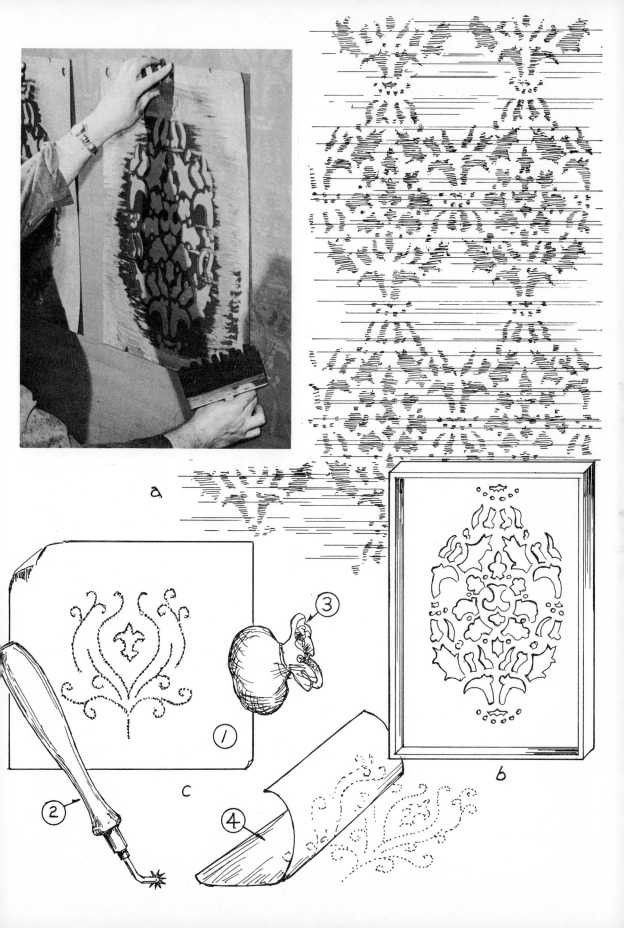

a

b

c

1

2

3

4

applied in about ¼-inch layers. While it is damp it may be roughed, combed, or grained for more texture. Sawdust, cork, or wood chips may be added to the mixture for extra texture. After the spackel coat dries (about 24 hours), it can be shellacked and detail painted.

SAWDUST COAT.   Sawdust or wood chips can be mixed directly with scenic paint and applied as a texture coat. The size should be stiffened a little to bind the sawdust firmly. A sawdust coat requires less preparation and dries quicker than spackel but does not have as deep a texture.

SAND COAT.   Prepared texture paint called "sand coat" combines sand with an oil or latex based paint. Flowtex, a latex-based sand coat, has been successfully used to prime wood and veneer surfaces with one coat. It gives the wood a texture close to that of scenery canvas and at the same time covers all blemishes, nail holes, and screw heads, thereby eliminating the necessity to cover the veneer with canvas or muslin. The resulting surface is excellent for scene paints as well as stopping the tendency of wood grain to bleed through subsequent coats of water-color paints.

SURFACE MATERIALS

Related to texturing a surface are the various materials that are used as a painting surface. Their varied uses are primarily for textural reasons. Each has its special handling and individual effect.

Irish linen has, of course, long since disappeared from the American theatre as the standard covering for framed scenery. Its durability and excellent texture have not quite been replaced by the scene canvas now in common use.

Canvas, which is eight-ounce cotton duck, has been discussed (pages 160-161) as a painting surface. It is the standard and most frequently used painting surface for all types of scenery. All other surfaces are limited in use to a special effect.

Muslin (unbleached) is the next most frequently used covering material. Although it lacks the texture and durability of canvas, its lightweight weave is useful for other purposes. As was mentioned, muslin is an excellent dye-painting surface for translucencies.

Scrim can be used as a painting surface outside of its general use as a dye-painted transparency. It can be used as a covering material if backed by canvas or some other opaque fabric.

Unbacked scrim can also be painted (dry brushed) with thin scenic colors. They are not as good as dyes for they tend to stiffen the scrim which is a disadvantage if it has to fold or roll. To paint large areas of scrim it is best to use a spray gun to avoid stretching it out of shape.

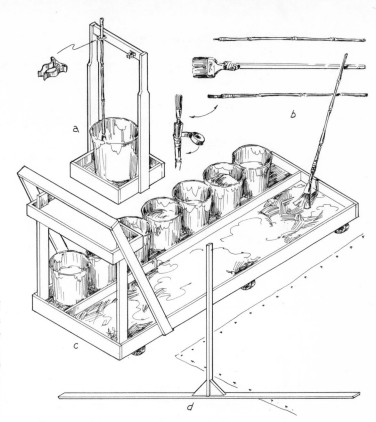

Figure 8–8. PAINTING ON THE FLOOR. Extensive floor painting is made easier with the use of proper tools and the right type of brushes. (a) Individual paint-bucket carrier. (b) Long handles for the brushes. (c) Paint cart with palette area for mixing paint. (d) Straight edge with handle.

Scrim mesh can be filled to create opaque areas with a mixture of latex and powdered chalk kept thin enough to spread, but thick enough to fill the mesh of the scrim.

Burlap is frequently used as a covering material chiefly for its texture. Burlap should be backed or fastened to a firm surface for it is jute and may stretch or sag under a heavy coat of paint. Sometimes it helps to paint and dry it horizontally.

Burlap needs to be heavily sized to keep the color from "striking in." However, this may be a desirable effect if it is to be an old tapestry or wall hanging.

METHODS OF PAINTING

Scenery is painted in two different positions: horizontally or vertically. The various methods of painting are devised to facilitate either way of painting.

HORIZONTAL PAINTING. Painting on the floor is the oldest and simplest method requiring the least mechanical assistance. Long handles on the brushes, charcoal holders, and straight edges help take the backache out of horizontal painting. The most essential requirement is lots of smooth floor space (preferably wood) and good overhead illumination (Figure 8–8).

Although some painting techniques are best employed horizontally, others are accomplished more easily in a vertical position.

STATIONARY FRAME AND BOOMERANG. It is easy to fasten scenery against a wall or on a stationary frame along a wall, but it is not so easy to reach all areas without using a ladder. A rolling platform or "boomerang" as it is called provides the painter with two or three painting levels (Figure 8–9b).

MOVING FRAME. The moving paint frame which raises or lowers past the working level brings the greatest flexibility to vertical painting (Figure 9a). The frame lowers into a well or to a second painting level. Some unusually high frames many times have two or three decks so that the painters can work at different levels at the same time.

TOOLS AND BRUSHES

The painter's most important tool is, of course, his brush. A good brush should have long bristles and a full shape (avoid hollow centers). Pure bristles are so expensive, especially in the larger sizes, that many painters have turned to nylon brushes. A nylon brush with sand-blasted tips is about half the price of the pure bristle brush of the same size. The difference in price offsets the slight disadvantage of nylon. Water color tends to run off the nylon, causing it to hold less paint than a pure bristle brush.

Because scene-painting brushes are used predominately in water colors, the bristles should be rubber set. Some brushes set in glue are suitable for oil paint, but will break down with continued use in water color.

TYPES OF BRUSHES. The types of brushes for scene painting are classified by the work they do, such as priming, base coating or "lay in," decorating, and lining (Figure 8–10).

The priming brush is the widest brush (6 inches to 8 inches). It holds a large quantity of paint which makes it good for spreading size and prime coats quickly and efficiently.

The lay-in brush is about 4 inches wide for the more careful painting of a base coat, blending, spattering, and similar techniques.

A decorating brush is from 3 inches to 1½ inches wide with a long handle. Sometimes called a foliage brush, it is used for most of the decorative painting, including the tree leaves. The foliage brush is a pure bristle brush made especially for scene painting and consequently is quite expensive. A sash tool, which is a long handled brush for painting window sashes, makes an inexpensive decorating brush.

Liners are also long-handled brushes varying in width from 1 inch to ¼ inch. Liners should have long pure bristles to perform well. A 1-inch sash tool can do limited lining, but there is no substitute for the smaller brushes.

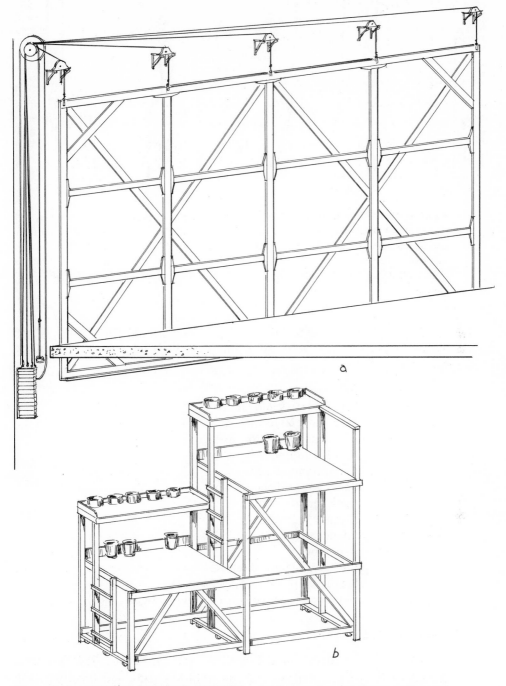

Figure 8–9. VERTICAL PAINTING METHODS. (a) The moving paint frame raises and lowers into a well extending below the main working-deck level. Scenery is attached to the frame and is painted in a vertical position by raising and lowering the frame. **(b)** The boomerang, a stepped-level platform on casters, provides a variety of working levels for the painter.

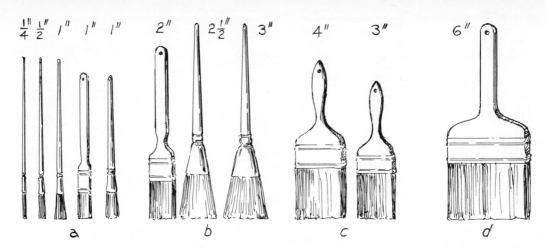

Figure 8–10. BRUSHES AND TOOLS. *Scene-painting brushes:* **(a)** Lining brushes, flat and oval. **(b)** Decorating brushes. **(c)** Lay-in brushes. **(d)** Priming brushes. *Painting tools and accessories:* (1) Beveled straight edge. (2) Yard stick. (3) Snap line. (4) Charcoal and holder. (5) Large compass. (6) Tank spray. (7) Spray gun and compressor. (8) Pounce wheel. (9) Plumb bob. (10) Bow snap line. (11) Burner and double boiler for glue. (12) Flogger.

PAINTING TOOLS. Besides brushes and paints, the painter uses other implements to prepare, lay out, and paint scenery. Other necessary painting tools are:

> Rule or steel tape
> Charcoal stick and holder
> Snap line (50 feet)
> Bow snap line (6 to 8 feet)
> Beveled straight edge (6 feet)
> Large compass (36 inches)
> Spray gun and compressor
> Tank sprays
> Flogger
> Pounce wheel
> Plumb bob
> Buckets (14 and 16 quart)
> Small pots or cans (No. 10 cans)
> Burner and double boiler for glue (Figure 8–10)

ANILINE DYES

Aniline dyes are available in almost all the standard colors. They are used for inking in outlines, thin wash glazes, translucencies, and for dip-dyeing fabrics.

Dyeing or painting with dyes is a different process than painting with scene paints. Scene paint changes the color of a surface by covering it with a pigment which is held in place by a binder. Dyeing, on the other hand, is

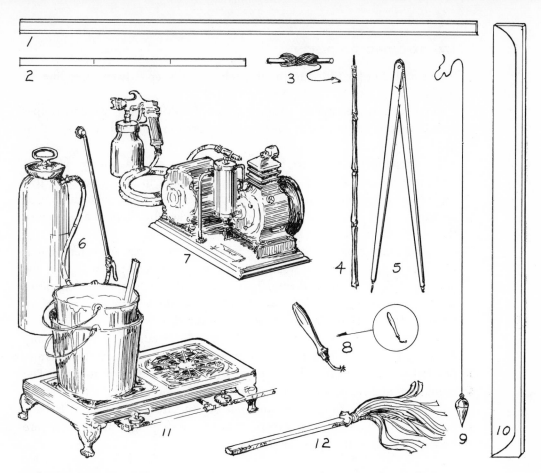

a chemical process. The dye color becomes a part of the material it is dyeing. It is important that the dye and material have an affinity for each other or a complete chemical action will not take place.

To dye cotton duck or muslin it is sometimes necessary to add a little acetic acid or vinegar to the dye solution. The acetic acid increases the affinity of the cotton for the dye causing the fabric to absorb more color from the dye bath. The addition of a little salt also helps to increase the amount of absorption. Salt counteracts the tendency of dye stuffs to go into solution, making it easier for the dye color to be absorbed by the material.

The presence of too much salt in the mixture, possibly from salted dyes or flameproofing compounds frequently mixed with the dye bath, can keep the dye from going into solution. It is important that all the crystals dissolve or streaks of concentrated color will appear on the surface of the canvas. If the dye is separating, the addition of some alcohol will insure a complete solution. Normally, the crystals go into solution in hot water without any trouble.

For extensive dye painting, as would occur in painting a translucent drop, the muslin is prepared with a starch size (page 160). If the painting is being done on a fabric that can't be starch sized, such as velour or silk, a little starch can be added to the dye mixture to keep it from spreading on the fabric.

Dip-dyeing is used mostly on small pieces of fabric such as window drapes or tablecloths. Occasionally, large gauze pieces are dipped with excellent results.

The preparation of the dye for dip-dyeing is the same as for dye painting except, of course, larger in quantity. It is important to be sure enough dye has been mixed, for to run out of dye mix in the middle of a dipping is disastrous. The color of the mix should be checked by dipping a sample of the fabric before preparing it for dipping.

In preparation for dip-dyeing, the fabric is first dipped in water. If it is new material, it should be washed to remove the size. After wringing, the still damp fabric is dipped into the dye mix. If it is a stage gauze, after squeezing or wringing out the excess dye, it should be stretched to dry, or hung in place and stretched back into shape as it dries.

An important thing to remember is that dip-dyeing will take out any flameproofing that might have been in the material. It has to be reflame-proofed later, or better still flameproofing mixed into the dye solution. The regular sal ammoniac and borax mixture (see Flameproofing) can be cut to half strength by adding water and still give a satisfactory test. It is best, however, to run some test experiments under dipping conditions before taking a chance with a large piece.

FLAMEPROOFING

Canvas and muslin can be purchased already flameproofed but if the scenery has been washed for reuse the canvas will have to be flameproofed again. A mixture of one pound of sal ammoniac, one pound of borax, and three quarts of water is an inexpensive flameproofing formula. It is brushed or sprayed onto previously dampened material for the best results. Sheer materials, such as scrim or bobbinet, should be dipped to insure a successful test.

As the flameproofing mixture is highly corrosive to metals, brushes and spray cans should, after use, be washed thoroughly in cold water. A small amount of acetic acid in the water helps to counteract the corrosive action.

ADDITIONAL SUPPLIES

There are some additional supplies that supplement the dry colors, glue, and dyes which are directly associated with scene painting. Some have been mentioned in relation to a particular painting technique. These supplies and their uses are:

White shellac —for glazes, water-repellent finishes, binder, and hardener.

Alcohol —solvent for shellac and speeds the dissolving of colors that are poor mixers.

Flat varnish —glaze finish and paint binder.

Turpentine —solvent for varnish and oil paints.

Liquid wax —glaze finish and paint binder.

Metallic paints—powder mixed with strong size for metallic surfaces. All right for scenery, but not for props. Spray cans (Crylon) have harder finish, good for props, more expensive.

Glycerin —added to paints to slow drying.

Formaldehyde —preservative.

Alum —for alum-size preparation.

Sal ammoniac —flameproofing chemical.

Borax —Formula—1 lb. borax, 1 lb. sal ammoniac to 3 qts. of water.

Oil paints —limited use in the theatre. When they are used they are the flat Japan color, or Coach colors.

9

THE HANDLING
OF SCENERY

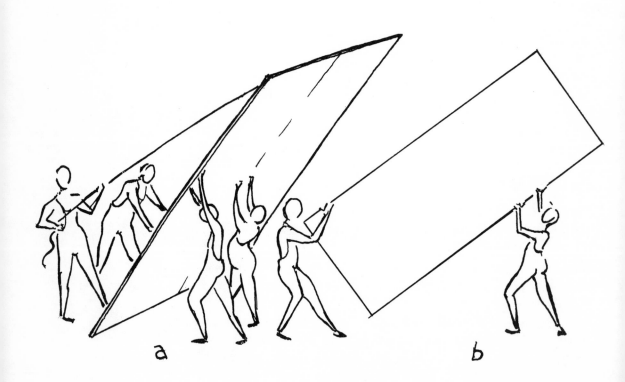

a   b

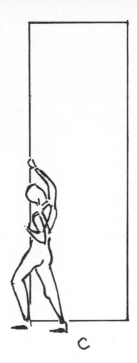

Figure 9–1. RUNNING SCENERY. The running or "gripping" of scenery is the simplest handling method although, occasionally, the awkward shape or extreme size of a piece may require experience to handle it successfully. (a) "Walking-up" a stiffened two-fold. (b) "Edging-up" a single flat. (c) Running or "gripping" a single flat. (d) Making a lash. *Page 178:* (e) Three men running a top-heavy piece. *Page 179:* (f) Running a two-fold. (g) "Floating" down a single flat.

c

d

When the designer is confronted with a multiscene play, he has to consider early in planning a method of handling the many settings. From the numerous ways of moving scenery he can develop a production scheme into his design concept. Consequently, the more he knows of the mechanics of the modern stage and theatrical techniques for moving scenery, the closer he can come to fully realizing his designs. This is especially true of theatre away from New York and its unlimited budgets, where the designer has to be clever not only to overcome limited funds but many times poorly equipped stages. Some hold the belief that too much technical knowledge inhibits a designer's imagination. To the contrary, it can help him solve his scenery-shifting problems with an ingenuity that often becomes inventively original.

INFLUENCING FACTORS

How scenery is to be handled is influenced by four major factors: the play, the theatre and its stage, the design of the production, and the budget.

PLAY STRUCTURE. The form of the play or its plot structure are the primary influences on the handling of scenery. A play, for instance, may have many unrelated episodic scenes, a "flash back" technique, several simultaneous scenes with continuous action, or the conventional three-act form. The structure of the play, besides determining the number of scenes or locale changes in their order of appearance or reappearance, also establishes the *kind* of change.

The most common interval for a change of scene is between acts. The "act change," which can be as short as three minutes or as long as fifteen minutes, presents no great problem under optimum conditions, assuming the stage has adequate flying and offstage space. Even under limited stage conditions, an act change usually allows enough time to maneuver the scenery although it may require more ingenuity and manpower.

A change within the act, or "scene change," can be as short as thirty seconds to as long as a minute and a half. If the time interval of a scene change is too long the continuity of the play is seriously interrupted.

A scene change, by necessity a fast change, can be handled several different ways. It may be a hidden change, taking place behind a curtain, or without a curtain, but hidden by a "blackout." It may be a *visible* change (avista) made in full view of the audience with a display of theatrical magic, or by actor–stagehands frankly moving elements of scenery as a part of the action.

In contrast to the other kinds of changes, the avista, or visible change, becomes more a part of the play, by calling attention to the movement of scenery. As a theatrical technique, it obviously fits only certain types of plays and production schemes.

THEATRE AND STAGE.   The shape of the theatre and the size of the stage, of course, have an important influence on the movement of scenery. The amount of flying space and equipment, the extent of offstage and wing space, the size of the proscenium opening, and sightline conditions obviously help determine the way scenery can be handled.

Some stages have more elaborate mechanical aids or stage machinery for

shifting scenery such as: built-in revolving stage, tracking and offstage space for full-stage wagons, or elevator stages. The existence of one or more of these mechanical aids in a theatre cannot help but influence scenery-handling techniques.

Other scenery-shifting considerations are those of a traveling production. Instead of one theatre and stage the designer has to consider the size and sightline conditions of many stages and auditoriums as well as the physical limitations and extreme portability expected of scenery for a "road show."

Elaborate scenery-moving devices such as turntables and treadmills are sometimes duplicated so as to reduce the setup time in each theatre. Two crews are used. The first specializes in assembling the shifting aid which might be a turntable, for example. They work in advance of the second crew who are running the show. The second crew, when the run is finished, moves the show from theatre "A" to theatre "B" onto the preassembled turntable No. 2, leaving behind turntable No. 1. The first crew then returns to theatre "A" and moves turntable No. 1 in leap-frog fashion to theatre "C," and so on.

DESIGN AND SCHEME OF PRODUCTION.   The scene designer combines the influences of the play and the stage and adds a third control, the scheme of production. The designer's production scheme stems from the kind of scene or locale change inherent in the play, the physical limitations of the stage, and his visual concept of the play's setting (Chapter 4). A designer cannot design a large production without thinking through, at least in basic terms, a method or scheme for handling the changes.

BUDGET.   The influence of budget on the handling of scenery is felt directly through the control of the scale of the set designs and general size of the

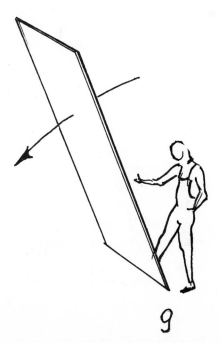

f

g

productions. Although the operational budget has little direct effect on the form of the physical stage, it does influence its operation in providing funds for an adequate production staff. A large stage with a small technical staff, for example, would limit the amount of scenery that could be efficiently handled.

An operational budget also is tied in with the estimated length of run. A Broadway show with a prolonged run, for example, can reduce its operational costs by spending more money on costly mechanical aids to shift the scenery, thereby cutting down the number of stagehands on the weekly payroll.

The operational budget of university or community theatre influences scenery handling in a slightly different way. The decision to use an extensive mechanical aid is based upon its reuse value for other productions so as to spread the cost throughout the season's operational budget.

BACKSTAGE ORGANIZATION

The layman who has seen a fast change from a backstage vantage point is often amazed by the teamwork and precision with which the large pieces of scenery, properties, lights, and actors seem to move. This is due, to some extent, to careful rehearsing, but largely it is the result of normal backstage organization and its division of responsibility. Under the coordinating management of the stage manager a production has two major divisions: acting and technical. The technical responsibilities are divided between the scenery, electrical, property, and costume departments.

STAGE MANAGER.   Once the production is on the stage, the stage manager becomes its field commander. The responsibility of the performance is in his hands. He starts each performance, gives all cues, calls the actors, and posts all daily calls. He is charged with maintaining production standards set by the director and company discipline onstage.

STAGE CARPENTER.   Although taking his cues from the stage manager, the master carpenter is in charge of the shifts, the rigging, and the general condition of the scenery. Responsible to him is the crew, which is made up of assistant carpenters, grips (stagehands), and flymen.

MASTER ELECTRICIAN.   The responsibilities of the master electrician include: the hanging and focusing of the lighting instruments, the maintenance of all electrical equipment, and operation of the switchboard for the lighting cues. Any movement of lighting equipment during a shift comes under the supervision of the stage carpenter but may be done by grips assigned to the electrical department.

MASTER PROPERTY MAN.   The property man's duties include the care and maintenance of the set and hand props, rugs, ground cloth, mechanical sound effects, and any trick device handled by the actors too small to be classified as scenery. He supervises the handling of props during a shift with the help of grips assigned to the property department.

Sometimes electrified props cause what may seem to be double handling. A living room lamp, for example, is placed on the set by a member of the prop crew, but it is connected and lighted by the light crew. The offstage storage and visual appearance of the lamp is the responsibility of property men, while all electrical maintenance is done by the electrician. The division of responsibility is clearly and logically defined.

SOUND MAN.   Although traditionally a member of the electrical department, the sound man is established in many theatre organizations as a separate department. The increasing use of high-fidelity recording for a major portion of the sound effects and incidental music warrants in many cases the creation of a sound department.

The sound man is responsible for the recording and editing of each show tape as well as the operation of sound equipment for sound cues. He supervises the placement and installation of speakers and microphones, maintains all sound equipment, the stage manager's inner-communication, and for a permanent producing group might organize and service a sound-recording library.

WARDROBE MISTRESS.   The care and maintenance of all costumes is the responsibility of the wardrobe mistress, as well as the assistance of actors during a fast costume change. The backstage organization of community and university theatres often places the supervision of make-up in the costume department.

METHODS OF HANDLING SCENERY

The four basic methods of handling scenery, in the order of their increasing complexity and additional construction are: first, the moving or running of scenery on the floor; second, the flying of scenery; third, the moving of scenery on casters, including such large units as wagons and revolving stages; fourth, the handling of scenery through the stage floor by elevators.

THE RUNNING OF SCENERY ON THE FLOOR

Running or "gripping" of scenery is the simplest handling method and requires the least additional construction. As the units are usually strong enough to support themselves, the only additional support that is needed is horizontal stiffening of two or more units; the vertical bracing of the piece in an upright position; and the quick and easy method of joining together the various parts of the set. Occasionally the extreme height of scenery combined with its traditional thinness makes it difficult to move, to anyone not experienced in handling scenery.

The designer frequently thinks through a method of handling a particular piece of scenery before deciding on the scale or fragileness of its design. Some of the many ways of handling single flats, two-folds, and partially assembled units of scenery on the floor are illustrated in Figure 9–1.

STIFFENING, BRACING, AND JOINING.   Because scenery has to travel in units of relatively small, lightweight sizes to get in and out of theatres, it depends on joining or unfolding these smaller units into larger shapes. The new larger shape requires stiffening to be safely handled in a shift.

A stiffener is usually a horizontal stiffening member (1 x 3 or 1 x 4 on edge) that is loose-pin-hinged into place as the set is assembled. A vertical stiffener is often called a "brace," especially if it is in the form of a "jack," to brace the unit in an upright position. Bracing and stiffening can take a variety of forms depending upon the shape and size of the scenery they are reinforcing (Figure 9–2).

Joining appears in three different categories again related to the portable nature of scenery and the degree of permanence of the joint. Elements of scenery may be joined together by fixed or permanent joining, by assembly joining, or by temporary joining. The kind of joint and its location is often important to the design as the designer seeks ways to avoid a crack or open joint in a conspicuous area of the setting.

Fixed joining occurs as the scenery is being built (with use of nails, screws, and so on). A fixed hinged joint is made with tight-pin hinges so that large units composed of several small pieces may unfold into larger sizes. The smaller pieces remain fixed together and travel or move from shop to stage folded, to be unfolded and stiffened into their final shape in the theatre (Figure 9–3a, b, c, d).

On the other hand, large areas of scenery may be made in separate small pieces to be assembled in the theatre. Loose-pin hinges, bolts and wing nuts, and turn buttons are some of the most frequently used methods of assembly joining pieces of scenery together into a larger unit. After it is stiffened and braced, the larger unit can be handled in its assembled form until time to leave the theatre (Figure 9–3e, f, m).

The temporary joining of scenery occurs during the striking and making of a set during an act or scene change. The lashed joint is the most common means of temporarily joining units of scenery. Loose-pin hinges, turn buttons, hooks and eyes are some additional ways that scenery may be temporarily joined (Figure 9–3e, j, k).

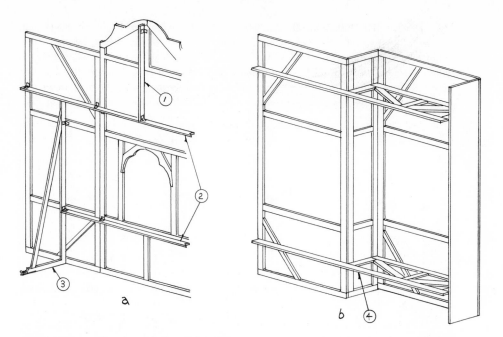

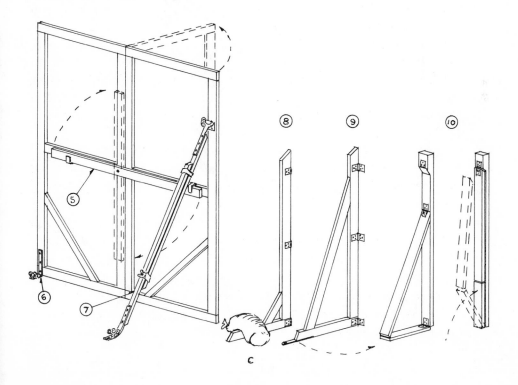

Figure 9–2. BRACING AND STIFFENING. **(a)** Stiffening a flat wall: (1) Vertical stiffener. (2) Horizontal stiffener. (3) Bracing or "jack." **(b)** Stiffening a jogged wall: (4) A framed stiffener which conforms to the shape of the wall. **(c)** Other bracing and stiffening techniques: (5) A swivel keeper bar and keeper hooks. (6) Bent footiron and stage screw. (7) Adjustable stage brace. (8) L-jack and sandbag (no stage screw). (9) Hinged jack. (10) Folding jack.

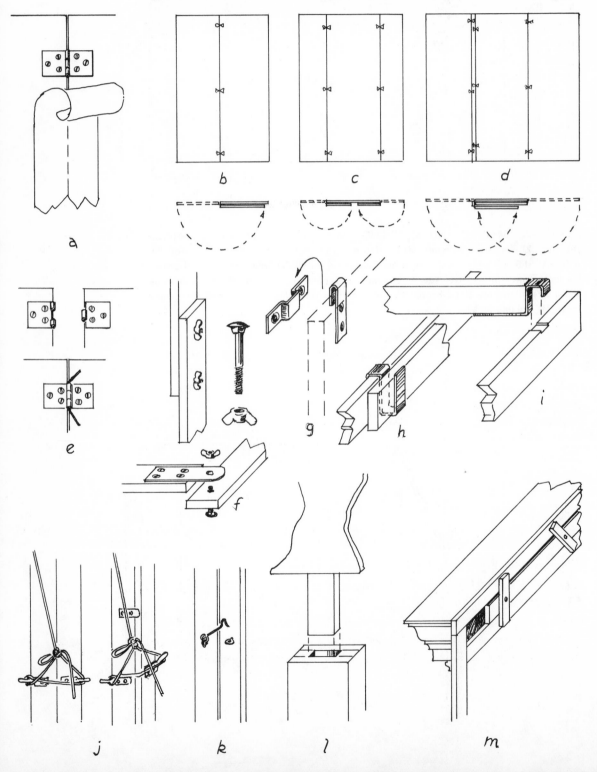

Figure 9–3. THE JOINING OF SCENERY. *Fixed joining:* **(a)** Tight-pin hinge and dutchman. **(b)** Two-fold, two flats tight-pin-hinged together. **(c)** Three-fold, two jogs, and a flat hinged together. **(d)** Three-fold and "tumbler" to hinge three full-width flats together. *Assembly joining:* **(e)** Loose-pin hinge. **(f)** Bolting. **(g)** Picture hanger. **(h)** S-batten hook. **(i)** Keeper hook on end of a spanner. *Temporary joining:* **(j)** Lashing, flush and around corner. Note stop cleat. **(k)** Hook and eye. **(l)** Tongue and socket. **(m)** Turn buttons.

FLYING SCENERY

The designer is always interested in the size of the stage house and the type of flying system, if any, over the stage, for the extent of flown scenery he may design depends upon their presence or absence. A good stage house that is designed to handle scenery in the air will have an adequate flying system and generous amount of hanging space, which means a high and wide loft. The two common methods of flying scenery are the pin-and-rail and counterweight systems. Both are based on the presence of a gridiron over the stage to support the sheaves or pulley blocks and the extended control of the line-sets to one of the side walls. They differ in the complexity of the rigging, cost of installation, and the flexibility of use.

GRIDIRON. As the name implies, the gridiron is a grid or open floor of iron high over the stage. The average gridiron has at least three and sometimes four or five channels which run up and down stage and are spaced at approximately ten-foot intervals across stage. Across each channel opening, which is about five inches wide, sit the sheaves that make up the line-sets. Each line as it runs over the sheave drops through the channel to the stage floor.

The space between the channels is floored with strips of 3-inch channel iron running parallel to the main channels. The channel-iron strips are set far enough apart to allow the spotting of additional sheaves for special spotlines (Figure 9–4c-1).

LINE-SETS. A line-set refers to the grouping of three or more lines into a set to be handled as one line. The sheaves of a line-set are usually placed over each channel opening and are all at the same distance from the proscenium, thus forming a line parallel to the footlights.

The number of lines in a line-set depends upon the number of channels in the individual gridiron. A stage with a wide proscenium opening might have as high as five lines in a set, while a small stage usually has only three lines to a set.

The lines are named by their length and position on the stage. The line nearest the control side (pinrail or lock rail) of the stage is the "short line" and the line to the far side of the stage is the "long line." The line in between is, of course, the "center line." A four line-set would have two center lines, a "long center," a "short center," and so on.

PIN AND RAIL. The pin-and-rail system is the older though more flexible of the two flying systems. It is a less costly installation but does, however, require more skill and greater manpower to operate. The "hemp" system, as it is sometimes called, uses ¾-inch manila rope for liftlines. As illustrated in Figure 9–4a, the individual line in a line-set (1), (2), (3) comes up from the stage, passes through the loft block, travels horizontally to one pulley in the head block (4) located on the left or right stage wall. From the head block in which the pulleys are mounted in tandem, the lines are brought together as a set and tied off at the pinrail (5). The lower rail of the pinrail is usually the trim tie for the drop in its "in" or working position, and the top rail receives the tie for the "out" or stored position. A line-set can be "clewed" or bound together (7) and sandbagged (6) to counterweight a heavy piece for easy handling.

As can be seen, the pin-and-rail system has great flexibility in its ability to use, as desired, only part of a line-set, add a spotline to a line-set, or, in some instances, cross line-sets. The adding of a spotline employs a single rope and loft sheave occasionally placed in a remote position on the gridiron to fly a "raked" or angled piece of scenery (Figure 9–4c-1).

The chief disadvantage of a "hemp house" is the amount of manpower that is required to run a show, as well as the professional skill necessary to rig and safely counterweight heavy pieces of scenery. To the designer, this disadvantage is far outweighed by the greater design possibilities inherent in the flexibility of the pin-and-rail system.

THE COUNTERWEIGHT SYSTEM. Unlike the pin-and-rail system which can separate or add a single line to the line-sets, the counterweight system uses fixed line-sets. Although the counterweight system was born in an era of box settings and raked scenery as theatrical styles, it is, paradoxically, rigidly based upon wing and backdrop staging. It keeps the lines in sets, fixed to a pipe batten parallel to the footlights.

The system, as illustrated in Figure 9–4b, begins at the pipe batten (1) and the permanently attached wire-cable liftlines (2). Lifting the batten, the lines pass through the individual loft blocks at each channel, over a multi-grooved, single-pulley headblock (3) and attach to the top of the counter-weight arbor (4). The arbor is guided by a "T" track (5), or guy wire, and controlled by a separate purchase line. The purchase line (6) is also attached to the top of the counterweight arbor and passes through the large groove in the headblock. It then turns toward the floor and after going through the

Figure 9–4. FLYING SYSTEMS. (a) Pin-and-rail or "hemp" system: (1) Short line. (2) Center line. (3) Long line. (4) Tandem head block. (5) Double pinrail on fly floor. (6) Sandbag counterweight. (7) Clew or "sunday" on a line-set. (b) Counterweight system: (1) Pipe batten, a fixed line set. (2) Hoisting cable for liftlines. (3) Head block, multi-grooved. (4) Trim chains at top of arbor. (5) "T" track. (6) Purchase line. (7) Lock and safety line on lock rail which may be on a fly floor or the stage deck. (8) Idler pulley. (c) A demonstration of the flexibility of the pin-and-rail system: (1) Spot sheaves used to fly a drop at an askew angle. The spotlines use the same or adjacent head blocks. (2) The separation of a single line from a line-set to use in a spot-sheave.

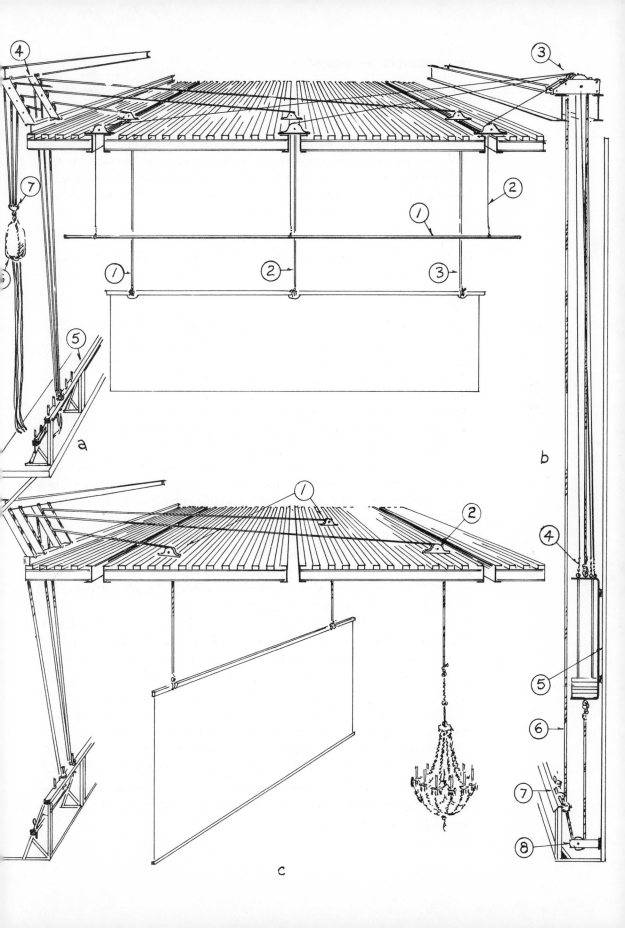

a

b

c

lock (7) on the lock rail and around the idler pulley (8) fastens to the bottom of the arbor.

Pulling down on the outside purchase line lifts the arbor and lowers the scenery hanging on the batten. A corresponding amount of weight placed on the arbor balances the weight of the scenery. Although the counterweight system is easy to run with parallel scenery, it is less flexible due to the fixed line-sets. Most of the rigging time used to hang an angled or raked piece is spent in overcoming rather than using the system.

THE SYNCHRONOUS-WINCH SYSTEM.   The newest method of flying scenery is the synchronous-winch system designed by George Izenour. It promises to give the theatre both the flexibility of the pin-and-rail and the weight-lifting capacity of the counterweight system, plus the added feature of a centralized electronic control.

There have been attempts in the past to electrify a flying system such as a single electric-motor winch lifting a battened line-set. All the lines in the set were wound upon a single drum which turned in only one direction to lift the batten. A mechanical clutching and braking device disengaged the drum from the motor allowing the weight of the attached scenery to bring the batten back down to the stage floor. Individual winches were sometimes employed but they operated independently and at a fixed speed. The synchronous-winch system is the first to apply winch power to the individual liftlines rather than a line-set. The liftlines can be placed in any pattern and still lift at a synchronized speed. The control instead of being located along one side of the stage is centralized in a portable console that can be placed in a convenient position on the stage floor.

With the winch system, the designer no longer has to think in terms of line-sets unless he specifically wants them. In a sense, every line is a spotline to be placed in any position or grouped into any pattern the floor plan may require. The designer has at his disposal all the flexibility of the pin-and-rail system in only a fraction of the rigging time.

Figure 9–5 is a schematic diagram of the synchronous-winch installation. The gridiron design of the winch system differs from the pin-and-rail and counterweight systems in respect to the number of channel openings that are provided. Although the channels (1) still run up and down stage, they are placed at four-foot intervals and extend wall to wall, over the entire stage area. Note that the individual loft blocks do not sit on the gridiron floor but are hung from a beam directly above the channel opening.

The winches (2) are mounted along the proscenium wall and back wall of the stage house. A basic system consists of thirty or more winches, each of which is powered by a one-horsepower synduction (synchronous and induction)-gear motor. The drum of the winch is vertical and the motor is reversible to raise or lower the line.

The liftline (3) which is ⅛-inch airplane strand-steel cable has a safe load capacity of 250 pounds. An individual line coming from a single winch is permanently threaded through a movable swivel loft block (4) which can be located over the desired pick-up point on the stage floor by sliding up- or downstage along its support beam. A pattern of lines (7) can be lifted at a synchronous speed in groups of winches up to eight.

The driver group (10) that powers the winch's motor is located in a remote position preferably out of the building because of the excessive noise and vibration it creates. The group consists of a variable frequency alternator which generates the current induced into all the winch motors that are connected to one of the two driver groups. As the frequency is varied, the winch motors synchronize and turn at the same speed (9A).

The alternator is driven by the prime mover of the driver group, a thirty-horse-power squirrel-cage motor which runs at a constant speed. (9C)

The speed or frequency output of the power group is controlled by dynamatic coupling between the prime mover and alternator (9B). The coupling by electrically clutching and braking produces a rapid response for precise acceleration and deceleration.

The electronic control of the two driver groups (9) is extended to the console on the stage floor. The console (8) is movable so as to be located in a convenient position for each show. On its face are switches for the selection of one of the two power groups designated as Red or Blue control channels and controls for varying the frequency or speed of the alternators and thus the speed of the winch's motors in the group. Further controls determine the forward or reverse direction of the winch's motor to raise or lower the liftline.

The selection and grouping of winches into a Red or Blue control channel is accomplished at the console's patch panel in much the same manner as the cross connecting of lighting-load circuits on the dimmers in a lighting-control system (see Chapter 18).

The telemeter or height indicator on the console tells the operator the exact position of each line or line group in both control channels as well as provides a means of setting the top and bottom trim of the hanging piece of scenery.

RIGGING

Whether a stage is equipped with a pin-and-rail, counterweight, or synchronous winch system, there are several flying and rigging techniques common to all systems. While many of the routine problems inherent in the older systems are eliminated in the winch system, certain specific problems pertaining to the movement of scenery in relationship to its hanging position and loft height will be forever present.

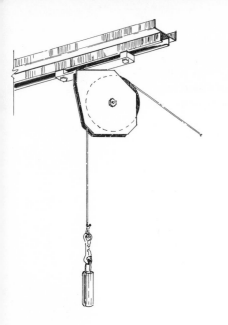

Figure 9–5. THE SYNCHRONOUS-WINCH SYSTEM (drawing, opposite page).   (1) Gridiron, channels running up and downstage. (2) Winches mounted on proscenium and back wall of stage (photograph of a winch with cover removed). (3) Liftlines, ⅛-inch airplane strand. (4) Swivel loft block (detail—left, top). (5) Cross section of channel beam holding loft block. (6) Truss batten to increase span and reduce the number of liftlines in a line-set. (7) A group of lines in operation. (8) The console (photograph—left, center). (9) Control group. (10) Driver group (photograph—below).

Scene-Control Console (left—center).   Right panel contains patch panel for grouping winches. Plugs control the winches and horizontal rows of jacks form the groups. Vertical row of switches in center of larger panel are selector switches which energize the groups; left for the red channel and right for the blue. To each side of the selector switches are the telemeters, or digital counters, which measure the cable paid out in feet and inches and can be preset to stop the scenery after it has been lowered or raised the desired distance. Below each telemeter is the speed-control knob for the separate channels. At left of each speed-control knob is the UP-DN switch which determines direction of travel. Above the red telemeter is the dimmer for console lights (not shown). Above the blue telemeter are push buttons which control the teaser and light pipe. The flexible conduit containing the electrical wires enters cabinet on lower right end and is not seen. "Scene Control" console by J. R. Clancy, Inc., Syracuse, N. Y.

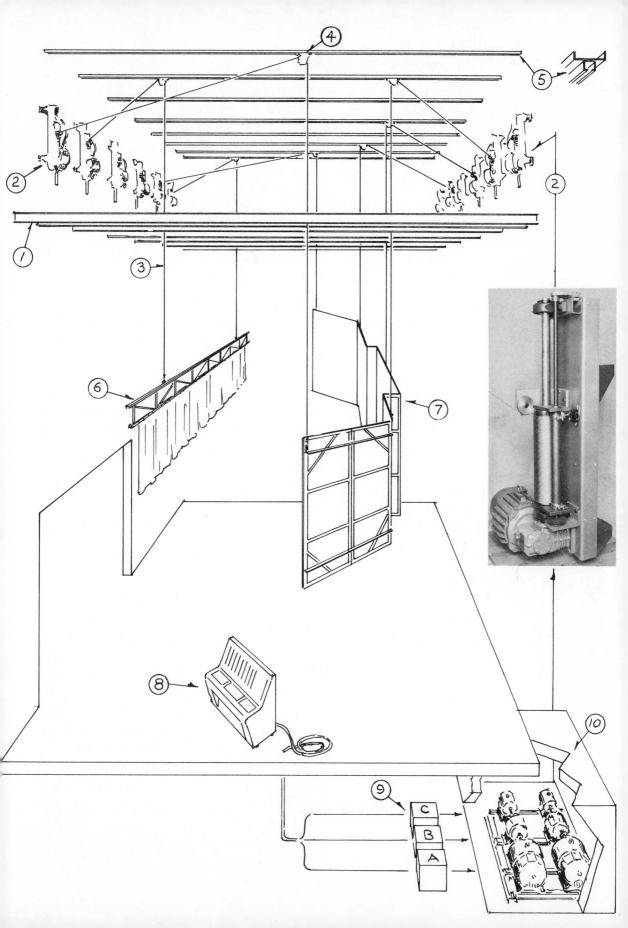

Stage rigging begins with the relatively simple process of hanging scenery and includes the more complicated maneuvers of breasting and tripping scenery elements. The handling of stage curtains (such as the traveler, tableau, and contour curtains) and the unframed drop are also a part of stage rigging.

HANGING SCENERY. An early step in rigging is the preparation of scenery to hang by providing hardware or some other means of attaching the lift-lines. Hanger irons or D-rings, which are used on framed scenery, should be bolted to a vertical member of the framing for greater strength. On extremely tall or heavy pieces two rings are used, the one at the top serving as a guide for the liftline which is attached to the bottom. To lift the load from the bottom is not only a safer procedure, but it also provides a convenient position to trim each line (Figure 9–6a, b). The use of the turn buckle or trimming hitch as illustrated is, of course, not necessary on the pin-and-rail system, for each line can be brought into trim from the flyfloor. The same is true of the winch system which can "inch" an individual line into exact trim.

Unframed pieces of scenery, such as drops and borders, are hung from their top battens and can be fastened to a pipe batten, or picked up by a set of lines in many ways (Figure 6c). The long thin batten requires numerous pick-up points, about every six feet (see Bridling, page 195), to keep it from sagging and thereby spoiling the trim of the drop.

KNOTS. Safe stage rigging requires the use of many familiar knots. The stage technician, and the designer who has to supervise his own rigging, should be skilled in the use of at least a few of the knots and hitches that appear in stage rigging. Some of the most frequently used knots are illustrated in Figure 9–7 along with notations of their uses for stage rigging. A more detailed and comprehensive manual of knots and splices can be found in the catalogue of cordage companies (see Bibliography).

BREASTING SCENERY. Two pieces of scenery, regardless of which flying system is being used, cannot occupy the same space at the same time, although the designer may wish they could. Consequently, it sometimes becomes necessary to hang a unit away from its working position and rely on breasting lines to bring it to its proper location. A breasting line (sometimes called a checkline or restraining line) is usually dead-tied at one end to the gridiron or side-stage position and fastened to the scenery at the opposite end. When the piece is in its flown position the breasting line is slack, but as the piece comes into its working position the breasting line becomes taut and breasts the unit off dead-center hanging. (Several breasting maneuvers are illustrated in Figure 9–8c, d, e, f.)

Figure 9–6.   THE HANGING OF SCENERY.   **(a)** Hanging hardware: (1) Top hanger iron, straight. (2) Bottom hanger iron, hooked. (3) Ceiling plate and ring. **(b)** Trim adjustments: (1) Trimming hitch using hemp rope of sash cord. (2) A snatch line. The snap hook on the end of the liftline makes it possible to unhook a flown piece of scenery. (3) Turnbuckle on wire cable, another way to adjust the trim of a flown piece of scenery. **(c)** Various methods of hanging a drop: (1) Tie around top batten. (2) Tie through batten. (3) Drop holder. (4) Tie-lines to pipe batten. (5 and 6) Floor stays.

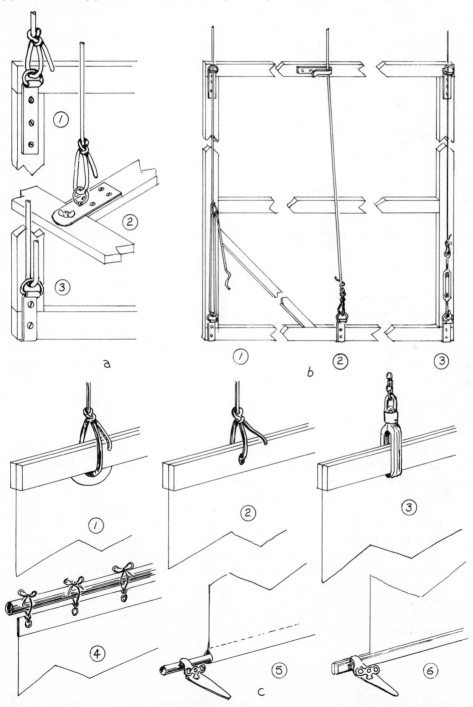

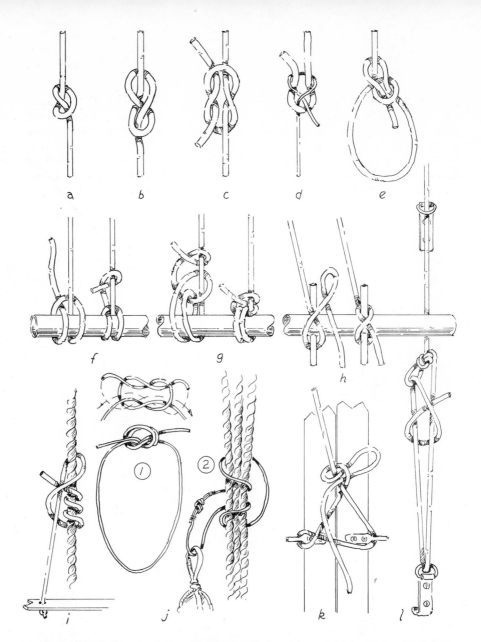

Figure 9–7. KNOTS USED IN STAGE RIGGING. (a) Half hitch or overhand knot.
(b) Figure eight, used to put a knot in the end of a line to keep it from running through
a pulley or eye. (c) Square knot, for joining ropes of the same size. (d) Sheetbend, for
joining ropes of different sizes. (e) Bowline. A fixed loop used on end of liftline through
ring. (f) Clove hitch on a batten, finished with a half hitch. It grips firmly under tension,
but is easy to adjust or untie. (g) Fisherman's bend. Excellent for a tie onto a batten. Not
as easy to adjust as the clove hitch. (h) Half hitch over a belaying pin. Used as tie-off on
pinrail. (i) Stopper hitch, made with a smaller line in the middle of a larger rope. The
safety line on the counterweight lock rail uses a stopper hitch on the purchase line. (j)
Sunday: (1) A method of joining the ends of a small loop of wire cable without putting
a sharp kink in the cable. (2) The loop is then used to clew a set of rope lines together
so as to counterweight them with a sandbag. (k) Lashline tie-off. (l) Trimming hitch, to
adjust the trim of a hanging piece of scenery.

BRIDLING.   The bridle is a simple rigging used to spread the load picked up on one line (Figure 9–8a, b). The number of lines in a set can be reduced, or the number of pick-up points increased by the bridling technique.

TRIPPING SCENERY.   Many rigging problems result from too low a loft or the complete absence of one. Tripping, which can only be used on soft or semi-soft scenery, is one way of flying scenery in a limited space (Figure 9–9d, e, f). By picking up the bottom of a drop as well as the top, it can be flown in half the height necessary to clear a full drop. The height can be further reduced by picking up the drop a third of the height off the floor and thereby tripping it in thirds.

An extreme variation of tripping a drop is to roll it on its bottom batten or drum at the bottom edge of the drop (Figure 9–9a, b, c). The old opera house "oleo" drop was rigged in this manner and it still is a good way of flying a drop on a stage with reduced flying space.

LEVITATION.   The flying of objects or persons, as if in defiance of gravity, requires special rigging. A designer, to create a workable setting for flying actors or objects, should be familiar with the special rigging that is required for a flying effect. The right kind of background, the properly planned exits and entrances and atmospheric lighting can serve to mask or camouflage any exposed support wires and dramatize the illusion.

An object, to create the illusion of floating in space, must be supported on as fine a wire as possible so that the support will disappear from view at a distance. Lightweight objects, such as a bat or bird, can be supported on fishing line (20-pound test) which becomes invisible at a very short distance. The size and strength of the support wire to fly an actor, however, is more critical.

The kind of wire used in the flying apparatus for an actor depends upon whether or not the wire has to go over a pulley. Wire rope, such as airplane strand, is extremely flexible and strong for its size—$\frac{1}{16}$-inch airplane strand tests at 500 pounds and has a recommended safe load of 100 pounds; 20-gauge (.045 inches) piano wire has great tensile strength (500 pounds) for its size but is a single strand and cannot be run through a pulley. Any sharp bend or kink quickly weakens piano wire to the point of breaking.

FLYING APPARATUS.   A flying apparatus begins with a harness for the actor. It is made of strong webbing and is fitted about the legs and chest like a parachute harness. The ring, to which the wire is attached, is placed approximately in the middle of the back, a little above the actor's center of gravity. The harness, of course, is worn under the costume with only the ring protruding.

Figure 9–8.   BRIDLING AND BREASTING TECHNIQUES.   (a) A simple bridle. **(b)** A bridle of a set of lines to support the overhang of an extra-long batten. **(c)** Breasting a drop up- and downstage: (1) Stored position. (2) Working position. **(d)** Breasting across stage. **(e)** Twisting a batten into an angled position. **(f)** Breast lines on the side-tab arms of a drape cyc.: (1) Stored position, arms hanging down. (2) Working position, arms pulled by breast lines into spread position.

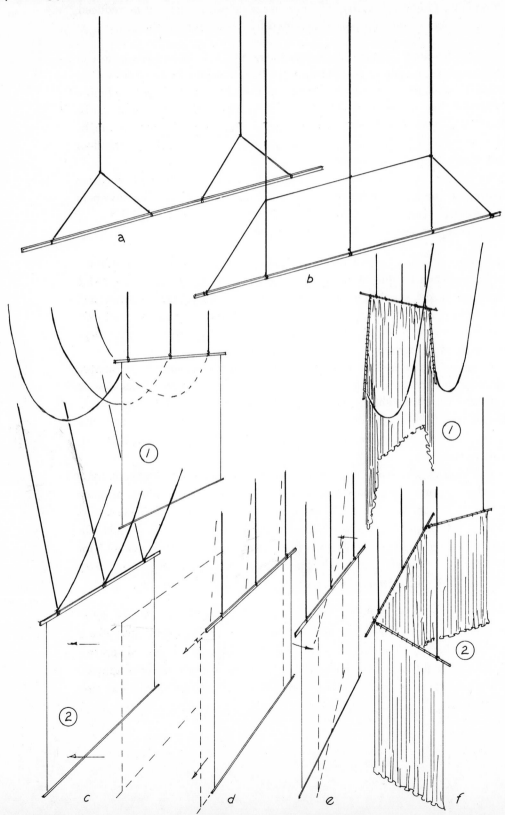

Figure 9–9. TRIPPING TECHNIQUES. (a) The "oleo" drop which rolls on the bottom batten or drum. Note: the rigging of the rope gives operator a mechanical advantage of two. Drop is made with horizontal seams to make roll flat. **(b)** An alternate rigging. Liftline has equal turns on the end of drum, in reverse direction of drop. When liftline is pulled, it unwinds as the drop winds onto the drum and thus rises. **(c)** Detail of drum construction: (1) Contour pieces. (2) Linear stiffeners. (3) Lattice slats. (4) Padding and final cover. **(d)** Tripping a drop; back set of lines is attached to bottom batten: (1) Working position. (2) Stored or tripped position. **(e)** Tripping in thirds. Upstage batten is attached at one-third height of the drop off the floor: (1) Working position. (2) Tripped position. **(f)** Tripping a drop which has the lower portion framed: (1) Working position. (2) Tripped position. **(g)** Book ceiling rigging: (1) Working position. (2) Booked position. **(h)** Carpet hoist, handling a variable load: (1) Free arbor (no batten attached) carrying counterweights. (2) Working arbor with batten that handles the variable load. (3) Free arbor is locked-off at top position allowing working arbor to run free of counterweight after load has been removed from batten (rigging is only usable on light loads of 100-150 pounds).

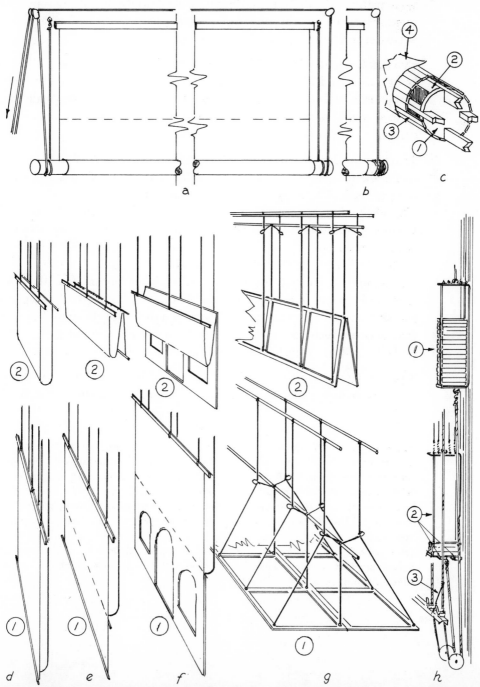

The type of rigging for levitation depends upon the movement of the actor both in the air and on the floor. For instance, the Rhine maidens in *Die Valküre* remain flying in a lateral pattern, back and forth across the stage. On the other hand, Peter Pan, beside flying in all directions, also lands and walks about on the floor.

Most flying apparatus is based upon a pendulum action whether the pattern of movement is lateral or in all directions. The pendulum is usually placed off center for a lateral movement and center stage for a free-movement pattern. Figure 9–10 illustrates, schematically, the various pendulum riggings as well as other methods of flying actors, some of which require two wires and more complicated apparatus.

CURTAIN RIGGING.   The actions or movements of a stage curtain, other than being raised and lowered on a batten, are classified into three groups. A curtain can be drawn horizontally from the sides, tripped diagonally into a tableau shape, or tripped vertically into the varied patterns of a contour curtain.

TRAVELER OR DRAW CURTAIN.   The conventional action of a traveler curtain is the drawing together of two curtain halves on two overlapping sections of track. The track guides the carriers which are attached to the top edge of the curtain at about one-foot intervals. The drawline is fastened to the first or *lead* carrier which pushes or pulls the rest of the carriers to open or close the curtain. The many track and carrier designs as well as the rigging of the drawline are illustrated in Figure 9–11.

Sometimes a one-way traveler is needed, which means that the curtain instead of coming from opposite sides of the stage is drawn on stage from one side on a single long track (Figure 9–11b). Also illustrated is a rear-fold device which causes all carriers to move at once rather than being pushed or pulled by the lead carrier (Figure 9–11c).

TABLEAU CURTAIN.   Like the traveler, the tableau curtain is made up of two curtain panels hung, with a center overlap, from a single batten. Each

Figure 9–10.   LEVITATION.   Types of rigging for flying objects or persons: **(a)** Pendulum and breast line: (1) Pendulum line, placed off center, has long arc when it is swinging free of breast line. (2) Breast line shortens arc and lifts object up and out of sight. **(b)** Pendulum and double breast line: (1) Pendulum line. (2) First breast line. (3) Second breast line. **(c)** Harness for actor. **(d)** Schematic diagram of Joseph Kerby's flying rig for Peter Pan: (1) Piano wire lead. (2) 1/8-inch wire cable feeds through swivel sheave at gridiron to a drum off stage. (3) Operating line turns large drum, thereby achieving a mechanical advantage and avoiding the use of counterweights. **(e)** Double-line counterweighted rigging provides a very flexible lateral movement although the actor has to remain attached to rig.

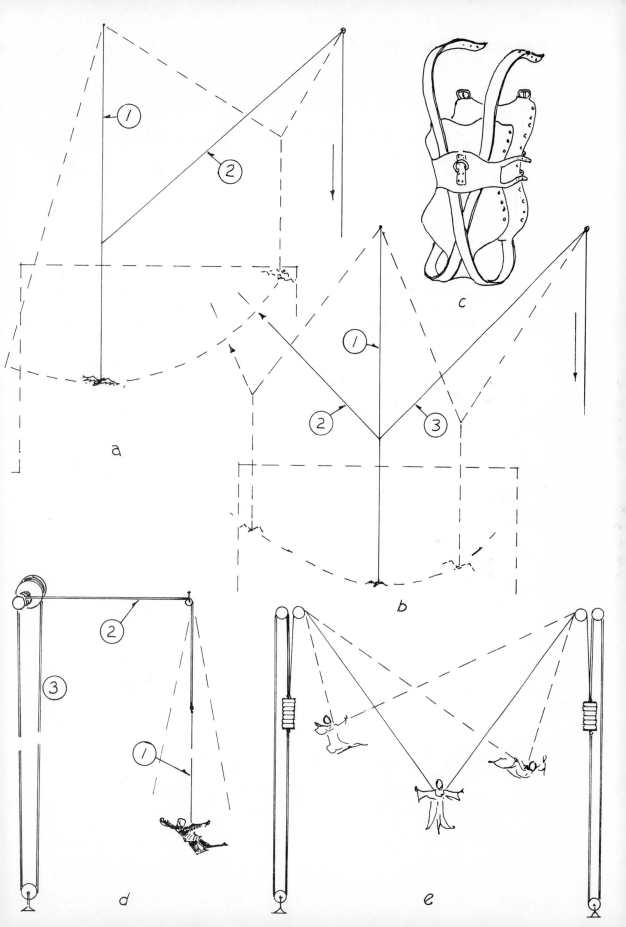

a

b

c

d

2

3

1

e

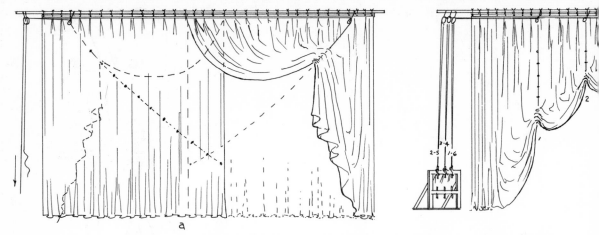

Figure 9–11. TRAVELER CURTAINS AND TRACKS. **(a)** Rigging of a draw curtain or two-way traveler: (1) Draw line. (2) Head block. (3) Lead carrier on downstage curtain, fastened to drawline. (4) Change-of-direction pulley. (5) Lead carrier on upstage curtain also fastened to drawline. (6) Floor block. **(b)** One-way traveler curtain. **(c)** Detail of rear-fold attachment. All carriers move at once with drawline and curtain folds offstage rather than bunching onstage. (1) Lead carrier. (2) Drawline. (3) Rear-fold attachment grips drawline until it is straightened up by bumping into the next carrier. (4) Drawline now passes through the rear-fold attachment. *Various Types of Traveler Tracks and Carriers* (opposite): **(d)** Wooden track with ball carriers. **(e)** Square steel track with double-wheel carrier. **(f)** Round steel track with ball carriers. **(g)** Triangular steel track with side opening and single-wheel carriers. (Vallen, Inc.)

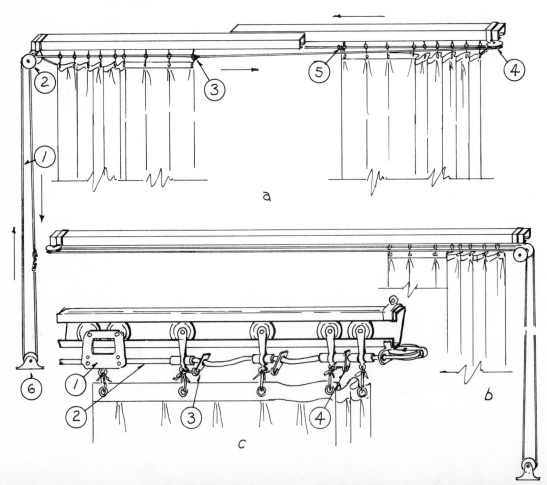

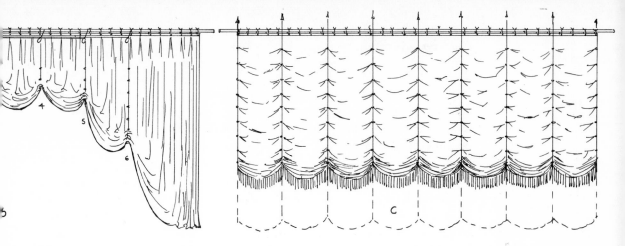

panel is lifted or tripped open by a diagonal drawline attached to the central edge, about a third of its height off the floor, and running through rings on the back of the curtain to a pulley on the batten (Figure 9–12a). The tableau has a quicker action than a traveler, but doesn't lift completely out of sight unless the batten is also raised at the final moment. Because of the picturesqueness of the tableau curtain drape it is frequently left in view as a decorative frame for the scene.

CONTOUR CURTAIN. The contour curtain is made in a single panel with great fullness, usually about 200 percent. The curtain, which is made of thin or soft material to drape well, is tripped by a series of vertical drawlines attached to the bottom edge of the curtain and running through rings on the back to pulleys attached to the batten. By varying the lift on certain lines the bottom ledge of the curtain takes on many different contours (Figure 9–12b).

The front curtain in a no-loft stage is sometimes rigged as a contour curtain to achieve a faster and more desirable lifting action than the slower side motion of a traveler curtain. In this case the amount of lift on each drawline is equal, eliminating the need for the abnormal fullness of a regular contour curtain. To add a decorative quality the curtain may have the horizontal fullness of a brail curtain, which is obtained by gathering material on the vertical seams thereby producing a series of soft swags (Figure 9–12c).

Figure 9–12. FRONT CURTAIN RIGGINGS (Top of opposite page). (a) Tableau curtain. (b) Contour curtain. (Above) (c) Brail curtain.

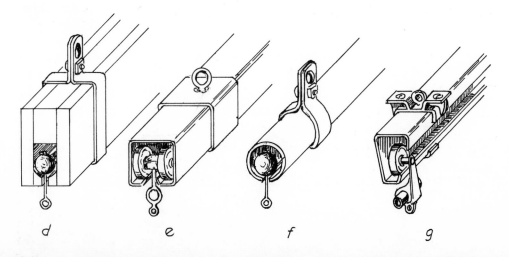

d   e   f   g

THE VARIABLE LOAD. Of the many rigging problems experienced with the conventional flying systems, the most annoying is the "variable load" or unbalanced condition resulting from the removal of part or all of the scenery load from a set of lines. The *deus ex machina,* descending with a live cargo of gods or goddesses and then ascending to the heavens empty, is an example of a variable load.

The carpet hoist is one way of compensating for the varying load if the weight variation is not too great (100-150 pounds). The counterbalancing weight to the variable load is not directly attached to the load-bearing batten but is handled on a separate purchase line. Figure 9–9h shows a carpet hoist rigging on a counterweight system. The counterbalancing weight is on the first arbor (1) which is a "free arbor" meaning that it is not attached to a batten or line-set.

The second arbor (2), which carries only enough weight to bring the arbor down, is attached to the batten handling the variable load. The extending hooks on the bottom of this arbor pass under and engage the first arbor to utilize its weights. It will be noted that when the first arbor is locked or tied-off in an up position at the moment the variable load is being removed, the second arbor is free to disengage and return to a down position. The counterbalancing weight can be returned to the second arbor by reversing the procedure and unlocking the first arbor.

Any larger weight variation has to be handled by an electric floor winch, or a hand winch which provides a mechanical advantage to offset the unbalanced load condition. The synchronous-winch system, of course, eliminates any variable load problem because it is based upon a direct lift and not a counterbalanced lift.

SCENERY ON CASTERS

The moving of a three-dimensional piece of scenery on the floor is made easier and faster if it is mounted on casters. The mounting of scenery on casters can vary from a single caster on the edge of a hinged wing to the large castered platform or wagon to move an entire set. In between are such techniques as castered tip and lift jacks, and out-rigger wagons for rolling three-dimensional units of scenery.

CASTERS. The stage places special demands on the kind of caster it uses. A good stage caster should first of all run quietly, which requires a rubber wheel or a rubber-tired wheel. Although more expensive, the rubber-tired wheel is a better long-time investment because the tires can be replaced as the rubber wears or fatigues.

Secondly, the caster wheel should have as large a diameter as possible

(3½″ to 4″). A wagon on 4-inch diameter caster wheels rolls with little effort and is not as easily stopped by small obstructions such as rugs, padding, ground cloth, or lighting cables.

Casters are of two general types: those made to move freely in any direction and those made to move in a fixed direction. The swivel caster has a free action that allows it to move in any direction, while the fixed caster is limited to one direction in a guided or tracked movement. Because both fixed and swivel-action casters are used on the stage, it is more economical to invest in swivel casters which, when necessary, can be blocked into a fixed position for a tracked movement (Figure 9–13).

TIP AND LIFT JACKS. The mounting of scenery on casters to make it move easily creates the paradoxical problem of anchoring, or keeping the unit from moving at an undesirable moment. The lift and tip jacks are methods of lifting or tipping a piece of scenery from a standing position onto casters to move (Figures 9–13d, 14e, f). The scenery, however, sits firmly on the floor when it is in its working position.

Another way to anchor a castered platform or bulky three-dimensional pieces of scenery is to attach it to units that are sitting on the floor, or by tipping the piece onto casters mounted on its offstage or upstage edge (Figure 9–14d).

OUTRIGGER WAGONS. An outrigger wagon is essentially a pattern of castered jacks or braces around the outside of a set or portion of a set. The scenery remains on casters. It is a skeleton wagon intended to brace and caster the scenery. The action of the scene is played not on a wagon but on the stage floor (Figure 9–13a).

WAGONS. The low-level platform (6″ to 8″) on casters, or wagon, can carry a large portion of a setting including the set props. Large wagons often carry an entire setting which can swiftly and easily move into place for a scene change. Although requiring ample floor space, the wagon is a flexible and efficient method of handling scenery.

WAGON CONSTRUCTION. Wagon construction is basically the same as platform construction. The caster in a sense becomes the post of the platform. If the casters are mounted on caster-planks (2′ x 6′ or 1⅛″ x 6′) the minimum span between supports can be increased. The caster-plank, besides providing a sturdy mount for the caster, serves as a cleat for the top to increase the overstrength of the wagon. Normally, unless the wagon is to carry an extremely heavy load, such as a piano, the spacing of casters at 3-foot intervals is sufficient to remove any noticeable deflection.

Stock wagon units made in a convenient size (3′ x 6′ or 4′ x 8′ modules) for handling are pin-hinged together to make larger units (Figure 9–15).

Figure 9–13. CASTERING TECHNIQUES. (a) Single caster mounted on rear of flat. (b) Single caster mounted in corner. (c) Outrigger wagon. (d) Tip jack: (1) Scenery tipped back to rest on casters. (2) Scenery upright, blocked-off caster in working position. (e) Castered jack: (1) Side view showing how scenery is held clear of floor. (2) Caster jack on a hinged or "wild" piece of scenery. (f) Flat-top swivel caster. (g) Flat-top fixed caster. (h) Stem-type swivel caster for furniture. (i) Small stem-type ball caster for furniture. (j) Large stem-type swivel caster. Mounts into bottom of scaffolding pipe.

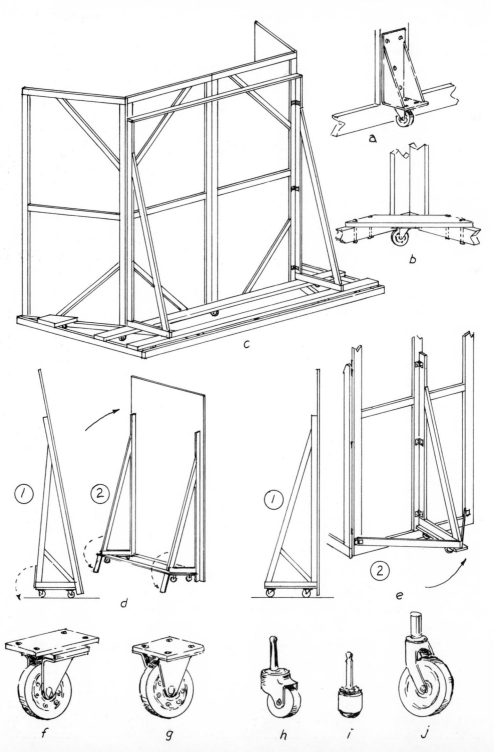

Figure 9–14.   METHODS OF STABILIZING CASTERED UNITS.   **(a)** Barrel bolt fits into hole in stage floor. **(b)** Hinged footiron and stage screw. **(c)** Portion of platform not on casters: (1) Steps hinged to castered platform folds on top for easy movement. (2) Unfolded and resting on the stage floor, the steps stabilize the platform unit. **(d)** Casters on offstage edge of platform: (1) Platform in working position, casters on back edge. (2) Platform is tipped onto casters to move. **(e)** Lift jack: (1) Pictorial view of lift jack. (2) Side view showing jack lifting scenery. (3) Jack released, scenery rests on floor. **(f)** Lift jack under a platform: (1) Jack released. (2) Jack depressed to lift platform on casters. (3) Sectional view.

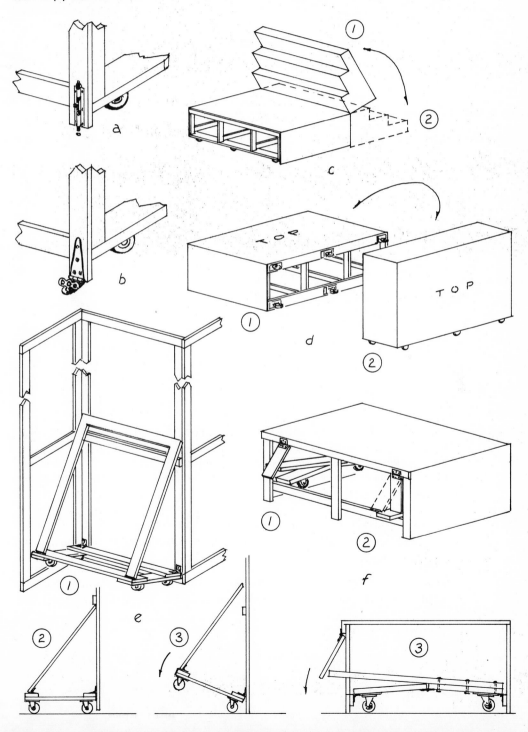

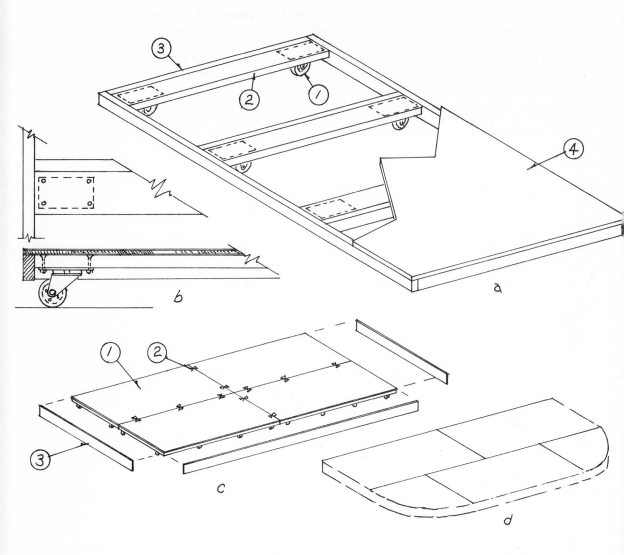

Figure 9–15.   THE WAGON UNIT.   **(a)** Construction of a stock wagon: (1) 2 x 3 frame. (2) 2 x 6 caster planks. (3) 4-inch swivel casters. (4) 4 x 8 foot, ¾-inch 5-ply top. **(b)** Cross section. **(c)** Large wagon made up of stock units: (1) Stock unit. (2) Units pin-hinged together. (3) Facing boards. **(d)** A different shape made of three stock wagons and two special corner pieces.

Although stock wagons use more casters than are necessary for the total area, the flexibility of arrangements, handling and storage ease justify the module system.

Wagon Movements.   Aside from the free movement of a wagon carrying a full or partial set, there are several controlled or tracked movements that can become a scheme of production for handling scenery entirely on casters. The scheme may be based upon a pair of alternating wagons that allow the scenery and props to be changed on the offstage wagon while the alternate wagon is in the playing position. The transverse, jackknife, and split-wagon movements operate on this principle (Figures 9–16, 17).

When there are many small sets in a production it is sometimes desirable to keep each set intact upon separate wagons. The stage then becomes packed with wagon sets and the shifting is accomplished by shuttling each wagon into position. The pattern of the movement varies with the size and shape of the sets and their order of appearance in the play.

THE REVOLVING STAGE

Another controlled movement of a castered unit is around a fixed center. A revolving stage that is not permanently built into the stage floor is similar to the wagon in structure. To remain portable, a turntable is made in small pie-shaped sections which are bolted or pin-hinged together (Figure 9–18). The casters are mounted in a pattern to properly support each unit and are fixed in a position perpendicular to a radius line drawn through the point of attachment. If the casters are carefully mounted, the turntable will revolve about its pivot point with very little effort.

SINGLE TURNTABLE. The revolving stage as a basic device can assume a variety of sizes and uses. The most familiar type is the large single turntable. Unless the stage is especially designed for a large turntable, its diameter is limited by the depth of the stage. If the stage happens to be shallow in proportion to the proscenium opening, a single turntable will leave an awkward corner in the downstage right and left positions. Attempts to fill the area with a show portal, or hinged pieces on the turntable which unfold and mask the corner, more or less negate the basic function of the single revolving stage (Figure 9–20a).

TWO TURNTABLES. A shallow stage is adaptable to the use of two turntables, either touching in the center or held slightly apart. This method removes the awkward corners of the single turntable, but it creates a design problem—that of joining all the sets in the center (Figure 9–20b).

THREE TURNTABLES. Occasionally, a large turntable is combined with two small disks in the downstage right and left positions. The small disks either carry scenery related to the large set in the center or are small independent sets. The production scheme for I Remember Mama designed by George Jenkins used this technique (Figure 20e).

Figure 9–16. TRACKED WAGON MOVEMENT. **(a)** Track on top of stage floor. **(b)** Section detail. **(c)** Section showing track sunk in floor. *Types of Tracked Wagon Movements:* **(d)** Transverse movement. **(e)** Split transverse wagons and a large single wagon moving up- and downstage. **(f)** Multimovements: transverse, diagonal, as well as up- and downstage.

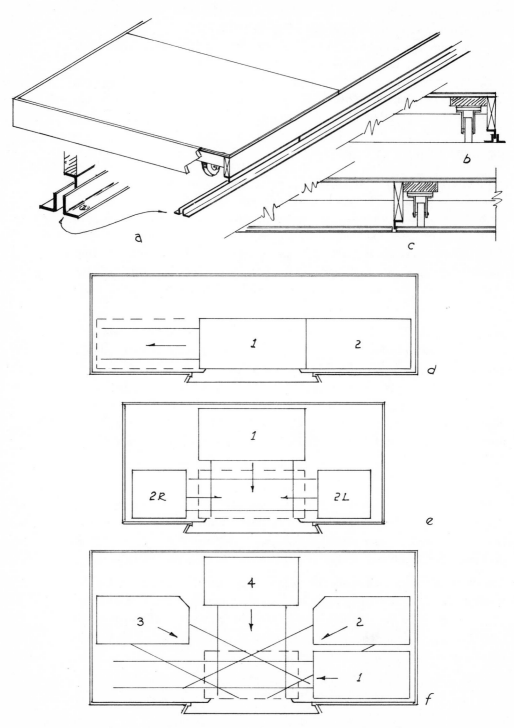

Figure 9–17.   PIVOTED WAGON MOVEMENT.   (a) Wagon moving about a pivot:
(1) Detail of pivot. (2) Casters blocked perpendicular to radius. (b) Jackknife wagons.
(c) Type of jackknife in combination with split wagons. (d) Pivoting a segment of a circle,
semi-revolving.

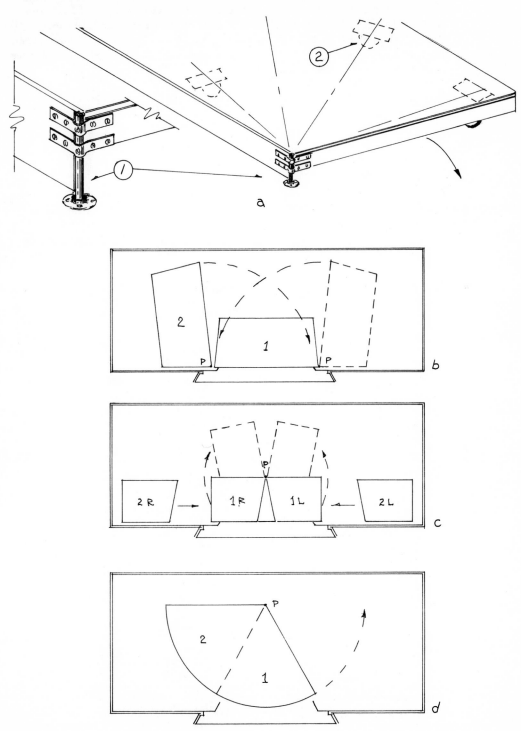

Figure 9–18. THE REVOLVING STAGE. A portable revolving stage or turntable can be built many ways. Shown here are two methods. **(a)** Turntable made up of stock wagon units with special-shaped wagons to form the curve of the outside edge: (1) Stock wagon. (2) Special wagon to complete circle. (3) Casters blocked perpendicular to radius. (4) Section. **(b)** Turntable made of wedge-shaped units around central core. Fewer casters are used creating less noise: (1) Basic wedge-shaped unit. (2) Top removed showing the position of casters. (3) Central core. (4) Section.

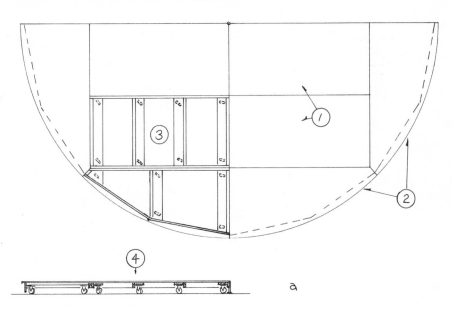

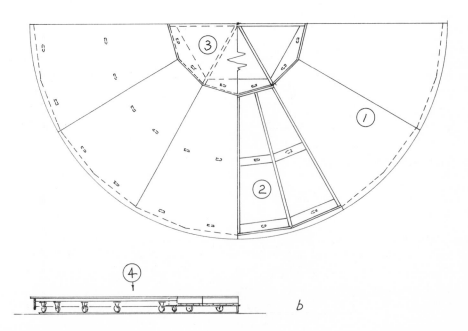

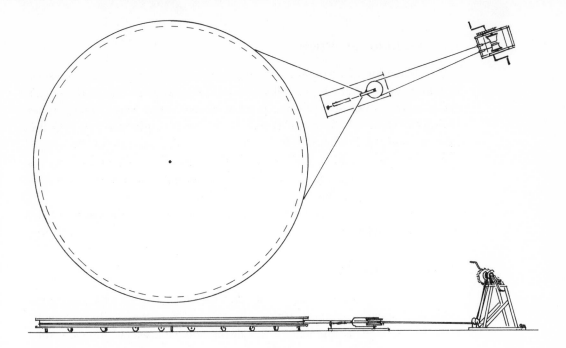

Figure 9–19. A METHOD OF POWERING A SINGLE TURNTABLE by cable around the
outside edge of turntable and a hand winch.

THE RING AND TURNTABLE. A great deal more variety of movement is
achieved by using a ring and turntable combination. The ring and turntable
are individually powered so that they can turn in the same direction at
identical or different speeds, or they may revolve in opposite directions. The
possible combinations of fixed units on the ring and turntable are almost
endless. If the changes are made avista it becomes a delightful scheme of
production. The settings for *Protective Custody* designed by Peter Larkin
were handled in this manner (Figure 9–20f).

TWO RINGS AND TWO TURNTABLES. Although less adaptable to revolving
fixed units than the single ring and turntable, two rings around two turntables are a very flexible method of changing elements of scenery and properties. This was demonstrated in the production of *Lady in the Dark*,
designed by Harry Horner. With the help of flown pieces of scenery, the
settings were able to blend from one scene to the next in full view of the
audience (Figure 9–20c).

SEMI-REVOLVES AND COMBINATIONS. The remaining variations of the revolving technique are the semi-revolving stage and the combination of a turntable and a wagon.

The semi-revolving stage is a portion of a ring or turntable tracked to
swing in half an arc and then return to its original position (Figure 9–20g).
The semi-revolving stage may be large or small, used singly or in pairs, or,
in some cases, combined with a turntable.

A combination of revolving and lateral movements can be accomplished by building a turntable into a full-stage transverse wagon (Figure 20d). This combination works best when a portion of one set is reused many times during the show. The lobby of *Grand Hotel*, for example, was saved in this manner. Most of the lobby setting remained on the left side of the wagon while a portion moved on the turntable. The smaller rooms and other scenes in the hotel occupied the remainder of the turntable and were moved in better sightlines by sliding the wagon to the left.

The scheme can be varied by setting the turntable into the center of the wagon and having elements of scenery on both sides instead of one side.

ELEVATOR STAGES

As a means of moving scenery, the elevator stage requires the maximum amount of stage machinery. Unless the theatre is in the position to make constant use of the equipment, or the elevators have a second function, such as a scenery and property lift to remote storage areas, the installation is extravagant. With few exceptions (Radio City Music Hall and similar presentation houses), the normal legitimate theatre in the United States has little use for the elevator stage as a method of changing scenery.

The financial organization and scale of production of numerous state theatres in Europe make the elaborate elevator stage a more feasible method of handling scenery than could be supported by the unsubsidized theatres of the United States.

SMALL ELEVATORS AND TRAPS.   Aside from the doubtful chance of using a full-stage elevator, the designer may encounter a limited use of elevators in the raising of small elements of scenery through the stage floor.

Although the average stage may not have an elevator system, it usually has a portion of the floor area made in sections or "traps." The traps can be removed to give access through the stage floor into the trap room below. Entrances by stairs or ladder can be made from below through such an opening. Trap openings are made between transverse beams that run parallel to the footlights. As a result the designer has great freedom in planning the size and position of an opening running across stage. Openings running up and downstage, however, are limited by the transverse beams.

Figure 9–20.   TURNTABLE AND RING COMBINATIONS.   (a) Single large turntable. (b) Two small turntables. (c) Two small turntables with rings. (d) Single turntable in a transverse wagon. (e) Large turntable with two small disks. (f) Large turntable with ring. (g) Semi-revolving ring-segment and small turntable. (h) A pair of rings.

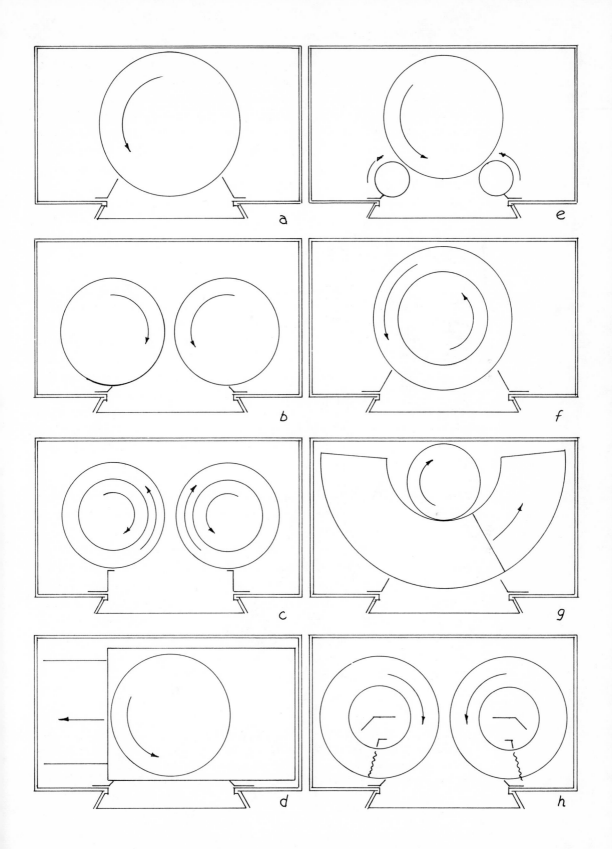

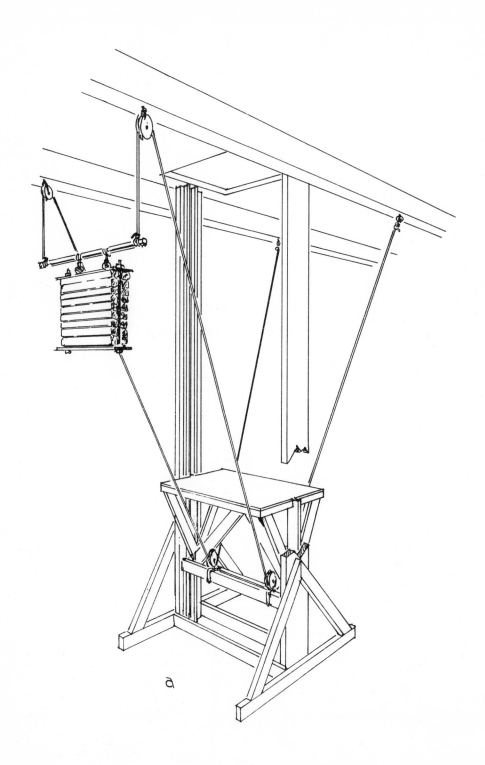

a

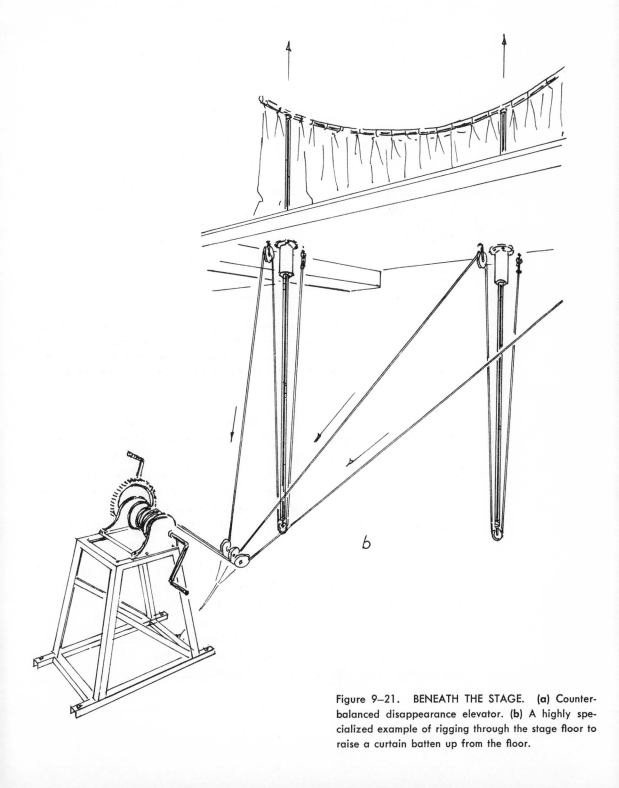

Figure 9–21. BENEATH THE STAGE. (a) Counter-balanced disappearance elevator. (b) A highly specialized example of rigging through the stage floor to raise a curtain batten up from the floor.

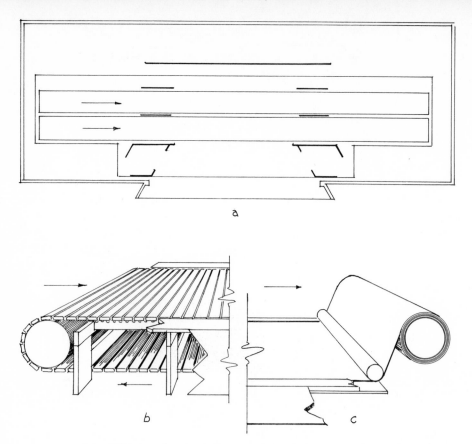

Figure 9–22.   THE TREADMILL.   (a) Plan of a pair of treadmills showing the amount of offstage space needed to use treadmills effectively. (b) Construction diagram of a treadmill with continuous action. (c) A simpler treadmill design, however, action is not continuous. The belt moves first to the left and then to the right as it winds or unwinds off the drums.

The construction of a temporary lift which can be used for scenery or actors is shown in Figure 9–21a. Although the elevator platform can be as large as a single trap opening, the example illustrated is smaller. A larger elevator would require more guides and liftlines. Figure 9–21b is an example of an elevatorlike mechanism under the stage floor designed to raise a small curved batten supporting a curtain. The technique is probably very similar to the methods used to raise a curtain out of the front pit of the Roman theatre.

THE ELEVATOR FLOOR.   The elevators designed to move scenery should not be confused with the short-run elevators used to shape the stage floor in some of the more recent theatres. In this instance, sections of the stage floor, which can be raised or lowered by elevators to make levels or pits, are not a method of moving scenery. They can, however, be considered as a means of changing the appearance or form of the stage floor, which in a sense creates a new scene although they are not literally moving scenery.

THE TREADMILL

Like transverse wagons, the treadmill has a lateral movement. It is a con-
veyer-belt method of moving light scenery and properties to the right or
left. It consists of an endless horizontal belt or flexible surface made of
narrow wooden slats, held apart by two drums on opposite sides of the
stage. Like a conveyer belt which is taut around the drums, the treadmill
surface will move to the right or left when the drum is turned. As the belt
has to return underneath itself, the space has to be kept clear of obstructions.
This limits the width or height of the platform, for the wider the belt the
higher the platform to allow for the framing of the span over the returning
belt. The usual belt is about four feet wide which keeps the platform about
a foot in height (Figure 9–22b).

A rather unique variation of the treadmill was developed by the Tobin
Lake Studios, South Lyon, Michigan, which allows the belt (vinyl plastic)
to rest on the floor. The belt is rolled onto motor-driven drums at opposite
sides of the stage. The action is limited in one direction by the length of
the belt which is not endless but rolls up on one drum or the other. Besides
not requiring extensive platforming, this type of treadmill has the added
advantage of being extremely simple to install (Figure 9–22c).

10

STAGE PROPERTIES
AND EFFECTS

Besides the large scenic background elements of the stage setting, the designer is responsible for the design and selection of stage properties and smaller bits of scenery more closely related to the actor. His responsibility for stage properties may vary from finding a marble-topped Louis XV console table to making an exotic sofa for a Turkish Cosy Corner; or from the borrowing of a Victorian tea set to the fashioning of tree leaves. Whether borrowed or constructed, each property is carefully coordinated into the design composition and adjusted to the production scheme, as well as being checked for size and ease of use by the actor.

Stage properties are in essence the design details of the over-all visual composition. Although the visual significance of properties applies more specifically to a realistic interior setting than to an exterior or abstract scene, their contribution cannot be overemphasized. Stage properties are, many times, the accent or artistic touch that makes or breaks the effectiveness of a stage setting.

Another visual consideration of a stage property of equal importance to its compositional value is its rightness for the play. Again applying more to the selection of furniture, the designer has to continually ask such questions as: Is this chair in the right historical period and nationality? Is the side board the kind Mama would choose? And so on. The selection and designing of furniture and properties is done in close collaboration with the director so as to insure not only its rightness for the play but also to check its part in the staging of the action. Reference is made to the specific size and position of furniture in the setting in relation to other properties and the movement of the actors. Large furniture may hinder movement between the pieces, or a high-backed chair may block off a view of upstage action.

Real furniture is, of course, used in the modern theatre although it is often altered to become stageworthy. Scale and color are sometimes changed to improve its relationship to the stage composition. Because of these alterations even real furniture takes on a theatrical look. It becomes a stage property suggesting, sometimes faintly, sometimes openly, that it is no longer real. The name, property or "prop," is often synonymous with the unreal or the theatrical.

Although discussed late in order, properties of a setting should be planned and built simultaneously with the rest of the scenic elements. Their importance to the design and production scheme is sometimes overlooked in the planning period. The construction of built properties is often started too late, or too many decisions in the selection of furniture or decorative features are postponed until the final hectic rehearsals. This often occurs when the designer, overworked and pressed for time, places the responsibility of organizing the properties on the shoulders of a willing but not-too-able apprentice.

To make better use of his time, the designer, besides having a competent background in historical furniture styles and period decorations, should be thoroughly acquainted with the traditional uses of properties in the theatre. He must also be able to evaluate a property in terms of its importance to the action of the play and its sheer decorative qualities.

PROPERTIES VERSUS SCENERY

What defines a prop? When does a small piece of scenery become a property, or a large property become scenery?

Stage properties are traditionally defined as: (1) all objects carried or handled by the actor; (2) separate portions of the set on which the actor may stand or sit such as rocks, stumps, or logs; (3) decorative features not permanently built or painted on the scenery (pictures, draperies, etc.); (4)

the ground cloth and rugs; and (5) all sound and visual effects that are not electrically powered.

In the average show, the categorical division of properties is based for the most part upon these traditional definitions of a property. An occasional exception or collaboration is made with the agreement of all concerned. Hence, a tree trunk may be scenery and the foliage a property; a pair of glasses discovered on the stage is a property while those brought on stage by the actors are costumes. Heavy properties often become scenery because of their size or necessity to be fastened to the scenery for movement.

Besides the distinction of properties from costumes and scenery there is the further classification of properties into groups related to their size and use. A property can be designated as either a hand, set, or dress property, or as a visual or sound-effect property.

HAND PROPERTY.   The small objects handled by the actor on the stage are hand props. They include such items as teacups, books, fans, letters, and many more similar articles.

SET PROPERTIES.   As the name implies, set properties are the larger elements more closely related to the scenery, but still used by the actor. This group includes furniture, stoves, sinks, rugs, ground cloth, and any domestic object used by the actor. Exterior set props consist of small rocks, stumps, bushes, foliage, real dirt (*Tobacco Road*), grass mats, and so on.

Set properties are in the care of the property man, who supervises the placing of the set prop on the stage and its removal to a stored position offstage.

DRESS PROPERTIES.   More closely related to the setting are the dress properties. Their chief function is decorating the set. They comprise all the elements not specifically used by the actor which serve to fill in and complete or dress the set. Window curtains, pictures, wall hangings, flower groupings are a few typical dress properties.

Dress properties, as a class, are not necessarily superficial. They can become a strong decorative feature in a setting. Because they are not used by the actor they can often be faked so as to be handled more easily or in a different way than the normal set property. Bookcases, for example, may have faked books and be attached to the scenery. A saloon back bar is often dressed with fake plastic or papier-mâché bottles to cut down the weight. A period piano or spinet, which is hard to find and harder to borrow, can be easily built and faked as a dress prop (Figure 10–1). These are, of course, just a few of the many, many types of faked dress properties.

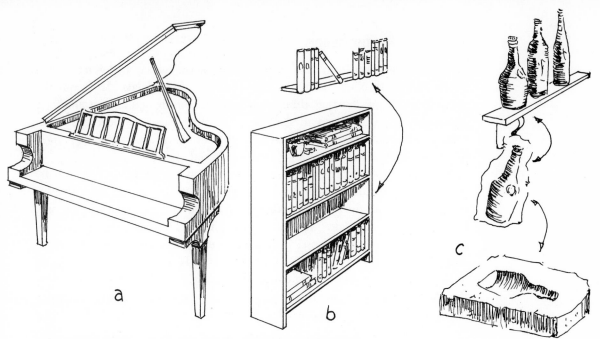

a

b

c

THE SELECTION OF SET AND DRESS PROPERTIES

The designer is responsible for the compositional unity, period continuity, and color relationships of the set and dress properties. Their first notation appears in the designer's sketch which may or may not be clear as to the indication of the real form. Once the general idea of the design has been accepted the designer can turn to a more careful study of period line and availability of each piece.

The final decision on each piece of furniture is made by the designer with the director's approval. To help reach this decision at an early stage in the planning, the designer uses individual sketches or illustrational clippings. The selection of set properties can be further facilitated by the use of a furniture plot and compositional elevations, as was suggested in Chapter 5, which give exact references to the size of the individual piece in relation to its surroundings.

PERIOD STYLES AND ORNAMENTATION. Needless to say, a scene designer must be well grounded not only in furniture styles, but also in period interior decoration and architecture. The more familiar the designer is with the historical background of a period style, the better able he is to design and select, and sometimes make-up, set and dress properties which bring a feeling of authenticity to the setting. This, of course, is more applicable to the naturalistic setting, but can be the springboard for abstraction.

Throughout the period of selecting or designing the properties and setting the designer draws heavily on a knowledge of period style. He cannot hope to recall at an instant the details of a certain period, but he should have a general sense of period style at the tip of his pencil. For detail and enrichment of the general form he depends on research. Research doesn't always mean leafing through reference books or old periodicals. It frequently involves study of the real thing in a museum or in actual surroundings. Again the designer resorts to sketches or photographs to collect this information. Although these are not presentation drawings they become important to the designer as personal reference material.

A designer soon learns to conserve energy and legwork on research by avoiding duplication. Generally much more material is gathered than is finally used. If all the research examples are filed and catalogued, they may come in handy at a later date on another show. The designer in this way soon finds himself in possession of an efficient reference library, to which should be added several inexpensive illustrated books, such as those listed in the bibliography, containing collections of furniture styles and ornamentation which also can serve as quick-and-easy reference. More extensive research, of course, may be needed to back any one style, depending upon the needs of the play.

DRAPERIES.   Of all the dress properties used onstage, draperies are the decorative detail that brings character to an interior setting. Their elegance or cheapness, style or lack of style, or complete absence contributes immeasurably to the visual expression of the kind of place and people in the play.

From historical references, the designer can plan his draperies which, depending upon the period, may include window, door, fireplace mantel, picture, and mirror draperies. The designing of draperies is based upon a knowledge of the way the material drapes or hangs and the methods of cutting and assembling the material into the desired effect.

A New York designer needs only to prepare a carefully scaled or dimensioned drawing of the assembled drapery, specifying the material and the action, if any. Window curtains, for example, may have to be drawn for a tableau during the action of the play.

For university and community theatre production, the designer is expected to guide the execution of the draperies and therefore needs to know something about drapery patterns and assembly techniques.

The Window Drapery.   Although draperies may occur in many positions other than at the windows of a setting, the fundamental parts making up the decorative portion are the same. The basic parts of window drapery, which may or may not be used all at the same time, are: glass curtains, shade, overdrapery, and valance. The overdrapery and the valance are the frame, so to speak, while the glass curtains and shade diffuse the light, or cut off the view into the room from the outside. Each is made of a different type of material.

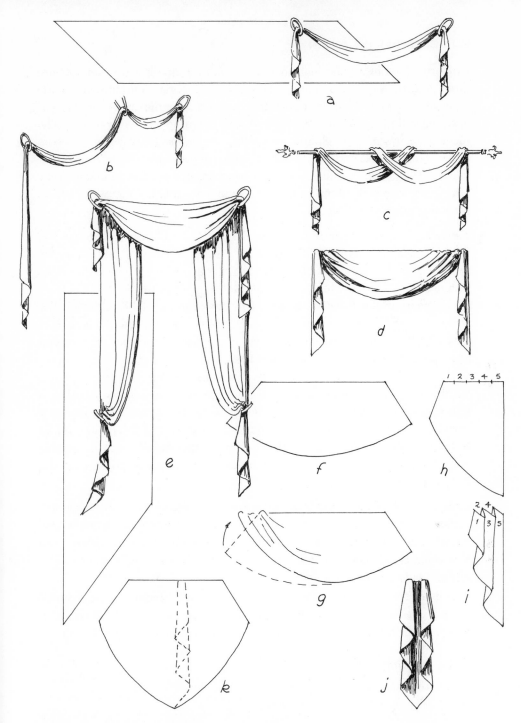

Figure 10–2. TYPES OF DRAPERIES AND VALANCES. **(a)** Festoon valance and pattern. **(b)** Eccentrically draped festoon valance. **(c)** Crossed festoons as valance. **(d)** Valance of swag and wing-pieces. **(e)** Festoon valance and side draperies showing pattern for side drapery. **(f)** Pattern of a swag. **(g)** Draping a swag. **(h)** Pattern of a wing-piece or tail. **(i)** Draping or folding a wing-piece. **(j)** A double or central tail. **(k)** Pattern of a central tail.

Drapery Materials.   The materials for window draperies are divided into three groups: the transparent or sheer fabrics for glass curtains and some types of draped shades; the translucent materials for the shade, unless it is opaque; and the opaque materials of the overdrapery and valance. The sheer materials may be chiffon, organdie, net, or theatrical gauze to name a few. Muslin, silk, and handkerchief linen are a sample of the translucent fabrics. Though the opaque materials for overdraperies are numerous, they usually are made of a fabric that will drape well such as velour, velveteen, corduroy, monk's cloth.

Types of Draperies.   As most of the decorative emphasis of a drapery is in the valance, it requires the greatest variety of draping techniques. A valance may be made up of plaits, swags, tails or wing pieces, or even festoons. The festoon, which is one continuous piece of material, is the basis for the more exaggerated shape found in the swag and tails. Although the swags and tails are cut separately they are frequently sewn together to look like a continuous piece of drapery. Examples of the types of draperies and their patterns are shown in Figure 10–2.

The side draperies, which are vertical members of the overdraperies, are usually a simple rectangular piece of material hung in fullness and drawn into a gentle or deep swag with a "tie-back" or decorative loop. Side draperies are sometimes shaped by cutting the bottoms on the diagonal similar to the festoon pattern (Figure 10–2e). Side draperies, although frequently draped symmetrically, can take on an eccentric draping depending upon the design and period style.

SHADES.   A shade normally is not included in a stage window unless there is action in raising or lowering it. Roll shades are fairly easy to make and install. A dye-painted shade of muslin or handkerchief linen can be attached to a commercial spring-loaded roller, which has been cut to fit any special size of window.

A more special type of shade for a very grand window is the festoon-draped shade, sometimes called a French Drape or Brail Curtain. It is pulled up from the bottom by a series of vertical liftlines, which have been threaded through rings on the back of the curtain like the rigging of a contour curtain (Figure 10–3). The bottom of the festoon-drape shade is shaped so that its top position becomes part of the valance design. The shade may work in front of or behind the side draperies.

BORROWING OR RENTING PROPERTIES.   Nonprofessional producing groups rely on renting and borrowing furniture or try to maintain in storage a collection of stock period furniture for continuous use. The storing of select period pieces is by far the most satisfactory method of securing properties

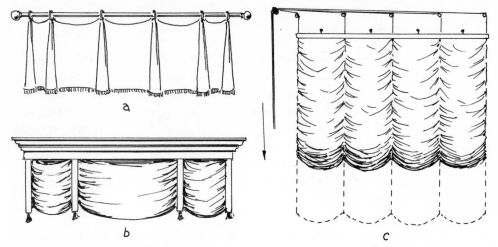

Figure 10–3. SHADES AND VALANCES. (a) Cafe-curtain valance. (b) Boxed-festoon drapery valance. (c) Festoon drapery shade.

for a repertory or stock company. Stock furniture can be varied with new upholstering and painted for reuse in many different productions.

A producing group which depends upon borrowing furniture and other articles must make an effort to maintain good will. Its members are part of the community, and if they want to continue to do business within the community, it pays to be businesslike when borrowing properties. Unfortunately, many a property room has been furnished with unreturned props, which is obviously not the way to build good will. A few simple rules for borrowing help to create a friendly, businesslike way of handling the loan.

1. Establish a method of recording each article borrowed, listing: name and address of owner; date borrowed, date to be returned; estimated value; description of article noting its condition (scratches, cracks, or parts missing); remuneration (cash, complimentary tickets, or program credit); and a signed receipt from the owner upon return of the article.

2. Centralize the responsibility. Handle all borrowing transactions through one person rather than selecting a different person to be responsible for each production.

3. Never borrow priceless heirlooms or irreplaceable antiques.

4. Take preferential care of borrowed properties on the stage, using dust covers and padding to prevent undue damage from movement of the scenery.

5. Return borrowed pieces promptly and on the date promised.

6. Secure a receipt and file it. If a record of the transaction is kept, it can become an excellent source for quickly locating and reborrowing for another production.

FLOOR COVERING. Floor covering serves two purposes, one esthetic and the other technical. First, any special floor covering helps to unify the stage composition by bringing colors and forms related to the setting into the floor. A painted ground cloth simulating wood planking, marble, or just a related hue help to anchor the setting to the floor. A setting on an unrelated or contrasting floor may appear to float in space. It loses stability and unity. This does not mean that every setting needs a special ground cloth, but rather that the designer, when using a stock ground cloth, consider its color so as to interrelate the setting to the floor covering. If the tone of the stock ground cloth is about a medium gray to low-light gray, it is not too difficult to relate the setting colors. Ideally, the presence of two stock ground cloths is more adaptable, especially if one is a warm neutral or brown tone and the other a gray shade.

Because regular scene paint will dust off when walked on, ground cloths are usually painted with dyes. The cloth can be folded for storage easily when it has been dye painted. Occasionally ground cloths are painted with oil paints, or casein paints, to obtain a harder water-repellent surface for scenes where water is spilled on the floor in the course of the action. Oil or casein paints, however, tend to shorten the life and effective reuse of the cloth.

The technical reasons for using a ground cloth are, first, to pad or cover padding and thereby deaden the sound of the actors' movements. For deep, permanent padding, ozite or ordinary rug padding is used. It is expensive but it can be reused indefinitely. A double layer of deadening felt, an inexpensive paper-pulp product found at most lumber yards, is used under the ground cloth for thin, temporary padding.

Second, if the show is traveling, the spike marks locating the working position of the scenery and properties are carried on the ground cloth. Once the cloth is laid to the center line in each stage the marks are located correctly, ready for setup.

There are many examples of unusual floor covering that go beyond the conventional ground cloth such as real dirt in *Tobacco Road* and *Bury the Dead*, artificial snow in *Ethan Frome*, grass mats in *Three Sisters*, masonite pavement in *Dead End*.

GROUND-CLOTH CONSTRUCTION. Ground cloths are made of heavy canvas (12- to 14-ounce duck) to withstand the wear of action and scenery. The seams which run parallel to the footlights, are double-stitched flat-felt seams for strength. The edges and corners are reinforced with webbing to take the tacks that fasten it to the floor. A convenient size is usually two or three feet wider than the proscenium opening and two-thirds the depth of the stage.

The shape is usually rectangular; however, a more flexible shape is achieved by adding to the long edge a tongue of one width of canvas (about 36 inches) slightly narrower than the proscenium opening. For a play with action on the apron, the ground cloth can be laid with tongue downstage

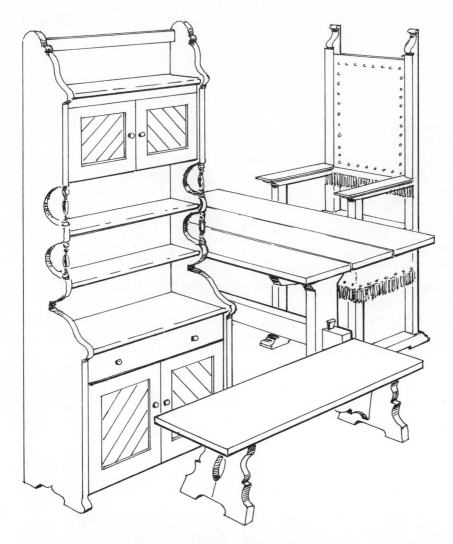

Figure 10–4. EXAMPLES OF CARPENTER-STYLE FURNITURE that are easy to make.

protruding through the proscenium opening to cover the apron. It can also be reversed with the tongue upstage and the straight edge downstage at the tormentor line in the more conventional position.

MAKING AND REMAKING FURNITURE

The making of cabinetmaker's styles of furniture is too difficult for the average scenery shop which is not equipped to finish or work hard woods. There are, however, several carpenter styles and rustic pieces of furniture that are more often easier to make than to find or borrow. Some of the unupholstered, carpenter-style pieces shown in Figure 10–4 can be made without too much trouble.

Figure 10-5. REMAKING FURNITURE. (a) *Remodeling a sofa:* (Above.) The original sofa before alterations. (Below.) Back removed, reupholstered, and freshly painted.

Figure 10–5, Continued.
(b) *Reupholstering, Tufting:*
(Above.) Tufting a sofa. (Below.) Rear view of ties used
to form tufts (Photos—Gene
Diskey).

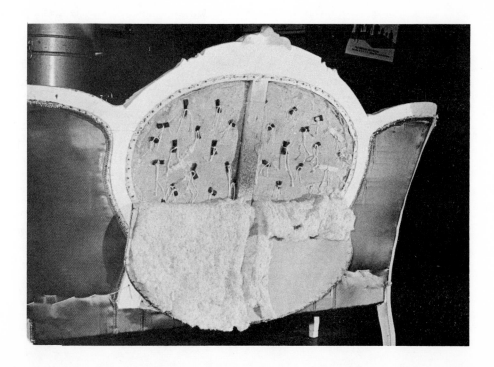

The alteration of furniture is often easier than making new, especially if the alteration is cutting down rather than adding to the original structure. The practiced eye of the designer can see in the otherwise hideous neo-Grand Rapids masterpiece, after a little painting, reupholstering, and trimming away of excess parts, a Louis XIV side chair that would fool Molière. Armed with a background of period style the designer frequently can turn a second-hand furniture store into a treasure house of antiquity (Figure 10–5a).

UPHOLSTERING.   Invariably when the sundry set properties are brought together on the stage for the first time, some or all may have to be upholstered for either color or compositional reasons. Extensive reupholstering is not recommended on borrowed pieces, although it is possible to cover the existing surface with a new material by catching it lightly with a needle and thread. This should not be attempted on antiques which might have old and therefore weak upholstering. Bright colors or shiny materials on a borrowed piece can be dulled by covering them with a black net.

To reupholster furniture that belongs to the theatre, it is best to follow the same method of covering used originally. If the old covering is removed carefully, the pieces can serve as a pattern for cutting the new material. While the upholstering is off, repairs can be made to the springs and webbing that holds the springs, as well as refreshing or altering the padding (Figure 10–5b).

If the piece of furniture is going to be kept in stock, the padding can be covered first with muslin which serves as a base for any future changes in upholstering.

Expert upholstering hides or covers the tacking. This is accomplished in many ways. The material can be tacked on a hidden edge in back or underneath; tacked to a surface that is later hidden by a covered panel; or the exposed tacks can be covered with a decorative gimp braid or fringe. Sometimes the tacks are studded and are left exposed as a decorative feature in themselves (Figure 10–6).

PAPIER-MÂCHÉ.   The term *mâché* work has grown to include all techniques and materials used to mold or fake carved relief detail on furniture or scenery. The original papier-mâché technique used paper or paper pulp,

Figure 10–6. UPHOLSTERING TECHNIQUES. **(a)** Tacking: (1) Hidden tacking. (2) Tacking covered by a panel. (3) Tacking kept on an unexposed surface. (4) Decorative tacking. (5) Tacking covered with gimp braid. (6) Tacking covered with fringe. (7) Upholstering tacks 4, 6, 12, and gimp tacks 3, 4. **(b)** Fringes and braid: (1) and (2) Ball fringes. (3) and (4) Tassel fringes. (5) Bullion fringe. (6) Braid. (7) Gimp braid. (8) Ruffle. **(c)** Plaits: (1) Pinch plait. (2) Box plait. (3) Accordion plaits. (4) Gathering.

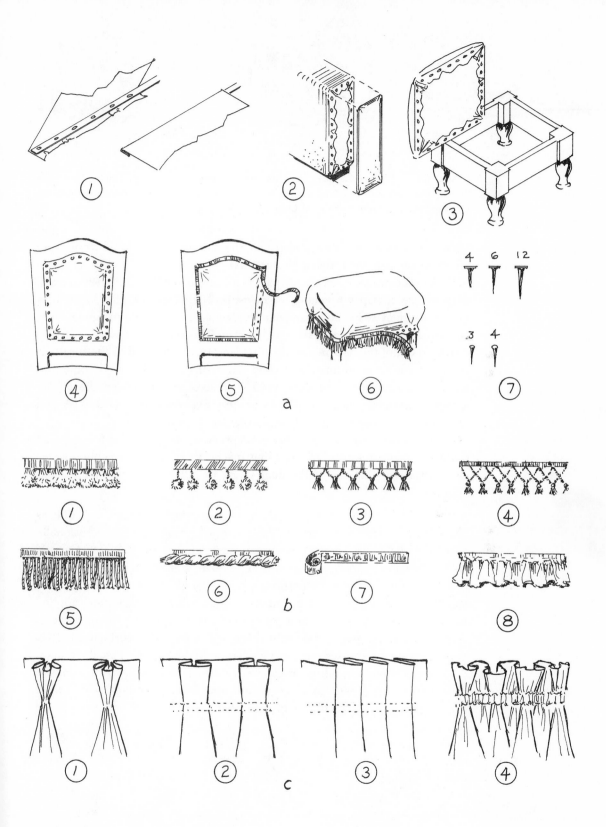

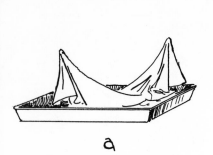
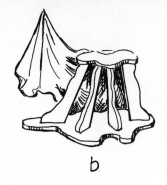
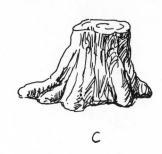

a

b

c

Figure 10–7. CELASTIC. (a) Fabric softened in special solvent. (b) Softened fabric is draped over prepared understructure. (c) Final form after Celastic has hardened. (d) Celastic used in negative mold. (e) Over a positive mold.

which was either modeled directly on the surface, or to duplicate a large number, was fashioned from a plaster mold.

When modeling directly with papier-mâché, a poriferous paper is used, such as tissue, paper toweling, or newsprint. The paper, after being torn into convenient strips and dampened in water, is dipped into binder consisting of wheat paste and strong glue size. The excessive binder is lightly squeezed out of the now near-pulp mass, and then is applied to the furniture surface to be modeled into the desired shape. If the relief is high, some preliminary modeling can be done with wire screening to which the mâché is applied as the final surface. The technique is very similar to that described in Chapter 5 for construction of large irregular shapes.

To duplicate identical forms, the same process can be applied to a greased positive or negative mold. In molding mâché there is a noticeable amount of shrinkage in the size of the final shape that has to be taken into consideration.

ASBESTOS PULP AND CELASTIC. Because papier-mâché-relief applique is rather fragile with excessive handling, a sturdier substitute is occasionally needed. Although more expensive, relief forms of asbestos pulp and Celastic are made more quickly and are stronger than papier-mâché. The process of molding and shaping asbestos pulp is slightly different. The pulp is moistened with size water to a consistency that can be modeled and applied to the furniture surface, or to a preshaped screen surface. Although taking longer to dry than papier-mâché, it dries with a very hard surface. The wet pulp also can be pressed into a negative mold to duplicate many shapes.

Celastic or Sculpt-o-fab is, of course, a different technique. It is a cheese cloth impregnated with cellulose nitrate and a fire retardant. This rather stiff fabric, when softened in a special solvent, becomes pliable, and can be

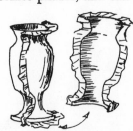

d

e

Figure 10–8.   MECHANICAL SOUND EFFECTS.   (a) Wind machine. (b) Rain, shot in rotating drum. (c) Rain, shot in tray with wire-screen bottom. (d) Thunder sheet. (e) Rumble cart. (f) Falling rubble after an explosion. (g) Wood crash. (h) Gun shots. (i) Slap stick. (j) Horses' hoofs.

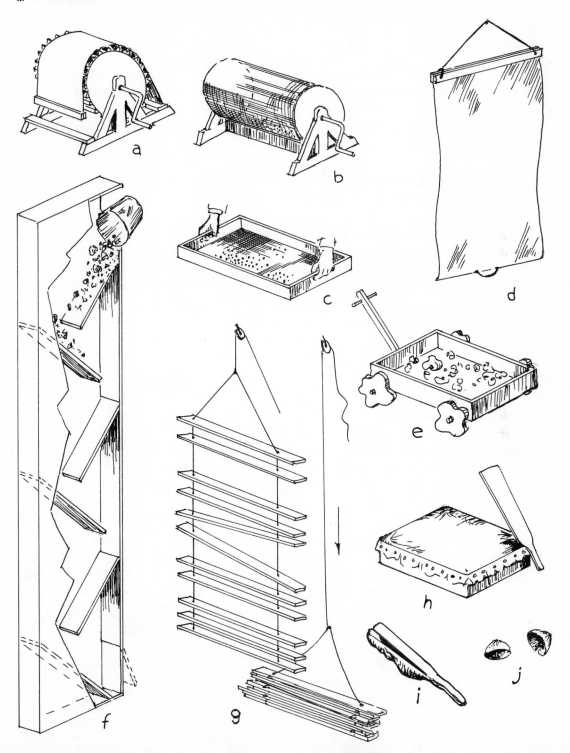

shaped or molded in a negative or positive mold. As the very volatile solvent evaporates, the cellulose nitrate hardens into the new shape. The Celastic form will separate easily from a mold that has been covered first with aluminum foil. There is very little shrinkage and the resulting shape is extremely sturdy (Figure 10–7).

EFFECT PROPERTIES

There was a time in theatre history when visual and sound effects were the major concern of the property department. Before the advent of high-fidelity recording many sound effects were created mechanically by the property man. Most of these machines are now gathering dust in the property room. An adequate sound system can bring any effect to the audience with a truer quality and a more sensitive control than the mechanical sound effect. There is one possible exception which is the effect of offstage gun fire. The recordings of distant battle scenes are fairly convincing, but close rifle

Figure 10–9. SMOKE EFFECTS. (a) Smoke bomb. (b) Dry ice and water. (c) Water mixed with titanium tetrachloride. (d) Heated sal ammoniac. (e) Heated mineral oil. (f) Squibb, means of electrically firing a flash or firecracker. (g) Flash box containing flash powder over low-amperage fuse wire for electrically firing flash and smoke.

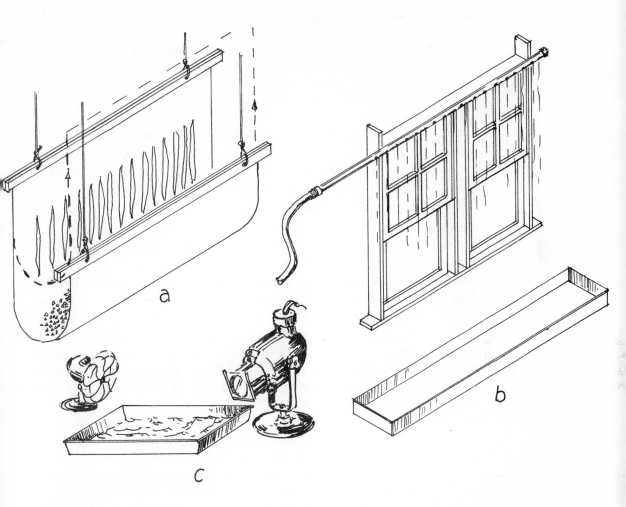

Figure 10–10. VISUAL EFFECTS. (a) Snow cradle. (b) Rain pipe. (c) Water reflection.

or revolver shots are better when a gun with blank cartridges is fired backstage.

More as historical record and less as modern practice, Figure 10–8 shows some of the mechanical sound effects that are a part of the property department.

Although some visual effects have become electrified, most of them have remained mechanical or partially so. Smoke, fire, and flash explosions are usually electrically controlled; however, smoke can be made nonelectrically if necessary (Figure 10–9).

Some familiar visual effects that are mechanical are the snow cradle and rain pipes which are shown in Figure 10–10 along with other special effects that call upon the ingenuity of the stage technician and property man to rig and trigger on cue.

BREAKAWAYS.   Many times pieces of furniture, dishes, or other objects have to break on stage. The chairs that collapse and the flag pole that falls down in *Cockadoodle Dandy,* the bullet fired through the windowpane in *Front Page,* or a railing that breaks during a fight scene are a few examples of properties or scenery breaking on cue and in a predetermined manner.

In Figure 10–11, a railing breakaway is prebroken and lightly glued together. Thin strips of "orange crating" are tacked on the back of the repair to give a convincing splintering sound as the railing breaks again. The pattern of the break is carefully planned so as to control the fall of the pieces in the same manner for each performance.

BREAKAWAY WINDOWPANES AND MIRRORS.   The breaking of real glass on the stage, although frequently done, is somewhat dangerous. Flying glass plus broken glass left on the floor can become a hazard. If the actor is too close to the breaking glass it is sometimes desirable to use other materials. One familiar substitute for glass used often in the motion picture industry is candy glass. Candy glass or hardened sugar and water is prepared like old-fashioned rock candy. After bringing a supersaturated solution of sugar and water to about 260 degrees Fahrenheit it is poured on a smooth surface into a thin sheet. The sheet hardens into a clear, transparent solid. Candy glass, however, has a low melting point and may soften under stage lights or excessive handling.

A clear-sheet breakaway can be made of powdered plastic. Santolite MHP, manufactured by Monsanto Chemical Company, can be easily melted and cast into transparent sheets, which upon hardening, break easily into dull-edged fragments. The best results are obtained by casting the sheets on a cellophane-covered, tempered Masonite surface. The MHP in sheet form also tends to soften easily but at a higher temperature than candy glass. Whenever possible it is wise to cast the plastic directly into the window or mirror frame to avoid excessive handling. A mirror is made by painting the back of a clear sheet with a metallic paint.

The fragments, as an added advantage, can be reclaimed and melted down again although the plastic begins to discolor after repeated remeltings.

Pottery Breakaways.   Opaque shapes, such as teacups, dishes, or small objects of art are much easier to make into breakaways. Because they are not transparent, inexpensive pottery or china pieces may be prebroken and lightly glued together again to insure their breaking onstage. As the second breaking usually shatters the piece beyond reclaiming, a breakaway should be prepared for each performance.

Special opaque breakaway shapes can be prepared by casting a mixture of plaster and Styrofoam into a mold of the shape. To keep the casting

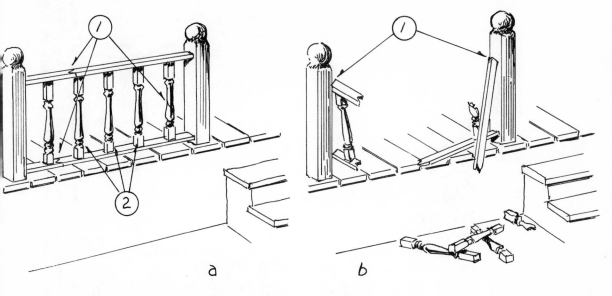

Figure 10–11. BREAKAWAY RAILING. **(a)** Railing prepared for breaking: (1) Pre-broken spots, lightly glued. (2) Loose spindles, lightly glued. **(b)** Railing after breaking: (1) prepared hinge points.

hollow for easy breaking requires a core mold which makes the whole casting process very complicated and time consuming.

If the authenticity, both in sound and looks, of the breakaway object is extremely important to the play a replica can be made in clay bisque. A clay slip or solution of powdered water clay and water is poured into a mold of the object and after allowing to set a few minutes is poured out. A thin shell of clay adheres to the mold making a hollow casting of the object. After drying thoroughly (48 hours) the raw-clay casting is fired in a ceramic kiln to bisque hardness. A great number can be prepared this way.

FOLIAGE

Artificial flowers and the foliage of hedges, bush pieces, and small trees are considered properties as well as live flowers, potted plants, and sprays of real leaves used to dress the setting. The expression "prop bush" besides meaning that the bush is not real, implies that it is shaped in three dimensions, as opposed to a flat, painted set-piece.

Lifelike artificial flowers can be obtained easily from display houses, local variety stores, or at the home-decorations section of a department store. Although they are more expensive than real flowers, with proper care they can be used over again.

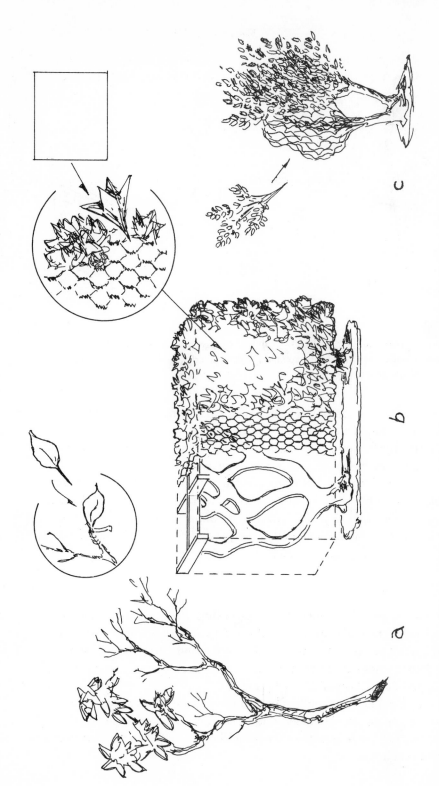

Figure 10–12. FOLIAGE. (a) Artificial leaves wired or taped to real tree branches or section. (b) Trimmed boxwood hedge made of frame covered with inch-mesh chicken wire. Crepe-paper or fabric squares are pushed into openings (color more convincing if two or three shades of green are used). (c) Untrimmed box or ilex bush; chicken wire shaped over basic frame and filled with sprays of artificial boxwood or ilex.

Stylized or caricatured blossoms have to be specially made. Their scale and design determine the material used. Exotic tropical flowers in a musical comedy, for example, have been made of velveteen or satin with leaves made of wire loops covered with sheer chiffon.

Banks of blossoms and box hedges can be made of shaped one-inch mesh chicken wire with ruffle-edged colored crepe paper or silk pushed into the openings. A more realistic box hedge can be made of chicken wire holding sprays of artificial boxwood or ilex leaves (Figure 10–12). Large mesh chicken wire can be used to support clumps of leaves on a tree branch, or as a hanging border related to a tree trunk. The leaf material, which can be either paper or fabric, should have sufficient stiffness to hold a leaflike shape, or it will have to be stiffened with wire. Window-shade stock, which comes in several shades of green, makes a good leaf fabric to staple onto a branch or chicken-wire frame.

PART 3

DESIGNING

THE LIGHTING

11

INTRODUCTION TO
STAGE-LIGHTING DESIGN

SCENE DESIGN AND STAGE LIGHTING

Scene design, unlike the other visual arts, is deeply dependent on the use of light as a part of the final composition—the dramatic picture. And stage lighting holds such importance in contributing to the total visual effect that no designer should neglect to familiarize himself with its techniques.

The design of lighting begins with the designer's sketch. Here he presents a suggestion of the light that will illuminate the scene. It may appear to be coming from such natural sources as the sun, the moon, or a fire—or from artificial sources as table lamps or ceiling fixtures. In contrast, the sources may be frankly arbitrary and depend on the position and color of the instruments used to build the composition. If the sketch is carefully done, the direction and color of the light will be apparent. To indicate any changes in brightness, color, or direction, the designer will prepare several sketches to show such altered composition and mood.

243

Such sketches, however, are only a start in the planning of stage lighting. Although a sketch represents an artistic concept, it must be technically sound to be properly realized. The floor plan that accompanies the sketch gives the first clues as to the credibility of the designer's lighting ideas. Many a beautiful sketch has been based on a floor plan that revealed, on closer study, impossible lighting angles and insufficient space for the lighting instruments.

Ideally the scene designer should also design the lighting for his conception. This is frequently the case in college and community theatre as well as in the commercial field. But some highly competent scene designers disclaim any ability in the field of lighting, and others seem to be just too busy to wish to bother. But whether the scene designer lights his own sets, or whether he depends on a lighting specialist to do it for him, he will certainly broaden his design concepts and save himself much distress if he learns the facts of stage lighting.

WHAT IS STAGE LIGHTING?

Everyone agrees that light is needed in order that the actors may be seen, that it is useful to differentiate between night and daytime scenes, and that it can, by virtue of some magic or other, create a mood. And this is as far as many people think on the subject. Good stage lighting must go well beyond these limited objectives.

Good lighting—and there is plenty that is not good—should tie together all the visual aspects of the stage. It is not enough to illuminate players, settings, properties, and costumes. Portions of the scenery may need to be subdued, certain properties may require accenting, handsome costumes must be enhanced. Briefly, all objects that appear on the stage must be focused by light into a picture that conveys sense and feeling to the viewing audience. And the actor himself, when he walks onto this stage, must be seen in a proper relationship to his background.

In fact, this might be considered the most important duty of light on the stage: to give the actor meaning in his surroundings, to provide him with an environment in which he may sensibly interpret his role, to assist him in every way to bring to the audience the full meaning and emotion of the playwright's script.

Naturally this statement negates the belief held by many that stage lighting is a succession of unusual pictures, beautiful patterns, visual excitement, each for its own sake. To be sure, scripts often call for startling effects: an explosion, a fog, a flashing sign, a fire on the hearth, a brilliant sunset. But each of these should have its definite part in advancing the plot, and even then it must not be allowed to steal the attention of the audience at the expense of the actors.

THE ARTIST AS LIGHT DESIGNER

A matter of taste is of paramount importance in lighting–taste and artistic judgment. And this means that the design of the lighting, and the control over how it is used, must be in the hands of an artist and not entrusted to an artisan, no matter how qualified such a person may be in the practice of safe wiring and the invention of gadgetry.

This is not to say that the stage electrician is not an extremely useful, in fact, an indispensable person, when it comes to mounting instruments, making connections, and, often, solving by ingenious methods the problems presented by inadequate equipment. And many such skilled technicians do possess great artistic taste as well. But all too often the reverse is true.

Before we go further, let us examine the aims of stage lighting, for without agreeing as to what its purposes are, we cannot discuss it with understanding.

THE FUNCTIONS OF LIGHT

VISIBILITY.   The first and obvious use for light on the stage is visibility: to allow each member of the audience to see clearly those things which he should see. By extension, this also means that the audience should not see, or not see as distinctly, certain other things. In some types of production this is extremely important; in others, less so.

By "seeing what should be seen" we do not mean merely making out that it is there and what it happens to be. The full, three-dimensional form should be revealed, the texture of the surface made apparent, and the variations in color disclosed. Nor is it enough to consider this sufficient when applied to an actor standing in one location on the stage. He should be equally well illuminated no matter where he moves, unless there is definite reason to the contrary.

PLAUSIBILITY.   The second aim for light on the stage is to give a feeling of plausibility: a reasonably accurate imitation of the light that one would naturally expect from whatever sources are apparent or suggested. For example: sunlight should enter a window in parallel rays that give a sharp pattern on whatever they strike, while the more general light of an overcast day would pour in the same window in a directionless flood. An interior room might seem to be washed with light from unseen, but plausible, sources. In other words, the audience must be able to accept the light that it sees on the stage as being in the realm of the possible, and must not be distracted by effects that cannot be accounted for by reasonable imagination.

On the other hand, in many modern plays the completely arbitrary is desired. In this situation the lighting should be so carried out as not to confuse the spectator into preoccupation with trying to identify what he sees with natural effects.

COMPOSITION.   The third function may be termed composition—the tying together of the stage picture into a meaningful and, frequently, a pleasing scene. This includes the subduing of certain less important features, the accenting of the more important, the smooth blending of light on those areas demanding an equality of illumination, the use of cast shadows, of high lights, and the like to lend emphasis and interest, and unobtrusively to focus the spectator's attention on areas where the critical action takes place.

MOOD.   And fourth there is mood—all too often the first and only aim of the inexperienced, but one which follows almost automatically if the other three purposes are properly effected. Perhaps mood is, in the end, the most important, but its realization usually results from the successful attainment of the others. Certainly no desirable mood can be achieved if either the visibility or the plausibility or the composition is neglected.

THE QUALITIES OF LIGHT

INTENSITY.   But what are the tools of light that enable us to effect these four functions, or purposes—what attributes of light may be used to attain visibility, plausibility, composition and mood? Again, these qualities are four in number.

The first and most obvious is intensity—the brightness of the light. This may vary over a vast range, from a mere glow to a burst of illumination of many hundred foot candles. The designer may utilize little more than the feeble flicker from a match for a scene played on an otherwise dark stage, or he may wash the action with such a brilliance that the spectator will vow that it outshines sunlight. Between these extremes he has the greatest of flexibility in selecting the exact amount of light needed for any portion of the stage picture at any time.

COLOR.   Color is the second property of light that is under the control of the designer. And quite literally every color of the visible spectrum is his to command and use. He can employ the most delicate tints to enhance the actors' faces, wash the setting in a sunny glow or a cool, evening shadow, or use his strongest colors for a nonrealistic effect on a backdrop. And color can be used skillfully to increase or emphasize the full dimension of solid objects, to enrich costumes, to modify the appearance of the painted setting.

DISTRIBUTION. Light has form and direction, giving us another tool in its effective use. A general wash of light over the whole stage is very different from a pencil-thin ray carefully focused on a specific object or actor, or from the sheet of light that illuminates equally all portions of a cyclorama or backdrop. A row of sources will give a general bath of light that seems to reveal no shadows, while a single source will etch shadows sharply wherever it falls. A spotlight angling in on an actor from above may give him a look of complete naturalness as though he were lighted from a street light or a household ceiling fixture. The same spotlight from below will distort his face with unusual shadows and high lights.

MOVEMENT. And each of these three properties—intensity, color and distribution—may be intensified, diminished, or otherwise altered by the fourth property, movement. Movement implies the change, whether subtly, or abruptly, of any of the other properties. We might take, for example, an ordinary room on a bright afternoon with sunbeams streaming in the window. As time passes and evening draws on, the room becomes darker (movement in intensity), the warmth of the sunbeams fade to the general cool of evening (movement in color), and the sunbeams themselves will dissolve and be replaced at the window by the more general light of dusk (movement in distribution).

LIGHTING THE ACTOR

By keeping the four functions of light in mind, and by the judicious use of its four properties, we may approach the matter of actually lighting the stage.

Certainly we want visibility. And we realize that lighting the actor's face from straight ahead is not the way to achieve it, as such light tends to wash out all the features of the human face, all its high lights and shadows, and renders it a blank, expressionless mask. We must seek some other direction from which light may fall to enhance the natural contours of the features.

It has long been a practice of artists, in sketching forms, to render their drawings as though light were falling on the subject at an angle of 45 degrees. And this same principle has been adopted by most stage-lighting designers as the best for their purposes as well. If this light is to have such direction, it is assumed that an instrument such as a spotlight must be used, so that all the rays may be directed in approximately one direction. And the 45-degree angle is sought in both the horizontal and vertical planes. This means that an actor standing in any part of the stage will see the spotlight trained on him at 45 degrees above him and 45 degrees to either his right or left.

Lighted by a single spotlight in this manner, the actor's face takes on great

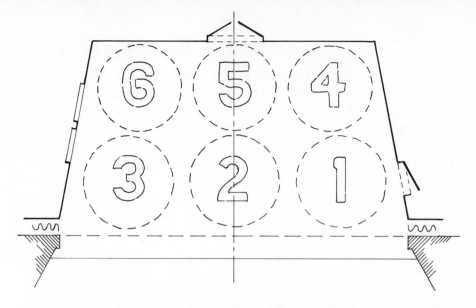

Figure 11–1. DIVISION OF VISIBLE STAGE SPACE INTO LIGHTING AREAS. Above: A conventional box setting. On opposite page: An irregularly shaped interior setting. In practice the individual beam patterns are larger and less regular, and overlap one another in all directions. Note the conventional numbering, from downstage left (the actor's left) to upstage right.

character, his features are clearly defined, his expressions are easily read. But, alas, only one side of his face is so effectively lighted, and the audience sitting in half the house will see mainly shadow. This may be dramatic for a few moments, but will not long be tolerated. It becomes necessary to place a second spotlight on the actor's other side, so that both sides of his face are illuminated.

Now this tends to wash out some of the definition that was established by the single light. To counteract this loss of plasticity, we can resort to the use of color, in very light shades (so as not to distort too greatly the natural tints of the face and costume). A familiar and popular combination is a very pale scarlet on one side and an equally light blue on the other. Which color is used on the right and which on the left will depend on the other aspects of the scene, the setting, the presumed source of light, and such considerations.

LIGHTING THE ACTING AREA

Of course we must place enough spotlights so that all portions of the stage in which the actor moves or stands for any length of time will receive nearly equal amounts of light, so that he will not pass through distracting changes as he moves about.

On a medium sized stage with a conventional box setting, twelve spotlights are usually sufficient. It is convenient and desirable to divide the visible stage space into six lesser areas, three in the downstage band, and

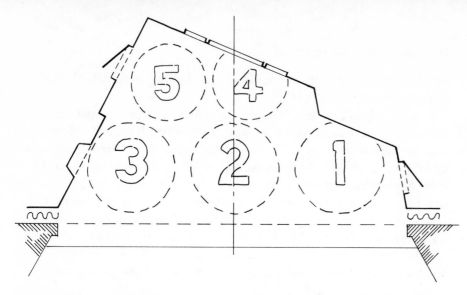

three in the upstage (see Figure 11–1). Larger stages or more open settings may call for more instruments. Irregularly shaped sets usually demand variation from the standard six areas. And when the available spotlights do not have sufficient intensity, or wide enough spread, it may be necessary to use more than six areas.

In recent years supplementary lighting of various sorts has become increasingly popular and often can be most effective in enhancing the illumination achieved by the "area lighting" described above. Side lighting, bursts of light in strong colors from spotlights ranged along the sides of the stage, is one of these. Of course, in a box setting, it is not possible to mount instruments along the sides, except, perhaps, in the extreme downstage corners. But in more open scenery, particularly of the wing-and-border varity, such lighting can be, and usually is, used.

The effect of a light directed across the stage, on an actor's face, creates a very plastic and dramatic picture. By using instruments along the sides of the playing area, in addition to the regular lighting, we can get some of the benefit from this. But certain precautions must be taken, or the actor closer to the side light may throw his shadow across an actor a little further away. Another difficulty frequently arises when an actor, near the side of the stage, finds himself in distractingly bright light, due to his proximity to a side-lighting instrument in the wings. For these two reasons it is desirable that all such lights be mounted fairly high and as well away from the playing area as the stage dimensions permit.

Another variation is "back lighting" or "top lighting." As the names indicate, instruments are mounted high above the stage and focused straight down or even a little forward, so that the beams fall on the actor's head and shoulders. The actor's face is by no means assisted by such light, of course, but the halo effects created about the head and upper body can make him stand out dramatically from his background. Excellent as such effects may

249

be, the importance of both back and side lighting should be considered secondary to basic area lighting.

Another adjunct of area lighting, but one not regarded with the same importance today as it once was, particularly when back and side lighting tend to usurp some of its duties, is blending light. This is traditionally done by means of striplights, hung as borders or "X-rays" overhead, as far downstage as possible, and also as the familiar footlights at the apron's edge. By using three color circuits with light shades of color, it is possible to get practically any tint that can reasonably be desired. Such light serves a dual purpose, tending to blend or smooth out any irregularities and unevenness left by the area spotlights, and throwing over the whole stage picture an atmosphere of color that can easily be modified through any scene.

LIGHTING THE BACKGROUNDS

So far we have been thinking primarily in terms of the acting areas, those portions of the stage where we expect the actors to stand, move, and speak. We have given no consideration to the scenery behind them, which though of less importance than the actors themselves, must be properly lighted to give the players a suitable location for their actions, an environment in which they may resolve the play.

In a conventional interior setting, the area lighting, arranged for the actors, will usually suffice to light the walls of the box set, particularly when borderstrips and footlights contribute their toning washes. But background areas are a different matter. Many times these are small, as the backing behind a doorway, rarely seen for more than a moment at a time, and then not very directly by most of the audience. No very elaborate device is needed to give these enough illumination so that an actor, when he leaves the stage, does not seem to be retiring into a dark closet.

But there are many larger areas, as a section of sky seen through a window, possibly with a ground row of distant hills or a hedge or a group of rooftops or even a solid wall representing a nearby building. Such scenes demand greater attention and flexibility of color control than is necessary with a small doorway presumably opening into a passage or adjacent room.

Most complicated of all are vast areas of sky, often with painted scenery on them, that are formed by large backdrops or cycloramas. These will demand rows of powerful instruments, above and below in order to give the proper amount of light, blended evenly over the whole surface. Great control of color is required to represent endless effects: sunny morning, approaching storm, star-studded evening, golden sunset, blackest midnight, or completely arbitrary washes of strong colors or of delicate tints. Many times these great cloth surfaces are partly translucent, requiring additional banks of light behind them.

SPECIAL EFFECTS

Motivating Lights. Lighting the acting areas and the background effectively and artistically is of course the primary duty of the light designer. This is the real meat of his work. But just as a child wants his dessert first, so it is very tempting for the inexperienced designer to become unduly involved and waste valuable time on the "fun" elements of stage lighting. These we may group together under the general heading of "special effects." Their number is infinite, but they seem to fall naturally into four basic classifications.

First are the motivating lights: sources that *seem* to be giving the light, or a portion of it, to the stage picture. Chandeliers, wall sconces, lanterns, fires are typical of this category. Usually each must be naturalistic enough to appear to be furnishing a plausible amount of light to the stage. Yet because such effects if completely realistic may be very distracting by their movement or their brilliance, they must be handled with extreme caution and taste.

Motivated Lights. The second category is motivated illumination—which seems to be emanating from some realistic source. We have already mentioned the burst of "sunlight" coming through the window as opposed to the more general, formless light that is typical of an overcast sky.

Other, and very common effects of this type are pools of light that presumably emanate from household fixtures. As was mentioned, audience comfort and attention will not permit the real thing in most cases, yet we must give the impression that these additional lights, whose sources are hidden from view of the spectators, are actually the result of the realistic fixtures on the stage. Other problems, such as the lights of a speeding car flashing past a window, a bottle that glows when approached, and the like, must be the product of ingenuity and inventiveness, and a source of genuine fun in their contriving.

Specially Defined Visibility. The third category might be considered as a variation in the regular area lighting. It is additional or specially defined visibility, and it takes several forms. A common concept, and one of the most difficult to achieve, is that of the lone actor on an otherwise completely darkened stage dramatically bathed in his private pool of light. Such lighting is purely arbitrary of course and should retain or suggest as little of the naturalistic as possible. A variation of this is the well-known follow-spot—

again an individual pool of light, but this time with movement added. It has long been used in musicals, revues, and other productions where realism is of minor importance. But it has come in recent years into a more general use in straight drama. Not so obtrusive in these, usually, but most effective when properly controlled.

In fact, the use of the follow spot in realistic drama is merely a variation of the long-established custom of accenting portions of the stage where especially important action takes place—the chair where a significant character sits, the table on which a vital object is placed, a hanging picture that bears a strong relationship to the play's meaning, doorways through which important entrances are made. Such lighting must be particularly unobtrusive: the audience should not be aware that an accent exists but only feel its effect.

PROJECTIONS.   The fourth group includes all instruments that project patterns of light or complete pictures, whether moving or motionless, on the scenery or occasionally on the actors as well. The problems encountered in the use of projections are discussed in Chapter 17. Despite their many limitations, such effects in the hands of knowledgeable designers are becoming increasingly important and valuable.

12

ELEMENTS OF
ELECTRICITY

The woods are full of competent electricians. Every group of high school age has its quota of boys—and girls—who can change a fuse, wire up a home-made striplight, or repair a rotary resistance dimmer. They may not use all the safety precautions of the professional electrician nor follow the requirements of the National Electrical Code, and why they don't electrocute themselves or burn down the schoolhouse twice a week, nobody knows. But they do work diligently and long hours to make possible the only stage lighting that is known to hundreds of dramatic groups across the country.

Unfortunately, their efforts are rarely of high esthetic quality. But, because we have no one to take their places, and they themselves are not usually aware of what constitutes good lighting, we must bear with their inartistic efforts. Nor should we blame them for the results. Rather it should be the interest of the designer to acquaint himself with the tools of the electrician that he may take over the execution of his own dreams and himself express his own esthetic tastes upon the stage.

For this reason we must instruct our artist in the nature of electricity and its laws, thus freeing him from his dependence on the artisan.

ATOMIC THEORY

All matter is made up of atoms. This is common knowledge. Each atom consists of several parts, the only one important to us in this discussion being the electron. The atom of each different element has, normally, a precise number of electrons: hydrogen has one electron, helium has two, lithium has three, and so forth. In the atoms of some elements the electrons are fairly stable—that is, they cannot be separated easily from the atom to which they belong.

However, in other elements it is reasonably easy to break an electron free from its atom. This may be done by chemical means, by friction, by a moving magnetic field, or by other means. When electrons are broken loose from their atoms, the process is called ionization.

Each electron carries a negative electrical charge. It is a tiny one, of course, but when many electrons are involved the result will be a considerable accumulation of negative charges. This is known as an electric potential and is what is produced by a battery to make the lamp of a flashlight glow, or by a generator to furnish the power necessary to run huge machines or to light many thousand lamps.

The electrons in such an accumulation are continually seeking to escape—to flow away to places where there is no accumulation, or at least a lesser accumulation. The more free electrons there are in the accumulation the greater is this effort to escape, or as it is called, the potential or electromotive force. This force is measured in terms of volts, and frequently the potential is referred to as "voltage." Now when electrons do move from their place of accumulation to some other place, this flow is called the "current," and the rate of flow of the current is measured in terms of amperes.

No material will allow a current of electrons to flow through it without offering some resistance, though there is an immense difference between the resistances of different materials. Obviously the longer the path the current must follow, the greater will be the resistance. On the other hand, the greater the cross section of the wire or other material providing the path, the less will be the resistance.

ELECTRIC MEASUREMENTS

OHM's LAW. There is a definite relationship between the electromotive force pushing the electrons through the conductor, the resistance the conductor offers, and the rate of flow of the electrons. This relationship is known as Ohm's law and states that in any electric circuit the intensity of the current (in amperes) is equal to the electromotive force (in volts) divided by the resistance (in ohms). Using the conventional symbols:

I = Intensity of current (amperes)
E = Electromotive force (volts)
R = Resistance (ohms)

we find that: $I = \dfrac{E}{R}$

THE PIE FORMULA. Ohm's law is an extremely important equation for every worker with electric circuits to keep in mind. But there is one more unit of measurement of equal importance, the rate of doing work. This is the watt, usually expressed by the symbol P (for power). Its relationship to the previously discussed units is that the total watts in a working circuit is equal to the product of the amperes and the volts. This can be easily remembered by use of the "pie" formula: P = IE.

Naturally these equations may be transposed or substituted one in the other to arrive at any arrangement suitable for solving any specific problem. Below are listed all the possible relationships of these four units:

$$I = \frac{E}{R} = \frac{P}{E} = \sqrt{\frac{P}{R}}$$

$$E = IR = \frac{P}{I} = \sqrt{PR}$$

$$R = \frac{E}{I} = \frac{E^2}{P} = \frac{P}{I^2}$$

$$P = IE = I^2R = \frac{E^2}{R}$$

DIRECT AND ALTERNATING CURRENT

Current can move through a conductor in either of two ways. Direct current, commonly referred to as dc, flows in one direction only, while alternating current, or ac, reverses its direction 120 times a second. This is known as 60-cycle current and is standard in most American installations, though many foreign countries use 50 cycles or even fewer.

Direct current is not a very efficient way to transport electricity for any long distance, but as it was the only way known in the early days, it was installed in larger cities and is still found in central areas of a few of these. Elsewhere it has been replaced by the more versatile ac.

Of the various household ac services in this country, 120-volt current

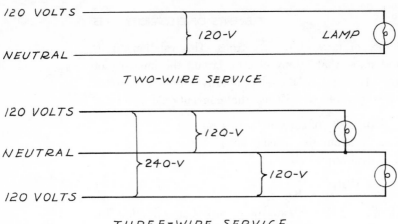

TWO-WIRE SERVICE

THREE-WIRE SERVICE

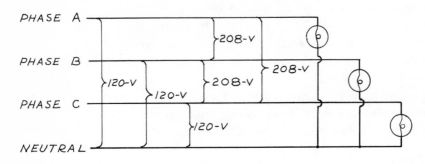

FOUR-WIRE (THREE-PHASE) SERVICE

Figure 12–1. THE THREE KINDS OF ELECTRICAL DISTRIBUTION SERVICE

accounts for almost two-thirds and 115 volts for practically all the rest. The few remaining d-c services are of 110 volts.

ELECTRIC SERVICES

It is essential that the stage electrician know by just what system of wiring the electricity is brought into the theatre or other area in which he may be working. This is especially true when a touring company moves into an unfamiliar building and must connect up its portable control board and other equipment. Without going into the intricacies of generator construction and distribution economics, let us glance briefly at the three forms of service in common use (Figure 12–1).

The first of these is the 2-wire system, carrying either dc or ac, in which one line is said to be "hot" and the other "neutral." The potential between them usually is 120 volts, though it could be 115 or 110 volts depending on the voltage supplied in that particular locality, as explained above. Practically all portable lighting equipment will operate almost equally well on any of these voltages.

The second form of service is the 3-wire system, which also may be either ac or dc. In this the two "outside" wires usually have a potential of 240 volts between them, but each has a potential of only 120 volts between it and the third wire, the common neutral. A familiar domestic application of this service is found in many homes where the electric lights are on two or more circuits of 120 volts each, while the electric range operates on 240 volts. Great care must be taken when working with such a system to avoid connecting any apparatus designed for 120 volts across the two hot lines. The 240 volts will blow the lamps at once, ruin other equipment promptly, and provide grave danger of fatal shock. The British, who use 240 volts for all their home lighting, must take precautions that would seem very irksome to us, who are used to our comparatively mild 120-volt service.

The third type of service, and one that is on the rapid increase due to its efficiency in distribution, is the a-c 120-208–volt, 4-wire system, also known as the "3-phase system." In this arrangement there are three hot lines and a neutral. Between any one hot line and the neutral there is the standard potential of 120 volts, but because the current in each hot line is alternating on a different time phase from the other two, there is a difference of 208 volts between any pair of them. This latter is of little concern to us except that we must be sure never to connect standard voltage equipment between two hot lines of a 3-phase service.

SERIES AND PARALLEL CIRCUITS

Once the current has been received from the supplying mains in any location, regardless of how it reaches the building (by 2-, 3-, or 4-wire systems), it is distributed in 2-wire systems, similar to the one diagrammed in Figure 12–1. And the various elements that work in these circuits—lamps, switches, dimmers, fuses, and the like—may be connected in either of two ways.

One of these is the series circuit in which the flow of current passes through the various elements successively. In the top diagram of Figure 12–2 it will be seen that the current must pass through each of the four lamps, one after the other, before returning by the neutral wire. But in the center diagram the same four lamps are connected "in parallel," and it is apparent that a portion of the total current can flow simultaneously through each lamp.

Almost all practical lighting circuits are a combination of these two. The bottom diagram of Figure 12–2 shows a typical example. The switch and fuse are in series, and they are also in series with each of the lamps. But the four lamps are in parallel with one another. Let the switch be opened or the fuse blown and all the lamps will be extinguished. But one of the lamps may be removed and the remaining three will not be affected. In other words, the series portion is used to control the circuit as a whole, while the parallel portion is valuable as a distributor of the current.

How does Ohm's law apply in relation to these two forms of circuitry? It is obvious that in a series circuit the current must force its way successively through the several resistances furnished by the four lamp filaments. As it must pass through all, the total resistance is the sum of all the individual resistances. The entire voltage will be used up in this process, with each lamp consuming a portion of the total potential in proportion to the resistance it offers. This will mean that no lamp will receive the full voltage on which it is designed to operate and hence no lamp will burn at full brightness.

It must be kept in mind that the current will distribute itself instantly in the proper proportions throughout the entire system, so it does not matter which element comes first in the circuit. A stable condition will be reached at once.

Now in the parallel circuit the full 120 volts is impressed on each lamp at the same time, so each may burn at its full brightness. This is the usual form of current distribution, and it is necessary to be able to calculate quickly the amperes flowing in a circuit of this sort. To do this we invert the pie formula to read: $I = P/E$. Now we know that E is 120 volts. Suppose that we have two 40-watt lamps, one 60-watt, and one 100-watt lamp in this circuit, this will give us a total of 240 watts. So, substituting these values in our formula we find that $I = \dfrac{240}{120}$, or $I = 2$ amperes. Every practical electrician should fully understand this formula above all others, and use it regularly.

CONDUCTORS AND INSULATORS

To allow electric current to flow through circuits of any kind it is necessary to provide a path through which the electrons may move as easily as possible. There is no material that will not offer some resistance to this movement, but silver offers the least of any substance known. Obviously the use of silver for extensive wiring is not very practical, and some less costly material must be used. Copper is this material: its conductivity is almost as good as silver's, it is relatively inexpensive, and it is easy to work—to form into wires and other parts. Aluminum is coming more and more into use in some applications, and brass is valuable for large, permanent parts that need to be especially rugged. Other materials are also used for special purposes, but by and large when we think of electric wires, switch parts, and the like, we think of copper.

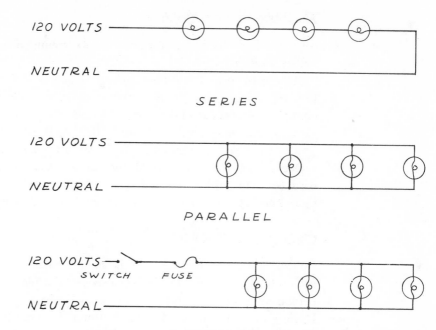

Figure 12–2. TYPES OF ELECTRIC CIRCUITS

Some sort of insulation is necessary to prevent the electrons that are flowing in a conductor from "short circuiting"—that is, escaping into other channels. This they will incline to do if the alternate path offers less resistance than the one that they were intended to travel. Obviously this would cause a lowering or even complete loss of available power. More important, this "short" may result in severe shock to anyone chancing to come in contact with the new and unprotected channel of flow. And because it may offer little resistance, it may allow a higher flow of current than the legitimate circuit was designed to carry, thereby causing damage to it.

Just as there is no material that is 100 percent conductive, so there is nothing that has 100 percent insulative properties, but there are many that can serve for various practical purposes. Glass and ceramics are excellent for small permanent parts such as sockets and switches, slate for larger switch and fuse panels, and asbestos where heat is involved. For wires and cables, rubber and fiber are used, while plastics are becoming increasingly common. The most useful insulator of all is dry air. If this were not so, every open socket or wall outlet would drain off current!

Permanent wiring, which should be laid by a licensed electrician only, may have a solid copper core through which the current flows, but the temporary wiring used on the stage always has a core made up of a number of small strands of wire. This is to provide proper flexibility in handling and laying. Standard stage cable consists of two such stranded cores, each surrounded by a strong rubber insulation. For physical strength, tough fiber cords are laid alongside, and the whole surrounded by either a rubber or a fiber sheathing.

Stage cable comes in different sizes, or gages, each of which is designed to carry a specific maximum amperage. These limits should never be exceeded. The most useful sizes are:

Size (gage number):	18	16	14	12	10	8	6
Capacity (amperes):	3	6	15	20	25	35	50

Occasionally, for a very small load and a very short run, ordinary lamp cord (or "zip cord"), which has an 18-gage core, may be used, but this should be kept to a minimum and carefully guarded against abuse.

CIRCUIT ACCESSORIES

CONNECTORS.   Because lights on the stage are temporary, being moved after each production, and often between scenes of a play, it is not wise to make permanent connections of the cables to the various lighting instruments. Devices that can be easily connected and disconnected are needed. Ordinary household plugs, with parallel blades, are used on some small stages, but because they are easily disconnected in error, are usually very fragile, and have limited capacities, they are not advisable. A departure from this style that is coming into popular use is the twist lock, roughly similar in appearance to a heavy-duty parallel blade plug, but with a design that permits the male and female caps to be locked together quite easily, yet firmly.

Probably used as much as any other devices are the pin connectors, heavy-duty fiber blocks with sturdy brass pins and sockets. They have the disadvantage of not always giving a firm electrical connection, and they can be easily pulled apart by mistake unless the two cables are tied together. As in the case with cables, all such connectors come in different sizes, each rated to carry specific maximum amperages. For the smaller stage it is wise to settle on a single-size connector, as well as a single type, to save confusion and wasted time—the 15-ampere pin connector or the 20-ampere twist lock being the usual choice.

SWITCHES.   A switch is a device, put into a circuit, to interrupt and to restore the flow of current as desired, or, as it is usually stated, "to open and close" the circuit. There are many types of mechanical switches, from the familiar domestic wall type to great knife-blade arrangements that handle many hundreds of amperes. Like everything else electrical, which type and size to use depends on the duty it is expected to perform and the load it is intended to carry. A contactor is an electrically-operated device whereby a small switch, located at some convenient place onstage, controls a magnet which operates a large-capacity switch in a remote spot. This has the double advantage of keeping the dangerously high current at a distance from the operator and allowing the heavy-duty portion, which is very noisy, to be placed where it cannot distract the audience.

FUSES AND CIRCUIT BREAKERS. No chain is stronger than its weakest link, and should an electric circuit suffer damage that permits a short circuit somewhere along the line, the ampere flow will increase to a point where *something* must burn out. The same thing will happen in the case of an overload—that is, if too many lamps are connected to the circuit. By using the pie formula we see that if six 500-watt lamps are connected to a 120-volt circuit, 25 amperes will flow through it. So if No. 14-gage wire, which has a capacity for only 15 amperes, is used, its limit will be greatly exceeded, and again something must burn out.

To protect against such occurrences, fuses of suitable capacities are inserted to form the weakest link in the electrical chain. Then, should the current flow grow dangerous, it will be the fuse that gives way, thus breaking the circuit and preventing more serious damage. The trouble is then located and corrected, and a new fuse is inserted with a minimum of trouble.

Today, in many installations, the fuse is being replaced by the circuit breaker. This, briefly, is a form of switch that is automatically opened when the current flow becomes higher than it should. For most installations the circuit breaker is a great convenience: it saves the trouble of keeping a supply of fuses on hand, it cannot be carelessly replaced by one of the wrong capacity, and, if of the magnetic variety, it can also serve as a switch for the circuit.

13

COLOR IN LIGHT

THE ELECTROMAGNETIC SPECTRUM

Light is caused by certain waves of radiant energy. The electromagnetic spectrum contains waves as long as 3100 miles: those of electric current produced by our standard sixty-cycle generators. It contains waves as short as one ten-thousandth of an angstrom unit (and 254,000,000 angstrom units make up only one inch!). These very short waves are cosmic rays which come to the earth from outer space. The waves which produce to our eyes the sensation we recognize as light range from 3800 to 7600 angstroms. Radiant energy in waves between these two limits make up the visible spectrum.

The shortest of such waves, 3800 to 4300 angstroms, produce what we call violet light. Next longer waves make blue light, followed by green, yellow, orange, and finally (between 6300 and 7600 angstroms) red light. All these together make white light.

Waves somewhat shorter than 3800 angstroms are called ultra-violet (*ultra* being Latin for "beyond"). Their effects are not visible to the human eye, but they have many uses, such as killing germs and creating photochemical, photoelectric, and fluorescent effects. Also they give to some a beautiful summer tan and, to the less fortunate, painful sunburn. The waves

262

longer than 7600 angstroms, also invisible, and called infrared (or "below red"), are likewise useful for heat therapy and commercial drying processes.

It is recommended that the designer read carefully the material on color in pigment, found in Chapter 8, before proceeding with this discussion of color in light.

PRIMARY COLORS IN LIGHT

As was stated, all the waves in the visible spectrum together form white light. But it is not necessary to use every single wave length for this result. White light can be produced quite effectively by mixing, in the proper proportions, red, blue, and green light. Red, blue, and green are, therefore, considered the primary colors in light, for no mixtures of other colors will produce these at full purity, but these three together, in varying proportions, can produce any color that can be conceived. This differs from the pigment colors in which red, blue, and yellow are the primaries, and it is sometimes difficult for painters to convince themselves that in light green takes the place of the familiar yellow as a primary.

COLOR MIXING. Now if we mix red and blue light together, we get a color that we call magenta; if green and blue are mixed the result is a blue-green that is referred to as cyan-blue or cyan; while red and green mixed will form a yellow light that is usually called amber. These are the secondary colors in light, and just as red, blue, and green can be mixed to form white light, so can magenta, amber, and cyan produce white. This should be obvious, for the secondaries are nothing but combinations of the primaries. In fact, by mixing the secondaries in varying proportions, we can achieve almost any color of the spectrum except those very close to the purest primaries themselves.

Likewise if we mix any secondary with the primary that has not gone into its making—say amber and blue—we again get white, for the amber already contains the red and green waves.

When we have used the word "mix" above, we have been employing it in the sense that the various beams of colored light were being focused, one on the other, against a common neutral surface and the resulting effect is what we see on this surface. This is additive mixing and is one of the two ways of producing and changing color in light and light effects.

COLOR FILTERING. There is a second way of altering the color of light, sometimes known as subtractive mixing, but more accurately called color filtering. It is best explained by examples. Suppose we have a beam of white light falling on a neutral surface. That surface will reflect to us white. Now, if we place a sheet of pure red glass or red gelatin in the path of this beam, the red sheet will absorb all the blue and green waves of the white light and allow only the red waves to pass through to the neutral surface which will now appear red. Or, if we put a sheet of pure blue in the beam, the red and green waves will be removed, the blue waves will pass through, and the neutral surface will appear blue.

But if we put both the red and the blue sheets before the beam, no light whatever will come through, for the red sheet will filter out the blue waves, the blue sheet will absorb the red waves, and both will remove the green waves—leaving nothing to strike the neutral surface!

If we put a piece of magenta glass and a piece of amber glass in the same beam, the magenta will filter out the green in the amber while the amber will stop the blue in the magenta. Result: red, which is common to each. Notice that this red is produced by the negative approach of filtering out the other colors, not the positive approach of adding or mixing colors to achieve it, so our statement that a primary cannot be produced by mixing other colors still holds.

USES OF MIXING AND FILTERING.   Both color mixing and color filtering are extremely important in stage lighting. Our lighting instruments give out beams of approximately white light and the only practical way to color these beams is to intercept them with a sheet of colored transparent material: color filtering. Then when we have produced our colors—say red and green— in this way, we may direct the two beams on a single surface producing an amber effect: color mixing.

We have been discussing the primaries and secondaries in light, for a thorough understanding of the mixing and filtering processes is most easily arrived at through a study of these six hues. But it must be clearly understood that the same principles apply to all colors, tints, and shades. But, because most of these are rather complex mixtures, the exact results of their mixing or filtering cannot be predicted with such precision.

However, it is most necessary to consider these other, less strong colors, for they are of vast importance on the stage. Were we to attempt to light our acting areas with strong colors, except possibly for brief and unreal effects, the actors would appear far too distorted and unnatural for an audience to accept. And if we bathe our stage scenery with too rich a tone, the eyes of the spectators will soon tire of it. Far more often only tints and hints of color are used, or two or more of the stronger shades may be used to blend with each other and thus approach a more tolerable white light. The human eye tends to neutralize all colors it sees, so a startlingly vivid effect at the opening of the curtain will soon lose its impression on the spectator, but meanwhile his eyes are being strained and his nerves exhausted.

WARM AND COOL COLORS

In general, most people recognize red as typifying anger and war, amber as warmth and comfort, blue as restraint and coolness, green as restfulness. These and similar identifications should always be foremost in the designer's mind when selecting his stage colors. But for us there is no advantage in going deeply into the psychology of color, about which there are many (and usually contradictory) theories.

There is one psychological aspect, however, that cannot well be ignored: the matter of the relative warmth and coolness of colors. Few people would deny that a bright red-orange suggests warmth; most would agree that a brittle blue-white gives an impression of cold. Whether these sensations arise from association with flames and ice respectively we cannot tell with any assurance.

Given samples of twenty different tints and shades, rarely will two people list them in exactly the same order from "most warm" to "most cool." But in general we can say that the reds, oranges, and ambers are considered in the warm group, while the blues, violets, and greens fall within the cool range. Some mixtures of hues from the opposing groups, seem on the border line, and the particular effect they give at any moment is in contrast to whatever other color is seen in relation to them.

As a matter of fact, the precise feeling given by most tints is purely a matter of contrast. A pale blue that seems positively icy in contrast to a strong amber will appear quite warm when placed next to a stronger shade of blue. Pink and lavender are frequently used on the stage as free-wheeling tints whose effects we can reverse merely by changing the hues used in association with them.

COLORED LIGHT AND THE ACTOR. In a later chapter, we will suggest actual colors to be used in different types of productions, but it may be advisable here to give a little thought to the general effects desired in the various portions of the stage picture. For the acting areas, for example, it is well to stay clear of startling and unnatural shades that will adversely effect the faces and costumes of the actors. Sometimes an actor finds it necessary to ask, "What colors are you using, so I can put on the proper make-up?" This is inexcusable. No lighting designer has any business, on whatever pretext, to use colors so strong as to distort the actors' faces or force them to use anything but the natural, restrained make-up that is common practice today.

Like their faces, the actors' costumes should not be adversely affected by the stage lighting. This is sometimes more difficult to handle. Often the acting areas are lighted with tints of pinks and ambers, flattering enough to the human face, but deadly to green materials. Because the scene may definitely call for such colors in the light, the light designer should warn the costumer ahead of time to save distress and tears.

Beware of Green! It should be noted that green light has limited use on the acting areas of the stage. Green on the human face is extremely unbecoming, muddying the natural healthy colors of cheeks and lips, deadening blonde and reddish hair, and exaggerating to the point of grotesqueness the slightest blemish in the complexion. This is pathetically true of the blue-green light filtered through the gelatin commonly advertised as "moonlight blue." It is difficult to conceive of anything more alien to romance.

COLORED LIGHT AND THE SCENERY.   Just as the actor is entitled to his own face, the scene designer has presumably painted his settings the way he wants them to appear. And it is the utmost impertinence for a lighting designer to attempt to improve on his artistry. Enhance it, yes, but strictly in accordance with the scene designer's wishes. Ideally, of course, the scene designer should light his own settings, and many of the finest do just that. But, if he does not do so, he and the lighting designer should work in the closest collaboration. The result will usually be that nearby scenery, as the walls of an interior setting will, like the acting areas, receive tints of light only. Strong colors, as we have made clear, will tire the audience and will alter the appearance of the painting. Furthermore, being so close to the acting areas, it is almost impossible to separate light on such scenery from other portions of the stage.

COLOR ON THE SKY.   It is on the deep backgrounds that the light designer can cut loose. These are usually skies or distant scenery, and much stronger colors can be used here to depict the different times of day, conditions of the weather, or purely arbitrary effects. Setting up the instruments, selecting his colors, and juggling the intensity of his lights for a rip-roaring sunset should go far to relieve the tensions of the otherwise frustrated light designer.

In connection with backdrops and cycloramas the question frequently arises: is it better to try to select a single color medium that will give the exact hue desired, or is a blending of several colors to achieve the wanted tint preferable? Of course, if there is to be a change in color effect during the scene, then more than one color must be provided to enable a smooth blend from one to another. Likewise more delicate and precise shadings can be achieved if several different colors are blended into one. However, on a stage with limited equipment, especially for intensity control, it may be far easier, if not essential, to pick a single tint and let it go at that.

COLOR MEDIA.   We have spoken of color media without stating just what these may be. There are three kinds in general use today.

Gelatin. The most common, and certainly the cheapest, gelatin comes in the form of very thin sheets that are relatively inexpensive and in a vast range of colors. It has to be cut with care to prevent tearing, it dries out and becomes brittle with age, and it loses all form when dampened. Some of its shades, particularly the blues and pinks, fade quite easily and must be replaced in the instruments frequently—sometimes after a single perform-ance, if used with one of the largest instruments burning at high intensity. But all in all, it is probably the most satisfactory for any designer who wants to achieve the utmost in artistic effects.

Plastic Media. Fairly new media are the plastics, which also come in sheet form, but are sturdier than gelatin. These stand up better under rough usage. They are completely unaffected by water and are therefore essential for outdoor productions or theatres in particularly damp localities. Plastics come in almost as many shades as gelatin, but are considerably more expen-sive. Despite some claims to the contrary, their resistance to intense heat and to fading is not much greater than that of gelatin.

One annoyance for anyone ordering either of these media is the matter of identification of colors. The names given certain hues have little accuracy of description. Generally a number code is used, but no two companies use the same system. A collection of sample books, experience, and an accurate memory are all needed by the light designer when he orders color media.

Colored Glass. The most expensive medium of all is glass. While gelatin and plastic may be cut to any size or shape desired, glass must be ordered for exactly the purpose required. It comes in few colors, is heavy and bulky to store, and though it never fades nor is affected by heat, and stands up well under ordinary usage, it can be smashed. It has one great advantage in addition to its heat-resisting qualities in that it can have molded into it markings and prismatic lines that diffuse the light or spread it in certain directions—very important features under many circumstances.

14

LIGHT SOURCES

THE INCANDESCENT LAMP

The most common source of light used on the stage today is the incandescent filament lamp: a gas-filled glass bulb containing a tungsten filament which emits light when a current is impressed through it by the prescribed voltage, 120 being the most common in this country. The three important parts (Figure 14–1) of an incandescent lamp are the bulb (the glass envelope that encloses the inert gas), the base (to hold the lamp in position and to make electrical contacts), and the filament (to pass the current, yet offer enough resistance to effect the transfer of electrical energy into light energy).

LAMP FILAMENTS. The filament is the most important part of the incandescent lamp. It is the tungsten wire which emits the light. To keep it compact, it is usually coiled. Its arrangement within the bulb is of great importance. Among the filament forms used in stage-lighting equipment are the corona (C–9) and the barrel (C–5). These are designed to throw out their light equally in all directions. On the other hand, the monoplane (C–13) and the biplane (C–13D) emit most of their light in two opposite

268

directions only, thereby permitting a larger proportion to be picked up and made useful by a reflector or a lens.

The LCL (or light-center-length) of a lamp is the distance from the center of the filament to some definite place in the base. With a screw-base lamp, the measurement is to the contact button at the end of the base (Figure 14–1). With a prefocus base it is to the fins, and with the bipost to the shoulder of the pins. It is particularly important to know the LCL when a lamp is to be used in conjunction with a reflector or a lens, for the center of the filament must be exactly aligned with the centers of such optical devices.

LAMP BULBS. Lamp bulbs vary greatly in three ways: their size, their shape, and the finish or color of their glass. Obviously a small, compact bulb would be preferred, but two factors cause the higher-wattage lamps to have bulbs of larger sizes: the dimensions of the larger filaments demand a more roomy envelope and a larger surface is necessary to dissipate the greater heat emitted by them. Bulb sizes are expressed in numbers representing eighths of an inch: thus a bulb of five-inch diameter would be called a "40."

The shape of the bulb is designated by a letter. The A (for arbitrary) and PS (for pear-shape with straight sides) are common forms seen in the general line of household lamps (Figure 14–2). Many lamps used in stage-

Figure 14–1. A TYPICAL INCANDESCENT LAMP

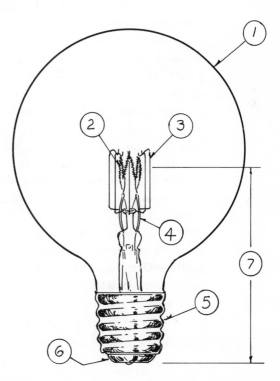

1. GAS-FILLED G-SHAPED BULB

2. BARREL FILAMENT

3. FILAMENT SUPPORTS

4. LEAD-IN WIRE

5. SCREW BASE

6. BOTTOM CONTACT BUTTON

7. L.C.L. (LIGHT CENTER LENGTH)

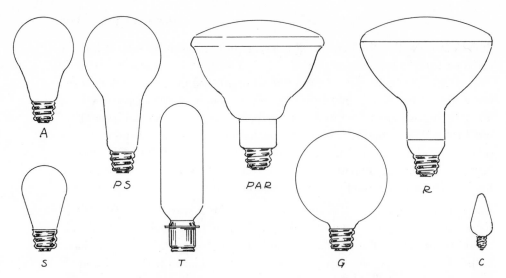

Figure 14—2. TYPICAL BULB SHAPES. (A) Arbitrary designation. (S) Straight side. (PS) Pear shape, straight neck. (T) Tubular. (PAR) Parabolic aluminized reflector. (G) Globular. (R) Reflector. (C) Cone shape.

lighting instruments are globe-shaped (G) to permit the even dissipation of heat, or tubular (T) to allow the filament to be brought closer to some optical feature. There are a number of other shapes, some of which are purely decorative. The line of reflector lamps will be discussed separately.

BULB FINISHES AND COLOR. Usually lamps used on the stage are made of clear glass, which is essential for any source used in an instrument with reflector or lens. But the smaller wattage A and PS lamps are more readily obtained with an inner frost finish that is intended to diffuse the light. If desired, these sizes can also be ordered in the clear-glass style, but this is seldom necessary as they are rarely used in stage lighting instruments of any precision. There are many kinds of finishes available, some purely decorative and others for some special application. The side-silvered showcase lamp that can be tucked away behind very little cover is often handy on the stage for throwing a little light in difficult corners.

Colored-glass lamps are obtainable in the smaller wattages only and are not very useful on the stage except in the smallest installations. There is one exception: the pale-blue "daylight" lamps which give off a color not much different from that seen outdoors on a slightly overcast day, or the light that comes through a north window. These can be used effectively to illuminate small backings or, in combination with other tones, larger areas, or to imitate general daylight (not sunbeams) pushing through a window. Daylight lamps come in sizes up to 1500 watts.

LAMP BASES. The base of a lamp is generally made of copper, though aluminum is now being used for many of the smaller wattages. The base may have any of several sizes, but medium (as the common household lamps) at 1-inch diameter and mogul with a diameter of 1½-inch have the most importance to us. While compactness is obviously desired, the bigger sizes are required for two reasons: the larger bulbs need the stability of the greater physical support, and the heavier currents demand larger electrical contacts.

The bases may also vary in type, with the common screw base (which comes in all sizes) being the simplest (Figure 14–3). Frequently this type is sufficient, but in certain cases it is necessary to provide some sort of locking device in the base so that the lamp and particularly its filament may be held in a precise relationship with some optical feature of the instrument in which it is designed to burn. Two such devices are used in the medium and mogul sizes. There is the bipost base which consists of two pins that push down into carefully aligned holes in the socket, and the prefocus base with side fins of different sizes that lock into the socket by a quarter turn. In the smaller sizes the bayonet, a variation of the prefocus base, is used. There are also a number of other forms, such as the screw base with a spring button at the end, the end prong, side prong, bipin, disk, and others too numerous to mention. In most cases these demand a special socket or contact; usually their mode of operation is apparent on inspection.

THE R AND PAR LAMPS

A feature in lamp design that is constantly gaining in importance is the "instrument-contained-in-the-lamp," marketed under the two lines of R (reflector) and PAR (parabolic aluminized reflector) lamps. Because all the light emitted by the filament is reflected out of these lamps in a useful direction and because this reflector is sealed into the bulb itself, these lamps are extremely efficient.

Figure 14–3. COMMON BASE SHAPES

  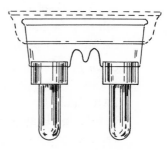

SCREW   PREFOCUS   BIPOST

The PAR's are presently available in wattages from 75 to 500, the R's from 30 to 1000, but the PAR 38's at 150 watts and the R 40's of 150 and 300 watts are of most importance to us. Of these, the PAR lamps are somewhat heavier, though smaller, than the R's, being made of molded, heat-resisting glass that can be burned outdoors with no shielding from the weather. The R lamp is blown in one piece, is lighter in weight, more fragile, and should not be used in the open without protection. PAR's cost almost twice as much as R's of the same wattage, but have definite advantages that make the extra expense worthwhile in certain circumstances.

Light Distribution from R and PAR Lamps.   In the wattages under discussion, both PAR and R lines come in two styles for each size: "spot" and "flood." The PAR-spot throws the most powerful beam, but has an uneven field. The R-spot has a slightly wider spread and a much smoother field, but there is less punch to its beam. The PAR-flood and the R-flood have smoother fields and much wider spreads than either of the spots, but quite low intensity compared to them, the R-flood being by far the weakest of them all in output. All have light diffusing marks on their faces, which should not be confused with true lenses.

Because of the great breadth of beam typical of these lamps, they can be very useful in striplights, where it is necessary to blend the light from different color-circuits smoothly and at short range. The reflectors being sealed into the bulbs, there is no worry over dirt or corrosion affecting their surfaces. Further, it is a simple matter to change from type to type, depending on the precise effect desired: as using PAR spots for a long, very intense throw—R floods for a short throw where smoothness is more important than brightness. Single lamps may also be useful as small floodlights.

Attempts have been made to use PAR and R spots as substitutes for conventional spotlights. For a small stage and a short throw they have enough punch, but it is impossible to control the very same side spill that makes them useful in striplights or as floods. A variety of hoods are advertised as answers to this problem, but the fact remains that there will be no real control over the unruly beam unless the lamp is placed in a hood at least two feet long—a very inefficient expedient as so little of the illumination will then be used. However, the smaller hoods can be handy for mounting the lamps, focusing them, and holding color media in place.

Color in the R and PAR Lamps.   Both types have recently added a line of colored bulbs. So far these are offered only in the 100-watt size for the PAR's and 150-watt for the R's. They seem to have distributional characteristics midway between their respective spot and flood models. Red, yellow, blue, green, pink, and blue-white are available, but it must be noted that even the full colors do not have the purity that is obtained from gelatin.

These colored lamps are particularly effective in striplights and other blend-ing arrangements, and the blue-whites have the same uses as the daylight-blue lamps described earlier.

It seems that future developments in these two lines of lamps may offer greater possibilities for the stage. At the present time, however, the R's and PAR's have limited uses in good dramatic lighting though they can be ex-tremely valuable on the low-budget stage if used with an appreciation of their limitations.

LAMP LIFE

The "rated-average life" of any type of lamp may be found listed in the catalogs. For the common household varieties, this is usually 750 burning hours, but for many stage-lighting lamps it is only 200 hours. This expected life is determined by many factors. It would be possible to build a lamp that never burns out, but such a lamp would give very little light for the current consumed. On the other hand, photo-flash lamps are simply those in which the sudden burst of intensity is more important than continued life.

A few of the G lamps come in two styles, designated, quite inaccurately, "spot" and "flood." Their difference lies in that the "spot" has a life of 200 hours but gives out much more light than the "flood" which is expected to burn for 800 hours. Their uses are identical, and which one to select depends on the comparative importance to the buyer of life versus output.

Rated-average life is presumed to apply under usual operating conditions. But a lamp's life may be shortened in a number of ways. It will give out more quickly if burned while enclosed in an excessively hot place such as one from which its own heat cannot escape. Rough handling may break some interior part, even though the outer appearance is not changed. If connected to a higher voltage than it was designed for, a lamp will burn out rapidly, even abruptly. And in the case of many lamps used in stage instru-ments, burning in the wrong position results in rapid failure. This is par-ticularly true of T lamps. The correct burning position, if important, will always be marked on the end of the bulb and should be consulted if any doubt exists.

PURCHASING LAMPS

When ordering lamps it is advisable to use the manufacturer's code number, found in his catalog, to be certain of receiving the exact type of lamp needed for your equipment. If there is any doubt, list all possible factors in making out your order: base size and shape, bulb size and shape, filament form and LCL, bulb color or finish, and so forth. The importance of being specific can be seen in the fact that the General Electric large-lamp catalog lists no fewer than thirty-seven different 100-watt lamps, all with a medium screw base, and twenty-seven different 500-watt lamps.

THE CARBON ARC LIGHT

One source of light that is not an incandescent lamp yet has a long history in stage use is the carbon arc. In this device a current is passed through two touching carbon pencils which are then drawn slightly apart forcing the electrons to leap (or arc) the gap. This bombardment of electrons burns into the receiving carbon a crater which emits an extremely intense light of slightly bluish tinge. Mounted in a hood, with a condensing lens, devices for shaping the beam, and a method of focusing the beam in different directions, the carbon arc becomes extremely useful as a follow spot for emphasizing portions of the stage or members of the cast.

The carbon-arc spotlight will be discussed in detail in Chapter 17.

THE FLUORESCENT TUBE, OTHER SOURCES, AND THE FUTURE

A different form of arc is that of the fluorescent tube which, despite great promise for the future, has distinctly limited stage use today due largely to the complexity of its installation and the fact that smooth dimming is almost impossible in its present state of development. The fluorescent tube has not yet lived down the stigma of the unpleasant color emitted by the earliest models. Much better color effects are now available, and continued improvement can be expected.

The gaseous discharge lamps, including the mercury vapor line, at this time offer little to the stage-lighting field. Whether the future will tell a different story cannot be predicted.

In the August 1961 issue of the *Journal* of the American Institute of Architects an article by Dr. Joel E. Rubin suggests some intriguing possibilities. He describes the small-source quartz-iodine cycle lamp, which has already been advertised for use in striplights and may soon be installed in spotlights. He suggests possible use of electroluminescent panels to provide a vast area of light, as a cyclorama with its own built-in glow. He mentions zenon and zirconium arcs and the extremely efficient cesium lamp as holding promise for the future, and anticipates important improvements as to wattage and control in the R and PAR lines of incandescent filament lamps.

15

REFLECTION, REFRACTION
AND ABSORPTION

When a beam of light, passing through air, encounters anything in its path, three things can happen. The light may be absorbed (as by a sheet of black material), it may be refracted (as through a lens), or it may be reflected (as by any opaque substance it strikes). Actually, none of these things will happen completely: a mirror or a lens will absorb a small portion of the light, the blackest of materials will still reflect some of it, a piece of colored glass will absorb certain light rays and allow others to pass through. By understanding the laws by which these phenomena operate, we can better understand how stage-lighting instruments work and why light behaves as it does when it strikes the stage and actors.

REFLECTION OF LIGHT

The law of regular reflection explains what happens to a light beam when it strikes a smooth, shiny surface, such as a mirror. It is reflected at an angle

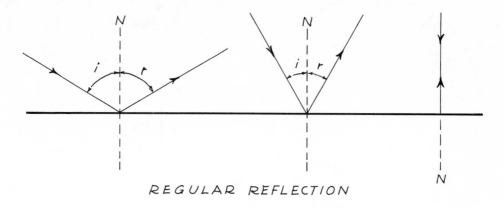

REGULAR REFLECTION

Figure 15–1 (above and below). TYPES OF REFLECTION

equal to the angle at which it struck, but in the opposite direction (Figure 15–1). A moment's contemplation of a mirror will make this clear. Of course, if the beam strikes the surface head on, it will reflect directly back over the same path.

If the beam strikes, not a mirror but a surface with slight irregularities, as etched aluminum or foil-paper that has been crumpled and smoothed out again, the same law applies, but due to the fact that there are now innumerable little surfaces, rather than a single, perfectly flat one, the reflected rays will tend to spread out somewhat, but will not diverge too greatly from a basic direction. This is known as spread reflection.

A piece of blotting paper, or soft, cotton cloth, will produce a diffuse reflection, due to the vast number and varied angles of the surface. In this case, there will be no single direction to the reflected light. Rather the whole surface will appear much the same from whatever angle it is viewed.

Last, we have mixed reflection, a combination of regular and diffuse. A piece of crockery with a high glaze will produce this: the rough surface of the ceramic will create diffusion, while the shiny glaze will act like a mirrored surface to give regular reflection. Furthermore, the diffused light will show the color of the material itself, while the regularly reflected light (or high light) will have the color of the source.

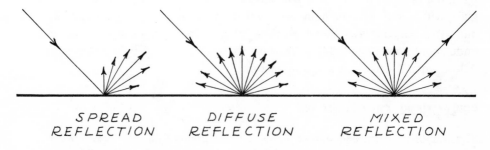

SPREAD
REFLECTION

DIFFUSE
REFLECTION

MIXED
REFLECTION

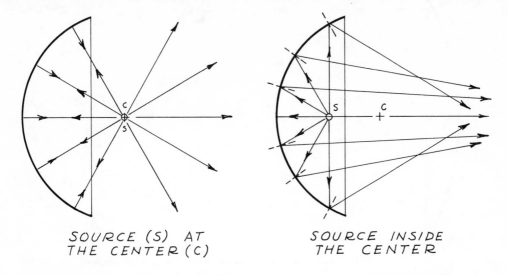

SOURCE (S) AT
THE CENTER (C)

SOURCE INSIDE
THE CENTER

Figure 15–2 (above and below).   REFLECTION FROM A SPHERICAL REFLECTOR UNDER
DIFFERENT CONDITIONS

THE SPHERICAL REFLECTOR.   Now, if polished metal is made into a reflector in the form of a part of a sphere and a source of light is placed at the center of the curvature of this form, each ray of light that strikes the reflecting surface will do so squarely. Therefore, it will be returned through the source and will augment the light emanating from the source in the opposite direction (Figure 15–2).

Naturally, it would be necessary for the source, say the filament of a lamp, to be precisely located in relation to the reflector, or its rays would not strike the reflector straight on but at various angles and would be reflected equally in various directions in accordance with the law of regular reflection.

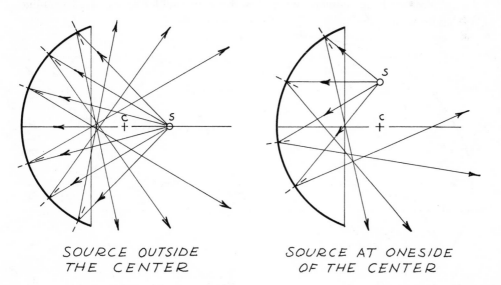

SOURCE OUTSIDE
THE CENTER

SOURCE AT ONESIDE
OF THE CENTER

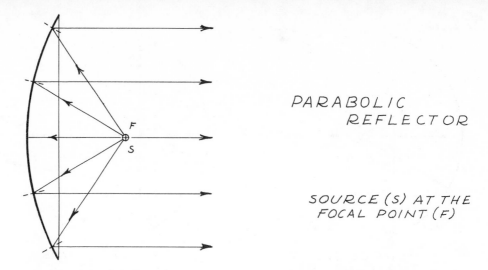

PARABOLIC
REFLECTOR

SOURCE (S) AT THE
FOCAL POINT (F)

Figure 15–3. REFLECTION (above) FROM A PARABOLIC AND (below) FROM AN ELLIPSOIDAL REFLECTOR

THE PARABOLIC REFLECTOR. Some stage-lighting instruments make use of reflectors with shapes other than the spherical. The nature of a parabolic reflector is such that if a light source is placed at its focal center, all rays that strike the reflective surface will emerge parallel one to another (Figure 15–3). This will naturally give a great concentration of light in a tight beam, rather than the spread effusion from a spherical reflector.

THE ELLIPSOIDAL REFLECTOR. A third form of reflector that has great use is the ellipsoidal. By mathematical definition an ellipsoid has two conjugate focal points. When a reflector is constructed in the form of half of an ellipsoid and a source is placed at the focal point at that end, all rays of light that strike the reflector will be diverted through the second focal point (Figure 15–3). The result is that an enormous percentage of the light from the source is directed in a manner that makes it easily usable, as we shall examine under Spotlights.

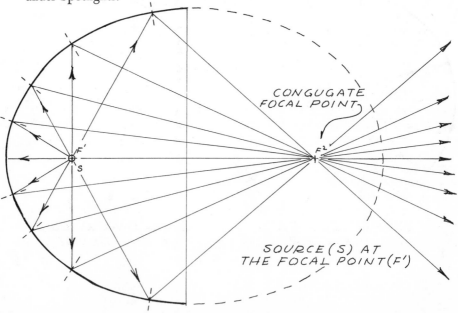

CONGUGATE
FOCAL POINT

SOURCE (S) AT
THE FOCAL POINT (F')

ELLIPSOIDAL REFLECTOR

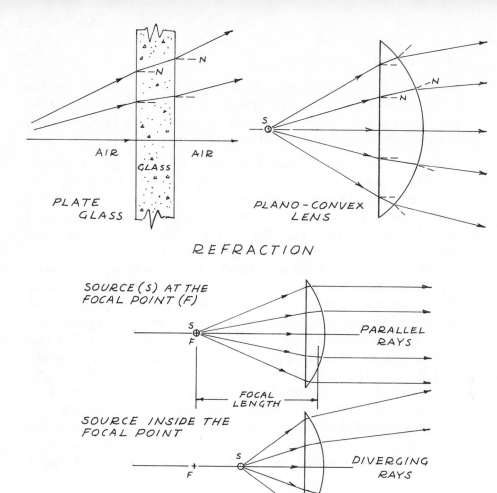

PLATE GLASS

PLANO-CONVEX LENS

REFRACTION

SOURCE (S) AT THE
FOCAL POINT (F)

PARALLEL
RAYS

FOCAL
LENGTH

SOURCE INSIDE THE
FOCAL POINT

DIVERGING
RAYS

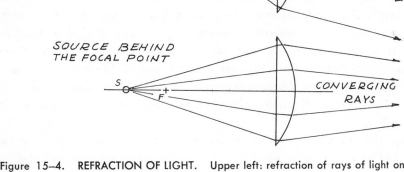

SOURCE BEHIND
THE FOCAL POINT

CONVERGING
RAYS

Figure 15–4.   REFRACTION OF LIGHT.   Upper left: refraction of rays of light on passing through a sheet of glass. Upper right: refraction of rays of light on passing through a plano-convex lens. Below: refraction of light passing through a plano-convex lens under different conditions.

REFRACTION OF LIGHT

Refraction is a phenomenon that has been observed by anyone who has ever looked into a pool of water and noticed how a straight stick will seem to bend sharply as it passes beneath the surface. The law of refraction states that when a ray of light passes into a denser medium (as from the air into the water) it is bent toward a perpendicular drawn to the surface at the point of entry, and when it emerges into the less dense medium again, it is bent away from the perpendicular drawn at that point.

THE PLANO-CONVEX LENS.   Now if the two surfaces of a sheet of glass are parallel, the path of an emerging ray will be parallel to its entering path, but slightly offset (Figure 15-4). But if the two surfaces are not parallel, then the emerging ray will take a different course depending on the angle at which it strikes each surface. This is the principle of all lenses, of which there are many forms, but the plano-convex lens, with one flat side and one curved surface (or modifications of this) is the only one of importance to us.

Every lens has a focal point. This should not be confused with the center of curvature of the surface. If a source of light is placed at the focal point of a lens, all the rays of light that emerge from the lens will be parallel one to another. Conversely, if parallel light rays (as from the sun) strike a lens, they will converge at the focal point. Lenses are identified by two numbers, the first of which states the diameter while the second gives the focal length: the distance from the focal point to a plane approximately two-thirds of the greatest thickness of the lens, measured from its plane face. Thus, a 6″ x 8″ lens would have a diameter of six inches and a focal length of eight inches. The greater the curve of the convex face, the greater the refracting power of a lens. Therefore, a thick lens will have a shorter focal length than a thin one.

FINDING THE FOCAL LENGTH.   As it is usually desirable to know what the focal length of a given lens happens to be, and as this information is rarely marked on it, a quick method of ascertaining this fact is good to keep in mind. If the sun is shining, the lens may be carried outdoors and held, plano side down, so that the sun's rays are concentrated on the ground. Then a ruler will measure the distance from the ground to the focal plane. For lenses used in stage-lighting equipment the focal lengths are always in even inches.

Often the sun is not available, in which case some indoors light must be used, but as far away as possible. The resulting measurement will be, in this case, somewhat longer than the true focal length, because the rays were not parallel but diverging, when they struck the curved surface. But this excess will be less than an inch; so by simply eliminating the fraction, we can calculate the exact focal length quite accurately. For example: if the measurement is 11½ inches, we know the focal length is 11 inches—if we measure 9¼ inches, we know the focal length is 9 inches.

Importance of Focal Lengths.   If a source of light be placed between the

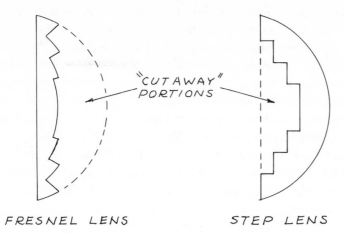

FRESNEL LENS   STEP LENS

Figure 15–5. SIMPLIFIED DIAGRAMS SHOWING HOW FRESNEL AND STEP LENSES ARE DERIVED FROM THE PLANO-CONVEX LENS

focal point and the lens, the emerging rays will diverge; if the source be placed further from the lens than the focal point, the rays will converge and eventually cross one another (Figure 15–4).

Because the light source may be placed closer to the lens when the focal length is short, it is obvious that such a lens will be able to gather and make use of a larger percentage of the emanating light and is therefore more efficient than a lens with a long focal length. But there is a drawback in that the thicker glass of the short focal-length lens will absorb more of the light and therefore crack more easily from the greater heat that results. In some lighting instruments this can be corrected by using two lenses of long focal length to form a lens train of total shorter focal length.

FRESNEL AND STEP LENSES. Because this is not always practical, two solutions have been developed, both using the technique of cutting away part of the thick glass, yet retaining the basic relationships between the curved and the plane surfaces. The first of these is the Fresnel (pronounced Fr'nel) lens, in which the plano face is retained, but the curved face is cut back in steps. More recent is the step-lens, in which the convex side retains its shape, while the plano face is cut back (Figure 15–5).

ABSORPTION

WHITE LIGHT. Absorption takes place to some degree whenever light strikes any object, no matter how mirrorlike or crystal clear it may seem. But absorption is more particularly important to us in connection with solid objects.

If a beam of ordinary white light strikes a white surface, most of it will be turned back by reflection, but 10 percent or more will be absorbed, regardless of how purely white the surface appears. If the same light is directed at a black object, it may reflect 5 percent or so, but the greater part of the light is absorbed. In each case, of course, the reflected light will be white light for nothing will have occurred to make any change in the color. In each case the reflecting surface will appear as it is: the white one white, the black one black, for nothing has happened to change their colors.

On the other hand, if this white light were to strike a pure-red surface, over 80 percent of the light will be absorbed but the balance will be reflected as red light. That is how we identify the surface as red. The only way we can tell the color of any object is by the color of the light that is reflected from it to our eyes.

COLORED LIGHT. Now suppose we direct a pure-blue light at this red surface, we will see it as black, for the red will reflect only red waves and no red waves were directed on it. This is similar, of course, to what we learned about white light and colored gelatins. Because pigments used to paint walls and dye cloth are seldom completely pure, we cannot count on a perfect demonstration of this phenomenon on every occasion, but the principle holds good and should be constantly kept in mind.

On the other hand, if we shine a red light on a neutral surface, whether white, gray, or black, we will find that the object will appear red, for that is the only light available for reflection. Further, if a red light is directed on two surfaces, one the same red and the other white, both these surfaces will seem to be almost exactly the same color to the viewer. This is a most important phenomenon to be kept in mind by the designer, lest, by use of strong tints, he may make large portions of the scenery or costumes appear just the same as something that had been intended to be a strong accent.

PROBLEMS OF ABSORPTION VERSUS REFLECTION

Other factors than pure colors enter into the picture of absorption versus reflection, the texture of the surface being of the utmost importance. Hard, shiny surfaces have a tendency to reflect light better than soft, woolly ones, even though both are apparently the same color. Such hard surfaces also may produce high lights when viewed from certain angles. These may be difficult to control on stage. For this reason metals, glass, and the like are usually confined to small adornments on costumes, or are soaped or otherwise clouded to prevent their disconcerting flashes and images. Likewise, enamel paint has little place in the theatre. Many times the light designer is blamed for distractions caused by shiny surfaces; but he should stand his ground and insist that the fault lies with the offending objects, which should be subdued in some way or eliminated.

Before we leave the subject of absorption, other warnings must be issued. White, or extremely pale colors, will always reflect a large portion of the light and are, therefore, inclined to be very obvious on stage. A white costume, beloved of all actresses, will draw attention away from more important action no matter how the stage is arranged. The best-lighted actors will appear as silhouettes before a very bright backdrop, and this effect can trouble the audience greatly. While on the other hand, no matter how black the scenery, of whatever material used, it will reflect a certain amount of light, even that which has been already once reflected from the stage floor! The "living darkness of the theatre" is one of its most difficult concepts to attain if, indeed, it can be achieved at all, except with charcoal on the scene designer's sketch pad.

16

STAGE-LIGHTING
INSTRUMENTS (1)

The term "stage-lighting instrument" is used to designate any device employed on the stage to hold a lamp in correct position, to direct and often to shape its output of light, and to hold color media in the resulting beam. Because stage workers have a habit of referring to whole classes of instruments by the trade names of certain manufacturers or other slang terminology, there seems to be a bewildering complexity of such instruments. Actually, there are just a few basic types, reasonably easy to comprehend.

SPOTLIGHTS

On the modern stage the spotlight is far and away the most important instrument of all. Fundamentally, the spotlight is a metal hood containing a high-powered source of light which is made more effective by use of a lens and usually a reflector as well. The resulting beam of high-intensity light can be shaped by various means to forms that may be useful in the stage picture.

THE PLANO-CONVEX SPOTLIGHT.   The first incandescent spotlight, and for many years the only kind, is what is known today as the plano-convex spot. In a simple hood a G-shaped lamp is mounted on a sliding carriage attached to which there is also a small spherical reflector that rides behind the lamp and is always in correct relationship to it (Figure 16–1). As was explained in Chapter 5, such a reflector sends all rays that strike it back through the original source, thus augmenting the forward emanation to a considerable degree.

In front of the lamp and carefully aligned with its filament is placed a plano-convex lens which refracts all the rays that strike it and bends them into a comparatively narrow beam. When the lamp is close to the lens in "flood" position the percentage of the total light that strikes the lens is quite high, but because this spreads into a wide angle after leaving the lens there is no great intensity to the beam at any distance from the instrument. When the lamp is moved back toward the focal point of the lens, the angle of acceptance of the lens is less and the beam much narrower. So, although a smaller percentage of the light is utilized, the beam then has greater intensity for all the light is concentrated in the narrower shaft. The inside of the hood is painted a flat black to absorb all rays of light that do not strike the lens directly.

Spotlight Accessories.   The lens of a plano-convex, indeed of any spotlight, is held in place by a strong metal spring-ring. Above and below the lens opening in the hood there are small troughs to hold color media frames. Every spotlight has some means of mounting it, usually a yoke held in place on side studs by large nuts or set-wheels. Ventilation must be supplied— both above to allow hot air to escape—and below to let cool air in. The ventilation holes or slots are fitted with baffles to prevent light spill. And except on the smallest models, an access door permits the electrician to inspect the interior of the hood and change the lamp without otherwise disturbing the instrument or its focus. Electric current enters all spotlights (indeed all lighting instruments for that matter) through a pair of wires with asbestos insulation to protect them against the intense heat.

Beam Characteristics of the Plano-Convex Spot.   When focused on a flat surface, the plano-convex spotlight's beam pattern is circular with a sharp, distinct edge. But the field is quite irregular in intensity, while aberrations in the form of rainbow effects are seen at the edges. When the lamp is moved back to the exact focal length of the lens, a precise image of the filament appears. The basic circular pattern can be easily changed by the insertion of mats (small metal or foil forms) into the color frame. This permits an exact shaping of the beam, often necessary to keep unwanted light off portions of the stage, to hold the light pattern to a precise location, and the like. Or an iris can be used to alter the size of the beam pattern without changing its circular shape.

Although the plano-convex spotlight does not have the importance it once held, it is still a useful instrument on many occasions, and it is far less expensive than the ellipsoidal-reflector spotlight, the other instrument that throws a sharply defined beam.

Plano-convex Sizes. The P.C., as it is frequently called, can be obtained in three sizes, the smallest and least powerful of which has a 5-inch lens and burns G-shaped lamps of 250 and 400 watts. It is useful for short throws, as on a very small stage and can be hidden in nooks where other instruments would prove too large. This little spotlight is usually referred to as a "baby."

Larger brothers are those with 6-inch and 8-inch plano-convex lenses. The various manufacturers furnish different lines of these, but in general it may be said that the 8-inch type burns 2000-watt lamps while the 6-inch models range from 500 to 1500 watts, all of the G-type. These cannot be recommended for the well-equipped stage ahead of the far more efficient Fresnels and ellipsoidal-reflector spotlights. But when nothing else is available, they can be used very effectively if the intensity demands are not too great.

THE FRESNEL SPOTLIGHT. Because its short focal length allows it to gather such a large percentage of the light from a source, the Fresnel lens has been incorporated into the spotlight line. Essentially the only difference between the hoods of the plano-convex and the Fresnel spots is that the latter is considerably shorter, as the short focal length of the Fresnel lens makes a long movement of the lamp unnecessary.

The Fresnel spot throws a beam of much greater intensity than does the plano-convex for the same current consumed. Moreover, the beam pattern of the Fresnel is far smoother and without a sharp edge. In fact, it is hard to find its limits at all, so gently does it drop off, thereby permitting easy blending of two or more beams without a noticeable break.

This same softness of beam edge makes matting the Fresnel not as sure and certain as with the plano-convex. But satisfactory jobs can be achieved with this softer edge that is often preferable as it keeps the drop-off from being too obvious.

Fresnel Sizes. Fresnel spotlights come in a number of sizes, the smallest of which has a 3-inch lens and burns a 150-watt G-shaped lamp. Like the

Figure 16–1. THE PLANO-CONVEX SPOTLIGHT. (1) Asbestos-covered lead wires. (2) Pin connector. (3) Vertical adjustment knob. (4) Spherical reflector. (5) G-shape lamp. (6) Yoke. (7) Pipe clamp. (8) Ventilation holes. (9) Lamp in flood focus position. (10) Spring ring to hold lens in position. (11) Color-frame holder. (12) Plano-convex lens. (13) Focus-adjustment knob. (14) Movable lamp socket.

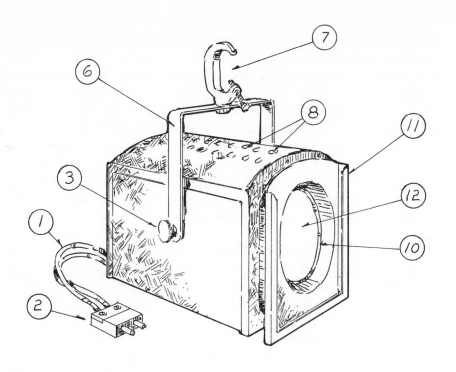

PLANO-CONVEX LENS
SPOTLIGHT

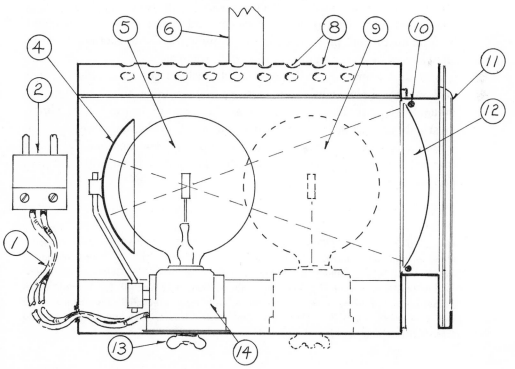

baby P.C., this little instrument though not possessing much punch is very handy for tucking into small corners. A streamlined version of the 3-inch Fresnel is sold in most camera-equipment shops for use in photographers' studios.

An extremely useful instrument on any stage is the 6-inch Fresnel, burning 500- and 750-watt T-shaped lamps. This spotlight is a true workhorse, being invaluable for the upstage acting areas where its soft-edged beam fades away on the scenery without leaving obvious and distracting lines and patterns. It throws a good punch with the typically smooth beam pattern. And for the larger stage the 8-inch Fresnel can be almost as valuable and with its 1000- and 1500-watt G-lamps has a powerful beam that can be put to many uses.

The Fresnel type of spotlight is also sold with lenses from 10 inches up to 20 inches in diameter. These have little importance for the conventional stage, being primarily designed for television and motion-picture studios. They might have significance for outdoor productions, where exceptionally long throws are often the rule. Another feature that has been introduced for television purposes is the Fresnel lens that throws an oval beam. This has no significance on the stage and should be avoided.

THE ELLIPSOIDAL SPOTLIGHT.   In Chapter 5 we saw that if a source of light be placed at one of the focal points of a reflector built in the shape of half an ellipsoid, all the light rays that strike this reflector are diverted through the conjugate focal point. By placing a lens just in front of this secondary focal point a spotlight of great efficiency and power can be constructed. Such an instrument, properly called an ellipsoidal-reflector spotlight, is more often known by one or another of its various trade names.

Because the primary focal point is extremely close to the reflector, it is necessary to employ only T-shaped lamps in order to get the filament placed precisely (Figure 16–2). Inasmuch as this type of instrument is almost invariably used with its nose tilted down about 45 degrees from the horizontal, lamps that are to be burned "base-up only" are used and the socket that holds them is uppermost when the spotlight is in its usual burning position.

Figure 16–2.   THE ELLIPSOIDAL-REFLECTOR SPOTLIGHT.   (1) Pin connector. (2) Monoplane (or biplane) filament, with its center at the focal point, "f." (3) Ellipsoidal-shaped reflector. (4) Bottom shutter, which shapes the top of beam. (5) Color frame holder. (6) Prefocus base socket. (7) T-shaped lamp, to burn base up. (8) Top shutter, which shapes the bottom of the beam. (9) The "gate," with typical reflected rays crossing at the conjugate focal point, "f¹." (10) Two plano-convex lenses. (11) Spring ring, to hold lens. (12) Alternate position of lens system.

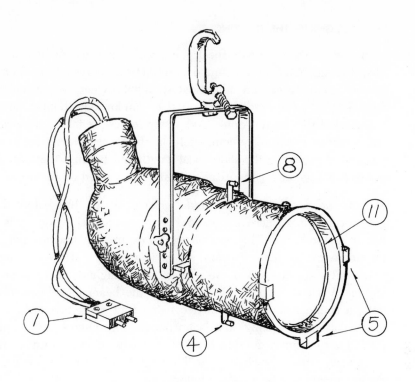

ELLIPSOIDAL REFLECTOR
SPOTLIGHT

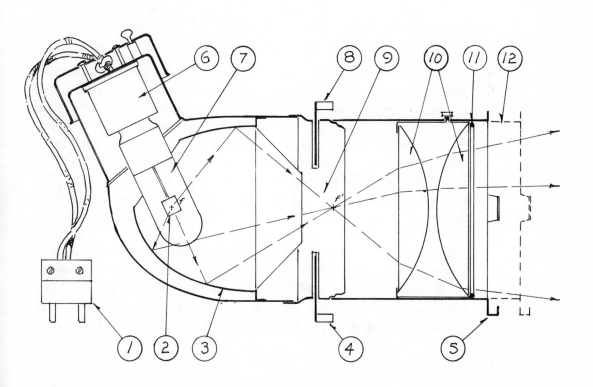

In front of the conjugate focal point, where the rays of light are starting to spread again, a lens is mounted to refract these rays into a comparatively narrow beam. In certain ellipsoidal spotlights, where a particularly short focal-length lens is needed, it is usual to employ two thinner lenses to get the effect of the one thick one. Today step lenses are taking the place of the plano-convex type pretty completely in these instruments for the double purpose of providing the short focal length and because these are less subject to breakage under the extreme heat concentrated on them.

Shaping the Beam of the Ellipsoidal-reflector Spot. Just before the conjugate focal point, where the various rays are still converging, is a baffle known as the "gate." This cuts off stray rays of light that are not useful in forming a well-controlled beam, and it is an image of the opening in this gate which appears when the ellipsoidal spotlight is focused on a plain surface. Various other features to shape the beam may be placed at the gate, a common and useful device being four shutters which, by proper manipulation, can change the beam pattern into almost any simple shape. An iris is sometimes inserted here, allowing the circular form of the beam to be made smaller or larger at will, though this is of more pertinence when the instrument is to be used as a follow spot.

Or special shapes may be cut from sheet metal and placed at the gate. The common term for one of these is a "gobo." Gobos are used extensively in television to throw vague patterns of light on a background that is never clearly in the focus of the cameras. This practice has occasionally been extended with excellent effect to the stage and some very ingenious uses made of the principle.

Other Beam Characteristics. The Ellipsoidal-reflector spotlight throws an extremely powerful beam of light with a firm, sharp edge to its pattern and is generally quite smooth in field. The beam cannot be shaped by external means such as placing mats in the color frame, but this is no problem because the internal shutters achieve the same results. Because the lamp, reflector, and lens are in static relationship, there is no flood and spot focus, as with the plano-convex and Fresnel spotlights. But the lenses may be moved a few inches, back and forth, thus allowing the beam pattern to be thrown out of focus and so softening to some extent the hard, sharp edge of the field.

Because of the delicate relationship between filament and reflector, it is easy for the instrument to get out of adjustment, particularly if an inexperienced electrician tampers with the adjusting devices on the socket cap. Often, especially in those instruments that use the prefocus lamp, the base has not been properly seated in the socket. At other times it is necessary to focus the spotlight on a plain surface and manipulate the adjusting devices until a firm, circular field is found again. Or the instrument may be dimmed down until the filament barely glows, the lenses removed, and an inspection of the alignment of the filament and the reflector made from the front.

Ellipsoidal-reflector Spotlight Sizes. The ellipsoidal-reflector spotlight comes in several sizes, from one with a 4½-inch lens that burns 250- and 500-watt lamps and throws a wide beam, suitable for small stages and auxiliary use on large, up to a 12-inch model that uses a 3000-watt lamp for a very narrow and extremely powerful beam intended primarily for follow-spotting from a distance. There are a number of models in the 6- and 8-inch sizes, some using 500- and 750-watt lamps and others those of 1000, 2000, or 3000 watts. The differences in design are too complex for analysis here, and are continually undergoing changes. But the buyer should study the latest catalogs carefully before placing his order and demand specific answers from the manufacturers as to the exact performance in the way of beam spread, foot-candle readings at various distances, and the like.

THE BEAM PROJECTOR

Despite its narrow and extremely intense output, the beam projector is not a true spotlight. It has no lens, and, more important, its beam pattern cannot be altered from the small and very bright circle that is its characteristic.

This instrument makes use of a parabolic reflector which sends all the rays that strike it forward and parallel one to the other. In order to eliminate diverging rays of light that would not contribute to the tight beam pattern, but would prove undesirable and distracting, a spherical reflector is often placed in front of the lamp to redirect such rays as may strike it back to the parabolic reflector, from which they may augment the other parallel rays (Figure 16–3). In some styles of beam projector baffles or louvres serve to intercept and absorb such diverging rays. Basically the beam projector is a searchlight adapted to the theatre. Its stage uses are largely confined to strong shafts of light of great intensity but confined to small areas, as sunlight through a window. For musical comedy and the like, great banks of beam projectors may be employed, but for the modest stage this instrument has more limited uses.

The beam projector comes in various sizes, from 10–16 inches in diameter. The 10-inch style may take a 250- to a 500- or a 750-watt T-lamp, while the larger types use 1000- to 2000-watt lamps, in some models G's and in others T-shaped. Because of the tremendous punch of the light, the beam projector is very hard on gelatins, burning the color out of some shades within minutes after replacement.

Figure 16–3.   THE BEAM PROJECTOR.   (1) G-shaped lamp. (2) Parabolic reflector. (3) Concentrated filament. (4) Lamp socket, adjustable. (5) Pin connector and lead wires. (6) Spherical reflector. (7) Color-frame holders.

THE FLOODLIGHT

A floodlight is, as its name suggests, a device for throwing a broad wash of light over a wide area. For many years the so-called Olivette was the standard instrument for such a purpose. Large and unwieldy, burning a 1000-watt G-lamp, the Olivette reflects a smooth wash of light from its box-like hood and white-painted interior.

Floodlights are now a little more sophisticated, and a lot easier to manipulate. Most of them employ the ellipsoidal-reflector principle, but with a matte finish that distributes the light smoothly, without a sharp edge to the beam. A single such instrument can be valuable for lighting a fair-sized window backing, while a bank of them may be used to illuminate a drop or cyclorama.

Most of these floodlights are about 15 or 16 inches in diameter and burn general-service PS lamps of up to 2000 watts in some types. There is also a small 10-inch model that uses 250 and 400 G-lamps, or, occasionally, gives good service with a 100-watt A-lamp when only a very low illumination is required.

THE STRIPLIGHT

One form of stage-lighting instrument that predates the invention of the incandescent lamp is the striplight, which produces the effect of a line of light by means of a number of sources—formerly candles or gas, but now electric—adjacent to each other. In its crudest form, the striplight is often found as footlights—the only light source on a small, ill-equipped stage—a row of bare bulbs, sometimes as far apart as 12 inches, extending the entire width of the proscenium opening.

While permanently installed footlights of better design may be useful on some stages, the more general approach today is to have striplights prepared in lengths of 4, 6, or 8 feet. These sections may then be placed about the stage, including the usual footlight position on the apron's edge, or hung from overhead, as needed by the requirements of the particular play and its design concept. This system allows far greater flexibility in the use of equipment than does permanently installed striplights at many locations.

Certain basic principles in striplight design must be understood. The lamps should be wired in several color circuits, three being the most common, though four have much to recommend them. Then, by using different

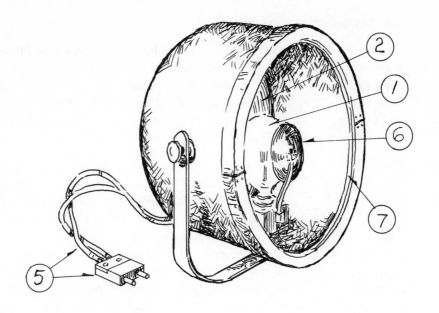

BEAM PROJECTOR

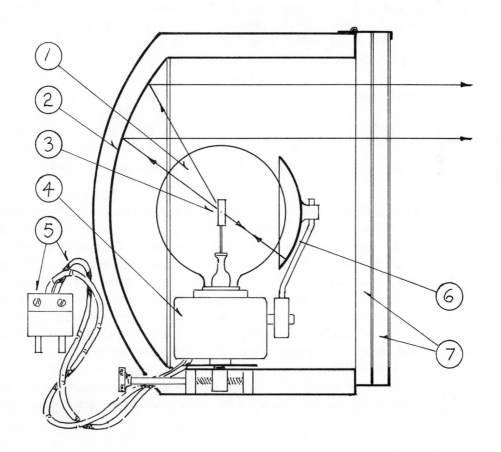

colors in each circuit and properly controlling their respective intensities, practically any color or tint of light may be attained. Obviously, the lamps should be closely spaced, so that their various beams will blend together more readily. Nothing is more ridiculous than the actor standing so near a badly designed footlight strip that his right foot is a rich magenta and his left a bright green.

TYPES OF STRIPLIGHTS. In the past various types of striplights were marketed and still are, unfortunately. The open trough is an abomination, as there is no possibility of using color media over the individual lamps. Only by employing the quite inefficient and unsatisfactory dipped-color lamps can any control over color be achieved.

An improvement over the open trough is the striplight in which each lamp has its own reflector, and various devices are provided for holding gelatin in front of it. The highly polished reflectors throw uneven light patterns, the matte finishes accumulate dirt. For the more powerful throws of light, larger lamps are necessary, and hence larger and more unwieldy instruments.

R and PAR Lamps in Striplights. The advent of the R and PAR lines of lamps has made all this obsolete. For the most elaborate establishments, only one style of striplight is needed: that with the lamps on 6-inch centers, as all the reflector lamps that are necessary for use have diameters of no more than 5 inches. Color frames that will accept both gelatin and glass should be employed. Because the R and PAR lamps have built-in reflectors, these strips do not need any of their own—a saving in money and nuisance. The strips should be wired in three- or four-color circuits, depending on the preference of the producers; probably three is sufficient in the great majority of cases. And the small, low-budget stage can do very nicely with the colored R's and PAR's as described in Chapter 13.

Color with Striplights. While gelatin will often be used, it is wise to have a good line of glass available as well, particularly as other media burn out readily when the strips are focused upward as at the foot of a backdrop. Glass roundels of the 55-degree-spread variety are particularly valuable and cost no more than other types. They have small prismlike ridges on the inner sides, and these serve to spread the light if the roundels are placed correctly: with the ridges running perpendicular to the long axis of the instrument. Certainly the primary colors should be stocked, as well as amber and blue-green. Such an inventory should prove sufficient for all but the most elaborate productions.

The 150-watt R and PAR lamps prove adequate for many stages, though occasionally the 300-watt R spots may be needed for extra punch, as in lighting a large cyclorama. The 150-watt PAR spots are almost as effective, however, but throw too narrow a beam for anything but a sheet of light focused up or down a flat surface. For a very broad, smooth field of medium intensity the flood types of either R or PAR lamps are the most useful. Recently the commercial theatre has been employing striplights specially designed to take the 300-watt PAR-56 and the 500-watt PAR-64 lamps. These have no application, of course, for the small stage, and their value on a medium-sized one is questionable. But the group that plays on a very large stage, with vast cyclorama or sky drops, might find them a good investment, if properly designed for their specific needs.

17

STAGE-LIGHTING INSTRUMENTS (2)

PROJECTED SCENERY

Probably nothing in the realm of stage lighting suggests more magic than the word "projection," which to many theatre workers guarantees marvelous scenic effects produced at very little cost and less effort—a dreamy substitute for the hours of hard work needed to build, paint, and rig the more structural types of scenery.

We wish it could be so. Unfortunately, there are as many problems surrounding the effective employment of projections as there are in the use of any other form of scenery. Valuable though this technique may be in many cases, it is essential that the designer be thoroughly aware of the many difficulties that are entailed.

Projected scenery should never be considered a mere substitute for painted scenery, but a medium in its own right. Inasmuch as a projected design consists of light, rather than of pigment, it has a different color range

and value scale than a painted design. And its colors are more intense—
and more dramatic.

Because of this heightened dramatic quality, projected scenery becomes,
in a sense, an actor, not just background. It is thus an integral part of the
play, and therefore usually functions best in nonrealistic types of production.

PLACING THE PROJECTION APPARATUS. Obviously, the mechanism that
throws a front projection should be hidden from the eyes of the audience.
This is frequently a tricky matter on a crowded stage. There must be a clear
throw from the instrument to the surface where the image is to appear. This
automatically eliminates a projection booth or other position in the front of
the house, for actors would pass through the projected light as they moved
about the stage.

Good locations on the stage itself are hard to find. Front projections mean
that actors must not pass through the projecting beam of light, nor stand
close to the screen on which the effect is to appear. Nor may scenery be
placed in these areas. The result is that large portions of the stage must be
left unused to accommodate the projection.

Further, if the projection apparatus cannot stand four-square in front of
the surface where the image is to be seen, then the picture that is thrown
on this surface will come in at an angle and be distorted accordingly. It
becomes necessary to calculate carefully the amount of distortion that will
be encountered in each instance and design the slide accordingly.

In the case of rear projections, a considerable area behind the screen must
be kept clear, an outright impossibility on many shallow stages. Further,
the bright source may be seen through the translucent material—an extremely
distracting situation. Rear projections call for large, unseamed surfaces, for
no one has yet found a way to eliminate the hard lines that appear where
narrow sheets of cloth have been stitched together to form a broad, translucent screen.

Also, the designer must keep in mind that the intensity of a rear projection falls off rapidly if not viewed from straight ahead, but at an angle. This
necessitates placing the projection screen parallel, or very nearly parallel,
to the apron of the stage, thus limiting, of course, any variety in floor plan.

KEEPING LIGHT OFF THE IMAGE. Another problem—and one that should be
perfectly obvious to anyone who has tried to look at television in a brightly
lighted room—is that no projection will be at all effective, perhaps not even
seen, unless all other light is kept off the image. On a shallow set, the actors
must be lighted even when they are quite close to the background, and some
of this light will strike the background washing out the projected pattern.
This can be partly remedied by the use of side-lighting exclusively, which

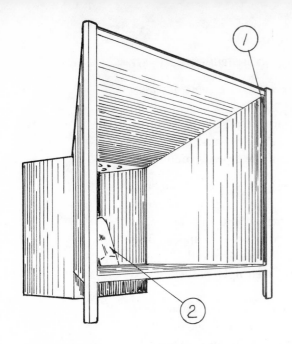

Figure 17–1. THE LINNEBACH PROJECTOR. (1) Slide holder. (2) Concentrated-filament T-shaped lamp.

LINNEBACH PROJECTOR

helps the projected effect, but may be very bad for the actors. Even when the background is far upstage of the acting areas a surprising amount of light will be reflected on it from the dingiest of stage floors to spoil the picture. Only the most careful planning and control over all light on the stage will allow a projected effect to be at all acceptable.

THE LINNEBACH PROJECTOR

There are two basic types of instruments for projecting an image. The first and simpler is straight-line projection, sometimes called shadow projection. In its least complex form it could be a single source of light allowed to fall on a plain surface with objects placed between it and the background, so the shadows fall on the latter. In practice it is more often a device known as a Linnebach projector (Figure 17–1), a large, plain hood with a source of light—sometimes an arc but today more often a high wattage incandescent lamp—before which a large frame is placed. This frame contains the picture that is to be projected. It may be in the nature of a cutout—plywood, cardboard, or the like—that will throw its shadow on the screen. It may be glass with opaque forms painted on it—again shadows will be thrown. Or translucent paints may be used on glass, or other transparent materials such as gelatins or plastic media may throw colored pictures or patterns. Ingenious combinations may be devised.

Distinctness of Linnebach Images. Whatever is used in the way of realistic or abstract patterns, it must be bold and simple, for the dimensions of the lamp filament prevent a sharp line from being projected effectively. No solid line will appear at all unless it is drawn half an inch wide on the slide; no opening will throw its image if it is less than an inch wide on the slide. All edges will be fuzzy and indistinct.

Many times this is completely satisfactory, or even desirable, as for distant and misty landscapes, or nonrealistic forms. But if sharp images, great detail, and clear pictures are necessary, then the simplicity of Linnebach projection cannot be used.

Recently Paramount Theatrical Supplies, New York, has put on the market a unique scenery projection system known as Multiscreen, the invention of Dr. Elemer Nagy. Based on the Linnebach principle, this system utilizes twin projectors carefully focused on screens as wide as 15 feet. By cross-dimming the two projectors, one scene can be changed to another with ease. By the use of a 6-volt, 18-ampere lamp with a small filament, the projected design has far greater clarity than it is possible to obtain with apparatus using the conventional standard-voltage lamp.

THE LENS PROJECTOR

The second and more complex type of image projection is the effect machine. The common slide projector is a commercially constructed example of this, but for stage use it is usually convenient to build exactly what is needed for each particular problem by means of a common spotlight hood and a few

Figure 17–2.   THE LENS PROJECTOR.   (1) G-shaped lamp. (2) Plano-convex lens. (3) Additional concentrating lens (or "Dutchman"). (4) Slide. (5) Objective-lens system.

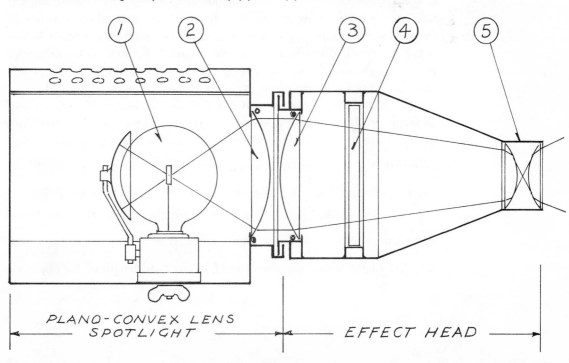

PLANO-CONVEX LENS SPOTLIGHT   EFFECT HEAD

additional pieces of apparatus that may be used time and again in various combinations for other projection problems.

This type of lens projector is shown in Figure 17–2. It is based on a large plano-convex spotlight with a lamp of 1000 watts or more. In front of its regular lens, a second lens called a "Dutchman" is placed. This is to pull down the beam spread and concentrate as much light as possible on the glass slide, which should be the largest that will be completely lighted by the beam from the two condensing system lenses.

PROJECTION LENSES. The image of the illuminated slide is focused on the screen or other surface by means of another lens (or lens train) called the "objective system." The lenses here are usually 3 inches in diameter and of various focal lengths. They are placed in a holder at the proper distance apart and the proper distance from the slide, and small adjustments are then made to bring the image of the slide's picture into a sharp focus.

Holders for the Dutchman lens, the slides, and the objective lenses are obtainable from the larger lighting-supply houses. The slides themselves can be made up of photographic pictures, prepared by any good photography shop, or of designs painted on the glass. The latter, of course, cannot be very detailed because of the small size of the slide. It is usually better for the designer to paint his picture to a convenient scale and then photograph it.

MATHEMATICS OF PROJECTION. To eliminate the trial-and-error methods of selecting and placing the objective systems, the use of certain formulas should be understood. The first of these gives the size of the image at any distance. It is: $S/I = s/i$ when S = the size of the slide, I = the size of the image, s = the distance between the slide and the objective system, and i = the distance from the objective system to the image. It must be remembered that all these distances must be expressed in the same units, usually inches. If the horizontal dimension of the slide is used, the horizontal dimension of the image will be obtained, while if the vertical measurement of the image is needed, one must use the vertical measurement of the slide.

For example, let us assume that our slide is 3 inches wide, and we need an image of 15 feet across when our projector is to be placed 20 feet away from the screen. How far must the slide be from the lens? Using the formula we find that $\dfrac{3}{180} = \dfrac{s}{240}$ (note that all figures are expressed in inches). Therefore $s = 4$ inches, and the lens must be placed 4 inches from the slide.

THE OBJECTIVE-LENS TRAIN. The second formula gives us the focal length of the lens required to give the proper effect. It is: $\dfrac{1}{s} + \dfrac{1}{i} = \dfrac{1}{f}$ when s and i have the same meanings as above and f = the focal length of the objective-lens train in inches. Continuing with the same problem as before, i is stated as 20 feet (or 240 inches) and we have found s to be 4 inches. Therefore: $\frac{1}{4} + \frac{1}{240} = \frac{1}{f}$ or $\frac{1}{f} = \frac{60 + 1}{240}$. Transposing, we find that $f = \frac{240}{61}$ or 3.934 inches, which is approximately 4 inches.

Now 4 inches is quite a short focal length for a lens, so we must try to achieve it by means of two lenses with longer focal lengths. Let us assume that we have two such, one of 6-inch focal length, the other of 8 inches. How can these be placed to make up a lens train of only 4-inch focal length?

Our third formula is as follows: $f = \dfrac{f_1 \times f_2}{f_1 + f_2 - d}$. As before, f is the focal length of the whole train, f_1 and f_2 are the focal lengths of the two lenses (which one is actually first and which is second has no significance), and d is the distance between these two. Now we can set up our formula as follows: $4 = \dfrac{6 \times 8}{6 + 8 - d} = \dfrac{48}{14 - d}$ or: $1 = \dfrac{12}{14 - d}$ or: $14 - d = 12$. Therefore, $d = 2$ inches, and the two lenses must be placed in their holder 2 inches apart.

Once these formulas are thoroughly understood, they can be utilized to solve any problem involving the effect machine.

MOVING EFFECTS.   An additional piece of apparatus that can be applied to effect machines is a drumlike device with a motor drive which provides for moving effects such as water ripples, flames, snowflakes, and the like. These are expensive, and the results are rather too obvious and distracting for today's tastes in most productions. Though it must be admitted that occasionally, for arbitrary and spectacular effects, they can be worthwhile.

THE ARC LIGHT

In Chapter 14 mention was made of the carbon arc as a source of light. When the two carbons and their associated apparatus are placed in a hood with a lens, it becomes essentially a plano-convex type of spotlight except for the source. The beam will have a sharp edge and, just as in the incandescent spotlight, the closer the source is to the lens, the more widespread the beam and the less intense the light. Then when the source is moved further back, the output narrows but becomes more brilliant.

It is not possible to control the intensity of the arc by conventional dimmers which alter the electric supply, for when the voltage drops, the arc simply goes out abruptly. But the *effect* of dimming can be achieved by moving the carbons toward the flood focus position, with the corresponding dropoff of intensity, and at the same time closing down the iris with which all good arc lights are equipped, so that the ultimate beam remains the same size. A skillful operator can do this so effectively that an observer cannot tell that mechanical means are employed, but it takes a great deal of practice and a piece of mechanism in fine repair.

With any carbon arc a "ballast" (or fixed resistance) of proper capacity must be used to prevent an unrestricted flow of current when the carbons touch. An operator must always be in attendance, as the carbons burn away quite rapidly and must be fed back into proper relationship with each other. The d-c arc light is inclined to be noisy, which can be very disturbing to any of the audience seated nearby.

THE NEWER ARCS.   Until recently the only forms of carbon-arc spotlights available operated solely on direct current and drew a very high amperage. But now effective arcs that draw little current, and that ac, have come into the market. These instruments are far more complete and include many accessories that the older types never had. They are expensive, but in any theatre where the throw must be over 75 feet, they are essential. In smaller houses with shorter throws the new 3000- and 5000-watt incandescent follow spots will do the job just as well and with far less trouble, while a new, low-voltage lamp follow spot has recently appeared on the market and promises fine results.

ULTRAVIOLET EFFECTS.   One field in which it is impossible to surpass the carbon arc is in the use of ultraviolet effects. Because the output from this instrument is rich in these very short waves, a "black light" filter that removes practically all the visible waves will still permit the ultraviolet ones to pass through in good quantity. Objects painted with a medium susceptible to such waves will glow under this stimulus and, if all other light is removed from the stage, weird and unworldly effects can be achieved.

FIRE EFFECTS

Open fires are rarely convincing on the stage. Yet play after play calls for them. If it is possible to design the setting so that the hearth is located in a side wall, reasonably good results can be attained by simply letting a flickering light move over the far corner of the fireplace. Even this must be kept at low intensity so as not to take attention from the actors.

All too often the demands of the script force the designer to put his fire in full view of the audience. Sometimes no flames are actually demanded, and then a mere glow, through crumpled gelatin (orange and red), broken glass splashed with translucent orange paint, or the like, will suffice. If it is essential to show "flames," then a glow on some form of rising smoke, or on thin streamers of chiffon, blown upward by a small fan, are often used. In every case, however, the designer is placed on the horns of this dilemma: to make the fire effects so realistic as to grab the attention of the audience— possibly to alarm them—or so phony as to arouse their ridicule. It must be stated emphatically that on the whole the less fire effect you can get away with, the more fortunate you and your production will be.

FLAMES.   These remarks apply equally to other open-flame devices such as torches, candles, oil-burning lanterns. Torches are a particular difficulty. Perhaps a flashlight hidden in the handle and focused on streamers of very light silk is as good a solution as any, but it is not very convincing, even when the torch is stationary and the silk can be blown upward by a hidden fan. Perhaps a smoke device can be incorporated and the flashlight trained on its fumes.

Oil-burning lanterns should never be used on the stage. To begin with, their use is strictly against all fire rules and insurance regulations. A real hazard is presented by their use, for in case of accident the stage becomes flooded with blazing oil. Fortunately oil lanterns conventionally have glass chimneys which can be realistically smoke stained to hide a small lamp bulb placed inside.

If the lantern is never moved during the action, it can be connected to the regular stage wiring and dimmed up and down from the control board. Of course, actors, when pretending to adjust the wick, or touch a match to it, or whatever, must always be careful to "mask" this fakery by placing their bodies between the lantern and the audience until the process of dimming has been completed. Nothing brings more gleeful snorts from an audience than a lantern that continues to "burn" despite a strong puff from the actor, and then fades away as he draws his breath for a second try. If a lantern is to be carried about the stage a battery must be hidden within it and a switch provided for the actor to use as he pretends to touch a match or blow out the "flame."

CANDLES.   Unlike oil lanterns, candles which usually extinguish themselves when dropped, are permissible on most stages if properly handled. In some locations they must be encased in transparent mica shields. It is advisable to clear this matter with your local authorities if any doubt exists. In no case should candles be placed near draperies or other easily flammable materials, including human hair and frilly costumes.

But despite the permissibility of candles, they are not advised if they can be avoided, as their bright spots of light and particularly their flickering at the smallest breath of air can be most distracting for the audience. Very effective faking of candles can be done by means of a small battery or pencil flashlight hidden in a white paper tube. A tiny lamp on the top, with a twist of colored gelatin about it gives a steady and quite convincing glow.

LIGHTING FIXTURES

Chandeliers, wall sconces, table lamps, and similar household-lighting fixtures offer no vast problems ordinarily except for the wattage of the lamps actually used in them. Such fixtures should never be counted on to produce all the light that seems to emanate from them. Frequently they are in quite the wrong locations to light the faces of the actors playing near them, so additional illumination must be provided by spotlights especially mounted for the purpose, or the acting area lights may be varied to give the effects desired.

This is particularly true when the fixtures have bulbs visible to the audience, for these, if at all bright, will throw a most annoying (even blinding) glare. Such bare bulbs must always be of extremely low wattage, and even then may have to be dimmed still further. Obviously little light will emanate from such fixtures, so the extra instruments become doubly important.

But if the bulbs are shielded by shades, then the glare is hidden and extra-large wattage lamps may be used to give a more realistic effect on an already bright stage. Such shades must be quite opaque, of course, or brown paper linings can be put inside them. Oftentimes an additional baffle of paper must be placed over the bulb to prevent an unsightly "hot spot" on the walls and ceiling of the setting. Basically then, it may be said that such household fixtures as chandeliers and sconces are more properly design features rather than functional lighting instruments on the well-appointed stage.

An interesting discussion on how the duties of handling and caring for such appliances are assigned in the commercial theatre will be found in Chapter 10.

MOON AND STARS

Someday a playwright will call for a realistic sun on the stage! Until then we can have quite enough trouble with the moon and stars so often necessary. If the background is in the form of a cloth drop or cyclorama, quite a realistic moon can be devised by cutting the desired shape—fully round or crescent—into a large sheet of thin material such as cardboard or plywood, which is then pressed firmly against the back of the drop and a small spotlight is focused on the cutout from the rear. If the background is not a cloth, then a projection from an effect machine in front must be used.

Stars can be quite effective, but are tricky to handle. The tiniest bulbs obtainable look like great blobs of light against a darkened sky. It is advisable to tape these over; a mere pin-prick will pass enough light. When the cyclorama is a permanent one of plaster or wood, tiny holes are often drilled through it and clips provided on the back to hold the little lamps in place. Usually for such effects it is advisable to get strings of low-voltage lamps that can be bought at any hobby shop together with an appropriate transformer. Even Christmas tree strings can be used.

Stars can be projected from the front but are rarely convincing as even the best slide equipment reproduces them as large and somewhat indistinct smudges of light. But for unrealistic, stylized effects, both stars and moon can be projected by a Linnebach with good results.

LIGHTNING

Lightning is a device in many plays. Fortunately it is usually not necessary to show forks springing from the sky, but only the sudden, rapid, and irregular bursts of high illumination as seen through windows or coming from the wings. By striking and breaking the contacts rapidly, a carbon arc can be used to give excellent results for this purpose. In fact a so-called "arc striker" that makes this even easier to handle is available commercially.

Another method is to switch on and off rapidly a number of small sources. It is better to use a striplight with many white and daylight-blue lamps of low wattage than a single large source which would respond more slowly to the irregular, staccato timing of typical lightning. A special switch may be devised to make the closing and the opening of the circuit easier to control, or the connectors themselves may be used to good advantage. Photoflash bulbs have also been used for offstage lightning.

If the lightning flash itself must be seen against the "sky," a projection must be used. Because of the slow response of the high-wattage lamp, it is well to have the instrument already turned on and an operator stationed at it, to reveal and conceal the beam of light by means of a cap or other masking device. And several different slides should be provided, rather than show the same shaped flash again and again. Scratches on black-painted slides can be drawn quite realistically for these.

EXPLOSIONS AND FLASHES

To produce these offstage, in the wings, the same general techniques can be applied as were suggested for lightning flashes, with the addition of mechanically produced noises when these are required. But for the same effects on the stage, in view of the audience, a flash pot is required.

A good flash pot consists of a metal pan with a tight-fitting wire screen over it. The bottom is covered by a piece of asbestos board, to which two electric terminals are fastened (small brass screws will do very nicely) but they must be carefully insulated from the box itself or a short circuit will develop. The two terminals may be about one inch apart. They are connected respectively to the two wires of a circuit that also contains a switch. Between the two terminals a single, very thin strand of copper wire is strung, wound firmly around each screw and lying flat on the asbestos board. A small quantity of flash powder is poured over this wire, covering all portions of it. When the switch is closed, the thin wire will burn out, igniting the powder. After each use the wire and powder must be replaced.

A variation of the flash box is a fuse of very low amperage set in an appropriate fuse clip or socket. The fuse is cut open—in the case of a plug fuse by prying out the isinglass window—with a cartridge fuse by cutting away part of the paper cover. Care is taken not to damage the fuse link. The resulting cavity is then filled with the flash powder. As with the flash box, the opened fuse and the powder must be renewed after each use.

Flash powder, when set off in this way, gives a good burst of light, but little smoke. If smoke is desired, some sal ammoniac powder may be mixed with the flash powder. In any case, the flash device must be well protected with a screen and should never be fired close to flammable materials or to persons. And an extra fuse, of higher amperage, should be placed in the circuit for additional protection.

And a most important warning: *very little powder should be used at one time—and it should never be tamped down,* but poured loosely into place.

FOG AND SMOKE EFFECTS

Many devices are used to produce smoke on the stage, but none is completely satisfactory. Perhaps the best known is sal ammoniac powder which after a few moments on a hot plate or in a heating cone will give off a good volume of white smoke. In ordinary quantities this is neither too odorous nor dangerous to breathe, but if allowed to become too dense, it can be very unpleasant. Cinnamon powder may be added to sweeten the smell for the actors. Of course it should never be permitted to creep down into the audience.

Sal ammoniac powder has disadvantages. It cannot be started suddenly, nor can it be stopped on cue. It is extremely corrosive on the producing elements.

Titanium tetrachloride combines with the moisture present in the air to give off a thin smoke that rises well. By adding a little water to it, or dropping a pinch of the powder into water, an instant response is produced that can be very effective, though the fumes are dangerous if breathed in quantity.

Dry ice can be dropped into water for a small quantity of "smoke," but this tends to fall instead of rise. Dry ice may be quite effective in a "fog machine" (a metal drum with a heating element to keep the water from freezing when the solid carbon dioxide is lowered into it). If the drum is provided with a cover, quite a flow of "fog" can be produced suddenly and directed around the stage by means of a hose.

Smoke bombs are very smelly, impossible to control, and leave a greasy coating on the scenery and costumes. Steam is clean, but requires special piping and produces a loud hissing that makes it impractical for quiet scenes.

One device that has recently appeared on the market may be obtained from Camera Equipment Co., 315 West 43rd Street, New York. It consists of a container which is filled with a special liquid. A heating coil is provided, a handle for easy carrying, and a plunger to pump the smoke about the stage at the desired rate and intensity. This mist tends to rise, but a cage is provided that may be filled with dry ice and fastened over the nozzle of the container. When this is done, the fumes hug the floor. Plastic hose, hidden about the stage has proved an easy way to make this mist appear wherever wanted.

A second fluid may be used to help disperse the smoke, and several essences are available to scent it pleasantly. The most remarkable feature of this device is that no actor has yet complained, even after playing a highly emotional scene in the midst of this fog!

18

INTENSITY CONTROL

Control of the intensity of stage-lighting instruments—customarily referred to as "dimming"—has two aspects. The first and more obvious is the changing of light in view of the audience, as for a shift of emphasis or to mark a difference in time or simply to darken the stage at the end of a scene. The second and equally important purpose is the setting of the various instruments at different intensities to achieve a precise effect in the complete stage picture such as subduing the cooler colors to give a feeling of sunny warmth or adding more blue on the backdrop to paint the "sky" a richer hue. It is understood of course that dimming includes making lights brighter as well as darkening them.

OBSOLETE FORMS OF DIMMING

The history of dimming is a long one. On seventeenth-century stages cans on cords were lowered over the candles to vary the light; and in the eighteenth century candles in the wings were frequently mounted on vertical boards that could be revolved to turn the light away from the stage or back onto it. In the nineteenth century the gas table—a complex of pipes and valves—adjusted the flow of gas to the various jets about the stage and provided quite a complete control over intensities.

With the advent of the incandescent lamp, crude forms of dimming control were introduced almost from the start. These all utilized the principle of placing in series with the lamp some sort of resistance that could be varied at will. The carbonpile and salt-water dimmers were among these. But the most popular of all and one that lingers on even today is the resistance-wire dimmer, often called a rheostat. That this method of control is still in common use in the commercial theatre is more a comment on Broadway production methods than any indication that this archaic device retains any real merit. The fact that the resistance dimmer operates on both dc and ac is no valid excuse in the majority of modern situations. But because the resistance dimmer is still in some theatres the only form of intensity control available, it is necessary for us to give it passing attention.

PRINCIPLES OF THE RESISTANCE DIMMER. We saw in Chapter 12 that $I = E/R$. Therefore, the greater the value given R, the less value will I have. Or, we might state it: by increasing the resistance in a circuit, we decrease the current flow. Thus, if there is also an incandescent lamp in the same circuit, it will be deprived of current as the resistance is increased, and the brightness of the lamp will vary as the current is varied.

In order to dim an incandescent lamp evenly from full up to full out, a resistance of approximately five times the resistance of the lamp itself must be introduced into the circuit in series with it. The dimmer therefore provides a length of wire long enough to furnish a resistance five times as great as that of the lamp it is designed to control. By moving a shoe over taps spaced along this wire the amount of current available to feed the lamp is varied from the full supply of the house down to an amount insufficient to cause the filament to glow. The electrical energy that has been consumed by the wire is dissipated as heat.

TYPES OF RESISTANCE DIMMERS. The resistance dimmer is found in two standard forms. The less complex of these contains two coils of resistance wire placed parallel to each other and a short distance apart. The circuit enters at the top end of one coil and leaves at the top end of the other. A conducting shoe slides up and down between the two coils making contact with each. When this shoe is at the top it bridges the gap in the circuit without introducing any resistance whatever. But when it has been moved to the bottom the full lengths of both coils have become part of the circuit. This so-called slider dimmer is quite simple in its operation but is so difficult to maneuver smoothly that the light tends "to jump" when its intensity is being changed. Further, it is impossible for one operator to manipulate more than two of these contraptions simultaneously.

The other form of resistance dimmer has its wire in the shape of a multi-pointed star, or as two stars, one within the other. The wire is fastened to a circular vitreous plate and is sometimes baked into it with only taps showing at the surface. The shoe is on the end of a pivoted sweep (when two coils are involved there is a shoe at each end of the sweep) and the sweep is moved by means of a projecting handle. Various refinements can be supplied with this type of rotary dimmer, such as a cutoff switch at the low end, provision for interlocking all the handles in a bank of them, and the like.

DISADVANTAGES OF THE RESISTANCE DIMMER. Because the resistance dimmer consumes full current as soon as it is switched on—whether the lamp burns full up or otherwise—it is extremely wasteful of electric power. And the heat generated by the coils can be quite overwhelming unless adequate ventilation is provided—a rare condition on most stages. But these are less important from the artistic point of view than the problem of fixed capacity. As was stated, the length of wire in each dimmer is determined by the exact wattage of the lamp it is expected to control. If a lamp of a smaller wattage is used instead, the dimmer will not put it out completely, and what dimming it does accomplish will be at a different rate than for those lamps of proper size on adjacent dimmers. This must be corrected by the expedient of connecting, in parallel with the stage light, a second lamp or "ghost load" —hidden offstage—and of sufficient wattage to make the total load on the dimmer approximate what it was designed to control. At best the resistance dimmer is an inefficient, uncomfortable, and inflexible device.

THE AUTOTRANSFORMER DIMMER

Many complaints about resistance control are answered by the autotransformer dimmer. This is an induction coil from which a brush draws off a varying voltage depending on where it makes contact with the bared turns of the wire in the coil. Because this tapped-off voltage does not depend on the relationship between the coil and the lamp, it will be the same regardless of what load is placed on it. Thus any lamp from the smallest to the highest allowable can be dimmed smoothly and effectively between full out and full up.

Because the only current drawn is that actually used by the load, the autotransformer is not wasteful of power nor does it create any appreciable amount of heat. It is a heavy device however, and it will operate only on ac —though this should be a problem today in only a few locations. Autotransformers are built in two styles. One of these has a knob control and